D0931166

Germanic Studies in America

(Supersedes German Studies in America)
Founded by Heinrich Meyer

Edited by Katharina Mommsen, Stanford, California

No. 48

PETER LANG
New York · Berne · Frankfort on the Main · Nancy

Randolph P. Shaffner

The Apprenticeship Novel

A Study of the «Bildungsroman» as a Regulative Type in Western Literature with a Focus on Three Classic Representatives by Goethe, Maugham, and Mann

Illustrated by Walter W. Hunt

PETER LANG
New York · Berne · Frankfort on the Main · Nancy

CIP-Kurztitelaufnahme der Deutschen Bibliothek

Shaffner, Randolph P.:
The apprenticeship novel: a study of the «Bildungs-roman» as a regulative type in western literature with a focus on three classic representatives by Goethe, Maugham and Mann / Randolph P. Shaffner. Ill. by Walter W. Hunt. – New York; Berne; Frankfort/M.; Nancy: Lang, 1984.
(Germanic Studies in America; No. 48)
ISBN 0-8204-0073-4

NE: GT

Library Congress Catalog Card Number:
83-49046
ISBN 0-8204-0073-4
ISSN 0721-3727

Printed by Lang Druck Inc., Liebefeld/Berne (Switzerland)

For Eric

and Ted

and Joe

The Child is Father of the Man

--William Wordsworth,
"My Heart Leaps Up"

CONTENTS

Preface

In an article that retains substantial validity, unaltered by prior or subsequent literary criticism, Charles E. Whitmore formulates a soundly reasoned apologia for the use of definitions in literary discussion. "Even after all legitimate reservations have been made," he claims, literary definitions perform "a theoretical office which they have both the right and the ability to discharge." Literary definitions are not so watertight as scientific formulas, nor so fillable as prescriptions: "the type," for example, "though it may tend to become a mean, is not a norm." However, in their attempt to provide the literary critic with clues, kinships, orders, and types, definitions do perform a practical service. Whitmore sees their serving the double purpose of making available "something which will assist us in surveying a particular field of literary endeavor" and "something which will express our sense of underlying kinships." In either case they derive their "raison d'être" ontologically from an essentially and solely "functional" nature.[1]

In full agreement with Whitmore, who acknowledges the individual difficulties involved in adhering to "normative" conceptions of "genre" and "period," I regard such classifications as common-denominator terms of purely regulative or functional value, rather than sacrosanct as such, and hence useful only to the description of modifiable temporal types.

My aim in this book, therefore, is to attempt a functional definition of the "apprenticeship novel." Except for Susanne Howe's, G. B. Tennyson's, and Jerome Buckley's accounts of the development of this type of novel in England and Martin Swales' study of the type in Germany, I know of no other English-language study that seeks to provide a serviceable definition on a scale comparable to articles and dissertations in French or German by such scholars as Christine Touaillon, E. L. Stahl, Berta Berger, Hans Borcherdt, Hans Rudolf Wagner, Fritz Martini, Lothar Köhn, François Jost, Jürgen Jacobs, and others.[2] Since critical literature in English rarely refers to the "apprenticeship novel," I have chosen to discuss my topic in a manner understandable to readers who comprehend no German or French. Quotations in the text are in English, but German or French sources are designated in the notes or in the text, even where English translations are available for quotation. Except in those cases where cognate words appear readily understandable in the original language, the titles of works are followed by their English equivalents, which are then underscored if the works have been translated.

I have approached the problem of a functional definition of the "apprenticeship novel" through studies of three constituent concerns: a derivation of the term, a consideration of the "apprenticeship novel" as a regulative type[3] in contrast with several kindred types of the novel in general, and a look at the fundamental principles of this particular type, including a discussion of its presuppositions, patterns, and goals. To conclude the theoretical part of this book, selective lists of apprenticeship novels are provided for several literatures. My rationale for the lists is that they are neither overly inclusive, nor overly exclusive. They rely instead on candidates selected by special studies of the type. I am thus content that they may serve to help concretize the abstract term "apprenticeship novel" as it is realized in several Western literatures.

Regarding the pretentions of these approaches to a definition, I wish to forestall a major objection: that definitions unjustifiably restrict a genre as protean as the novel. The first part of this book will attempt only the adumbration of a theoretical stance. It does not intend to promulgate a norm but rather a purely regulative or functional description of a variable temporal type. In it I have sought to avoid the pitfall of prescription while performing a practical service through the combination of a theoretical stance with concrete manifestations of the type that it seeks to describe. Such a stance will contribute, by way of hypothetical introduction, to a clear understanding of the potential values, themes, and motifs inherent in, through modified by, particular novels under consideration. In support of this argument I have devoted two-thirds of the book to a particular focus on three significant representatives from the lists, namely, the "archetype" and the "last" of the popularly and critically applauded German masterpieces in the apprenticeship tradition, along with the "best" of the modern English apprenticeship novels.

"Steile Gegenden lassen sich nur durch Umwege erklimmen" (Steep regions cannot be surmounted save by winding paths). In Wilhelm Meister's Apprenticeship these words are directed at Wilhelm, who has just received his indenture from the abbot as completion of his formal apprenticeship. Certainly the evolution of this book has followed such a course. An earlier version was submitted as a dissertation to the faculty of the University of North Carolina at Chapel Hill. I take this occasion to express my thanks to Professors James O. Bailey, Eugene H. Falk, Richard H. Fogle, Werner P. Friederich, Siegfried E. Mews, and Christoph E. Schweitzer for their scholarly advice and encouragement while this work was evolving. I have rewritten the text extensively, but without altering the general argument or major topics and with an appeal to the linguistic preference of an English audience, all because I consider the study of significant enough import to warrant wider circulation. And to this end I am indebted to Professors Henry H. H. Remak and Katharina Mommsen for their invaluable aid in assuring its publication.

R.P.S.

Highlands, N.C.
May 1, 1983

I

DEFINITIONS AND DISTINCTIONS

In this work, when it shall be found that much is omitted, let it not be forgotten that much likewise is performed.

--Samuel Johnson, Preface to *A Dictionary of the English Language*

1. THE ORIGIN OF THE TERM

The terms "Bildung," "apprenticeship," and "apprentissage" in their respective languages have all shared a relationship with one specific type of novel. Since other expressions in these and other languages have been employed to designate the type best represented by the prototypal Wilhelm Meister's Apprenticeship, a discussion restricted to these three terms may reflect only a matter of preference. It is the intent of the present chapter, therefore, to consider several alternatives but to focus primarily on the coinage and popularization of "Bildungsroman," "apprenticeship novel," and "le roman d'apprentissage" as terms that best characterize the type herein defined.

The Reallexikon der deutschen Literaturgeschichte (Encyclopedia of German Literary History) claims that the eminent philosopher and literary historian Wilhelm Dilthey coined the German term "Bildungsroman" in his 1870 biography of Friedrich Schleiermacher, Das Leben Schleiermachers.[1] To this Fritz Martini takes exception. Karl von Morgenstern, he argues, had planned as early as 1803 a study of the "Bildungsroman," a term he created for a course at the University of Dorpat in 1810, "Über den Geist und Zusammenhang einer Reihe philosophischer Romane" ("On the Spirit and Relationship of a Succession of Philosophical Novels").[2] He again used it in titles of his theoretical and practical lectures, "Über das Wesen des Bildungsromans" ("On the Essence of the Bildungsroman")[3] and "Zur Geschichte des Bildungsromans" ("Toward a History of the Bildungsroman"),[4] in 1819 and 1820, respectively. Furthermore, Friedrich von Blankenburg had already defined the concept of the "Bildungsroman" in his Versuch über den Roman (Essay on the Novel) as early as 1774.[5]

Despite Martini's discovery of the actual origin of the German term, François Jost has sought to retain Dilthey as at least its popularizer. Since Morgenstern's influence has remained noticeably limited, Dilthey is credited with being indeed "the first to have broadcast the idea," for it was subsequent to his 1870 designation of the type in his well-known biography "that 'Bildungsroman' became part of the terminology employed by the literary world."[6]

The English equivalent of the term "Bildungsroman" poses a linguistic problem: the English language lacks an exact expression for the German concept.[7] Furthermore, only a few literary critics devote any consideration to the type itself as a subclass of the English novel. And these few critics who do recognize the type offer a variety of identifying tags, ranging from William Frierson's chapter on the "life-novel" in his study of the genre in England[8] to René Wellek's focus on the "educational novel" in his discussion of the type in Germany,[9] and including Susanne Howe's references to an "apprentice novel" or later, in the same study, to the "apprenticeship novel."[10]

Wellek's adoption of the English term "educational novel" invites the same vagueness that characterizes obscuring the boundaries between the "Bildungsroman" and its kindred types: the educational, "Erziehungs-," and the developmental, "Entwicklungs-," novels.[11] His option supports, by at least this one significant instance, Howe's observation that a "preference for vagueness" in English critics[12] distinguishes them from the Germans, whose "passion for categories" demands more precision.[13] On the other hand, Howe represents the exception to her own claim concerning the English, for she adopts the specific term "apprenticeship novel" instead of the generic alternative, "educational novel."[14]

My own preference derives from a process of elimination. I consider the term "life-novel" too general, since it obscures proper emphasis on the lone individual who discovers life through education and other formative influences.[15] Moreover, the term's implications extend beyond the age between youth and adulthood. My objections to "life-novel" apply equally to the "novel of culture"; and the term "educational novel," as noted above, encourages a vagueness that "Bildungsroman" does not convey.

We may justifiably assume that Carlyle's 1824 translation of Goethe's masterpiece, which he entitled Wilhelm Meister's Apprenticeship and which Howe discusses in her chapter on Carlyle, inspired Howe herself to select the term "apprenticeship" to characterize this particular type of novel.[16] Subsequent English translations--by R. D. Boylan, 1855; Eleonor Grove, 1873; Dr. Jjalmar Boyesen, 1885; or, most recently, H. M. Waidson, 1979; and others--whose titles retained Carlyle's use of the term "apprenticeship," further established its popular association with Goethe's type.

In essential agreement with Howe's choice, I accept "apprenticeship novel" as the nearest English equivalent for the German term "Bildungsroman."[17] The exact literal translation of "Bildungsroman"--"novel of formation"[18]--is defined as tracing the "formation and development of individual character."[19] But if the English literal translation, "formational novel," fails to designate the type represented by Wilhelm Meisters Lehrjahre, as it apparently does, we may wonder why literary critics from Morgenstern and Dilthey to the present have eschewed coining a German alternative to "Bildungsroman," namely, "Lehrjahre-Roman," for the English term "apprenticeship novel" is no more than a specific rendering of the title in translation of Goethe's prototype.

The French terms "le roman d'éducation" and "le roman d'apprentissage"[20] embody, respectively, the supposed English and German preferences for vagueness and precision. In 1830 the French Revue encyclopédique appears to have valued the latter term, for it strongly criticized Toussenel à Ratisbonne for having omitted from the title of his 1829 translation of Wilhelm Meister the essential phrase, "Les Années d'apprentissage."[21] According to Fernand Baldensperger whose comparative study, Goethe en France (Goethe in France), traces the progress of this term, the French language itself was "decisively enriched with the expression by which Goethe designated this series of experiences, and the term 'les années d'apprentissage' has improved the vocabulary of our psychologists and of our critics."

A particular problem inherent in the term "l'apprentissage" in French usage, however, as Baldensperger admits, derives from the negative reception of Goethe's book by the French, who regarded "this idea of 'l'apprentissage' and the word that expressed it" as designating a confused and incoherent type of novel, if such "a confused assemblage of trivial adventures, of base characters, of mysticism without intelligence and without restraint" could be said to comprise a type at all. Both the idea and the term seemed to represent "the very essence . . . of this kind of psychological and social biography";[22] and perhaps the French preference for established or set conventional types precluded their early reception of a flexible or developing type, such as that which characterizes the novel of "Bildung." Certainly, the type has never achieved in France the popularity that it has enjoyed in Germany or in England.[23]

A latent objection to this discussion of the origin of the specific terms "Bildungsroman," "apprenticeship novel," and "roman d'apprentissage" may constitute the charge that all three terms rely exclusively on Goethe's Wilhelm Meister's Apprenticeship for their model of origin. We shall see in more comprehensive detail, in the fourth chapter's focus on concrete manifestations of the type, Wilhelm Meister's essential position as the prototype rather than the first genuine "Bildungsroman." For the present discussion, however, suffice it to say that a heterogeneous assembly of literary critics--among them Anthony Thorlby, François Jost, Susanne Howe, Thomas Mann, M. L. Kornbluth, Joseph Shipley, Gero von Wilpert, Werner P. Friederich, Max Wundt, and others[24]--unequivacally designate Wilhelm Meister as "le prototype," "the archetype," "der Urtyp" of a kind of novel which René Wellek claims it actually established.[25] As Howe points out, the type did not originate with Goethe in Germany, but with Goethe it "took an especially comprehensive sweep";[26] and the terms that have sought to categorize this comprehensive type have inevitably focused on the celebrated work that definitively shaped its character.

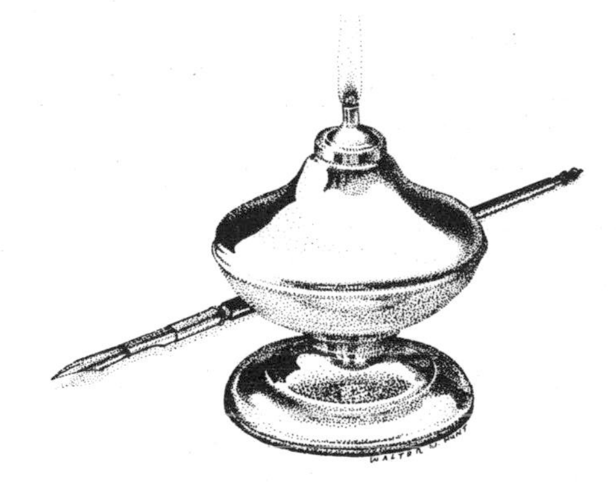

2. THE CONCEPT OF THE TYPE

Born of various earlier types of the extended narrative, ranging from the ancient epic to the medieval romance, the European "roman," and the Italian "novella," and including the picaresque narrative of Spain, the pastoral romance, the character sketch, and others, the novel now represents "a great variety of writings that have in common only the attribute of being extended works of prose 'fiction.'"[1] Since its flowering in the late eighteenth and the nineteenth centuries, it has engendered such a proliferation of new types of its own that one finds it difficult now to define exactly what comprises a novel.

I do not propose in this chapter to define the novel nor to create a formal definition of any of its forms. I wish instead to provide a seminal survey of a few commonly recognized types of the novel in general, to note several types that relate to the apprenticeship novel in particular, and to differentiate the latter from the former. Chapter three, then, will concern itself with the major principles of the apprenticeship type in isolation.

Attempting to classify many of the novel's specialized concerns, Joseph Shipley's Dictionary of World Literary Terms delineates and then subdivides several common types. Included under the heading "sociological novel" are the problem, propaganda, and proletarian novels and the novel of the soil. Under "historical novel" are the period novel, historical romance, and confessional novel (compared with the "livre à clef"), the Gothic novel, detective story, and science fiction. Structurally, the panoramic novel (or epic) is distinguished from the dramatic (scenic or well-made) novel, while such common classifications as the bourgeois, psychological, criminal (cf. detective story above), and sentimental novels abound, in addition to the novel of local color.[2]

Focusing primarily on German classifications, Hanns Eppelsheimer in his Handbuch der Weltliteratur (Handbook of World Literature) lists under the heading "Abenteurerroman" (novel of adventure) examples of the "Ritterroman" (epic of chivalry) and "Räuberroman" (robber novel) and of the "Schauerroman" (the tale of terror or "le roman noir"). He also notes the "Bauern Roman" (pastoral novel or "le roman rustique"), the "Entwicklungs-" (developmental) and "Bildungsroman" (apprenticeship novel), the "Exotische Roman" (exotic novel) and the "Geschichts-" (historical or "Historischer Roman"), concluding with the "Reise-" (travel), "Schelmen-" (picaresque) and "Zeitungsroman" (serialized novel or "le feuilleton-roman").[3]

One readily observes that both the English and the German listings exclude a host of common types of the novel, so that any comparable endeavor to subdivide the genre formally cannot presume to represent a comprehensive study. Neither do I propose in the present chapter to indicate all the commonly recognized subdivisions of a creation that Harry Levin describes as "the most protean of literary forms," in contrast to the stricter and more conventional forms of drama and poetry.[4] I wish instead to reemphasize the purely regulative value of common-denominator classifications, which should not be taken as either normative or inviolable. The essential nature of these labels should be considered solely functional in the description of modifiable temporal types of a genre.

Having thus ruled out inclusiveness in this brief survey of several commonly recognized types of the novel in general, we cannot presume at the other extreme to exhaust in particular the variety of possible types directly akin to the apprenticeship novel itself. Max Wundt in his thorough consideration of Goethe's Wilhelm Meister isolates several traits that the archetypal apprenticeship novel shared with its predecessors. Then in his chapter on the novel of the eighteenth century he concludes that the apprenticeship novel, on the crest of a wave of contemporaneous tendencies, united "all the otherwise separate types of the novel." He distinguishes the salient types with which the apprenticeship novel shared the following five traits: "the focus on inner life," which relates it to the novel of sentiment; itself an outgrowth of the romantic novel, the "Liebesroman"; "the striving for knowledge of the world" of the novel of travel, itself a later development of the novel of adventure; "the critical attitude toward the world" of the satirical novel; the "presentation of individual development" of the psychological and the biographical novels; and the "colorful portrayal of life and the world" of the broader novel of culture. Through an effective synthesis of all these traits of eighteenth-century German types of the novel, the apprenticeship novel in the example achieved by Wilhelm Meister "made use of all the types of the genre."[5]

When extended to include Wilhelm Meister's successors, a consideration of kindred types reveals a wealth of additional shared traits and differences. The apprenticeship novel certainly bears comparison with, but also distinction from, the novel of adventure as well as the more specialized picaresque, sentimental, pedagogical, developmental or psychological, autobiographical, and artist novels.

For example, the central distinction between the novel of adventure and the apprenticeship novel is conceptually clarified in the difference between the notions of being and becoming. Erich Jenisch argues that the novel of adventure experiences life as an existence, "ein Sein," whereas the apprenticeship novel portrays it as a development, "ein Werden." The concept of life as a succession of disconnected moments, which further identifies the novel of adventure, contrasts sharply with the view in the apprenticeship novel of life as a series of interconnected links in a chain. The one implies chance, "Zufall"; the other, arrangement, "Ordnung."

For Jenisch the chief cause of these differences resides in the nature of the novel of adventure, to which the "notion of character," seems utterly foreign. The character of the hero remains throughout unaltered: he is "the same at the outset and at the end of the novel." His quixotic life indeed recognizes no goal. He asks not for life's meaning in the moment, but for his own gain.[6]

In essence, E. L. Stahl reiterates Jenisch's distinction between the two types. He sees the idea of becoming permeating the apprenticeship novel to the extent that it portrays itself in stages, "Etappen," in the hero's development, unfolding his life from infancy to maturity "until that form is attained which the author intends." The apprenticeship novel, he insists, must presuppose as fundamental, "als Grundlegendes," the idea of becoming, both in a definite sense and with a definite goal in mind. It is not "static" but "dynamic." Its interest lies primarily in "descent, birth, change, metamorphosis, development."[7]

And in a similar manner François Jost concludes that the apprentice, unlike the adventurer, profits from the lessons of the world. From the beginning of the novel he has changed into a different entity by the end. In "the novel of adventure the events test and age the hero." But in the apprenticeship novel events mark the hero, defintively forming and crystallizing his character: "the confrontation of the hero with his environment--that is the Goethean culture principle."[8]

Literary critics often blur or ignore the distinction between the novel of adventure and the more specialized picaresque novel, for the latter constitutes but a subtype of the former.[9] The picaresque novel, however, warrants differentiation from the apprenticeship novel on separate grounds. H. L. Yelland's Handbook of Literary Terms applies the label "picaresque" to two separate types of the novel. The word itself derives etymologically from the Spanish term "picaro," meaning rogue. Originally it designated "a novel in which a character, picturesque though villainous, describes his experiences as a social parasite, satirizing the society which he depicts, e.g., the French Gil Blas." A wider usage of the term, however, regards as picaresque a novel whose events "revolve around a single character" and which freely develops "with the telling of his adventures," e.g., the English Tom Jones. The protagonist provides both the center of interest and the mainstay of the plot.[10]

In both types of the novel to which the term picaresque applies, even when the interest focuses principally on the hero, the background against which the hero moves--including satire, characters of low life, and "social parasites"--commands primary attention; and the hero's secondary function as an objective observer either subordinates or ignores his subjective experience as a tertiary concern. As Jost observes, the novel whose hero does not develop at all--"a psychologically indolent, static hero, as it were"--is rare. Nevertheless, the picaresque novel belongs singularly within this category. "Le roman picaresque," which the Germans designate as "der Schelmenroman" and whose events exercise no actual control over the souls of its characters, appears at the "antipodes" of the apprenticeship novel.[11]

Werner Freiderich in his Outline of Comparative Literature also distinguishes these two types judging from the active or passive function of the hero. The German apprenticeship novel, we are told, because of its lyrical subjectivity, "violates the supposedly objective and epic character of the average novel and does not delineate a broad canvas of human society with the hero serving merely as an observer of that society as we find, for example, in the Spanish picaresque novel."[12] Thus, regardless of whether the interest of the picaresque novel centers on the protagonist or on the society which he or she depicts, the same argument that isolates the apprenticeship novel from the novel of adventure serves also to distinguish it sufficiently from the picaresque novel. The concepts of being and becoming again characterize the picaro and the apprentice, respectively.

As noted above, the apprenticeship and the sentimental novels share a "focus on inner life." But these two types differ in the nature of their subjectivity. The sentimental novel centers on self-revelation in contrast to the apprenticeship novel's focus on self-development or, as Jost describes it, "the how and the why of a development."[13] Certainly, moments of revelation, similar to James Joyce's "epiphanies," quicken the awareness and change the attitudes of the apprentice as he grows into an expanded and deeper consciousness of human experience. "Exquisite pauses in time," as Pater defined such moments, designate definite phases in the apprentice's increased awareness of living. But these moments of revelation represent only the progressive achievements of a process of culture, and in the apprenticeship novel the process attracts more attention than do the special products of the process. Jost contends that the apprenticeship novel, from a perspective of becoming, comprises essentially "the account of an evolution, of a gradual development or, as the Germans love to say, of a 'Werdegang.'" The apprentice is judged, not according to "his actions"--a judgment that necessitates in the sentimental novel an apology for his life--but according to "his intention" of utilizing events to further his progress toward some lofty "ideal of perfection." Thus he cannot bear responsibility for the validity of his self-revelations as the sentimental hero must.[14] The focus of the apprenticeship novel, as opposed to the novel of sentiment, concerns itself not with the what of self-revelation but with the how and the why of self-development.

Literary critics have sporadically employed the term "educational novel" as an all-embracing English translation of the two specialized German terms: "Erziehungsroman" (educational novel) and "Bildungsroman" (apprenticeship novel). Fewer critics have gone so far as to include as an equivalent the novel of development or psychological novel, the "Entwicklungsroman." Gero von Wilpert in his Sachwörterbuch der Literatur (Encyclopedia of Literature) accurately characterizes the boundaries that delimit these three types of the novel as "fluid." In practice, he admits, they frequently coalesce. It is the German passion for categories, which Wilpert ultimately reflects in his own endeavor to distinguish the apprenticeship novel from the novel of development, that here demands precise differentiation.[15] E. L. Stahl insists that these two types warrant separation not only from the novel of education but also from each other,[16] unlike Shipley, whose English approach in his Dictionary of World Literary Terms, defines the apprenticeship form simply as an "educational novel."[17]

A preference for either stance, to my mind, will not alter the functional validity of both the German and the English attempts at literary definition. A consideration of several essentially German distinctions may prove useful; but I do not regard the English attempt at inclusiveness as absolutely comprehensive any more than I consider the Teutonic delimitations inviolable. The problem here of definition, as Helmut Germer points out, originates in part from an early vagueness by German critics themselves. "The German novel of the late eighteenth century," he contends, "in spite of the excellent models of Wieland, Heinse and Goethe and the treatises on the genre by Blankenburg, Sulzer, Adelung and J. J. Engel, was not a clearly defined genre." He cites the popular Journal der Romane (Journal of Novels) as one example of critical laxity, for although purporting to publish novels, "Romane," it printed all fiction whether long or short, narrative or poetry.[18]

Germer's dissertation itself represents a recent German endeavor to delimit conclusively within a restricted historical period (1792-1805) the type of genre that he terms "The German Novel of Education,"[19] which Henrich Meyer makes it a point to qualify even more definitively "as 'Erziehungsroman' [educational novel] and not 'Bildungsroman' [apprenticeship novel]."[20] One of the earliest German attempts to draw this boundary clearly was made by Nicolas Tetens in 1777. Distinguishing "culture" or "natural development" from "education" or "artificial academic development," he sought to separate developmental from pedagogic influences.[21] Compare Heinrich Pestalozzi's distinction between the product of culture, as influenced by accidental situations and events, and the product of education, as influenced by man's moral will.[22]

Granted that both types, the apprenticeship and the educational novels, present the development, or "Werdegang," of a hero "from childhood through life to maturity," a further distinction by Stahl contends that in the novel of education one or more teachers directly guide the maturing youth. But in the apprenticeship novel, as also in the novel of development, the whole world with all its manifold influences serves as a surrogate guide.[23] The idea of the world as environment, "Umgebung"--including human educators--characterizes the expanded range of influences that from one perspective isolates the apprenticeship novel from the novel of education. Also concerned with education, it assures that its hero nevertheless "learns from life as a whole."[24]

These German characterizations of the novel of education as distinct from the apprenticeship novel agree fundamentally with Jost's conception, which further posits a basic difference. The hero of the novel of education submits to "the influence of a tutor, of a school, of a force, if not an exterior constraint, artificially instituted with a view to attaining a result."[25] Such a formation as a matter of willful, external, and often moral, purpose identifies the novel of education.[26] Admittedly, formation in the apprenticeship novel also becomes a matter of purpose. However, the hero of this type of novel in his "natural habitat," as Jost describes him, educates himself. He "strives for a goal that he glimpses or that he has assigned himself and, in so doing, forms himself." The reader construes purpose here as internal. Jost even suggests the term "novel of self-education," "Selbsterziehungsroman," as a more appropriate synonym for apprenticeship novel, to distinguish it clearly in the above perspective from the novel of education. From the view of literary history, therefore, he redefines the apprenticeship novel as "the literary expression of a new ideal of education," discerning at the center of this ideal the impression that a youth must form himself, rather than submit to formation: "instead of educating a child, it is necessary to allow him to educate himself."[27]

Self-formation against a background of all the influences that the world can offer, therefore, identifies the apprenticeship novel. Indeed, Hermann Weigand regards as crucial the concept of self-formation, which pervades his analysis of Thomas Mann's twentieth-century apprentice Hans Castorp. The hero of Mann's Zauberberg (Magic Mountain) "develops, not according to the lines of a pattern imposed from without, but according to an inner law of his own personality that becomes manifest by degrees." Weigand concludes that "we are in reality dealing, then, with a novel of self-development rather than a pedagogical novel."[28]

Although literary critics regard the attempt to isolate the novel of education from the apprenticeship novel as more readily defensible than an endeavor to distinguish the latter from the novel of development, Stahl's demand for just such a distinction finds support among English as well as German scholars.[29] Mario Pei and Frank Gaynor in the Liberal Arts Dictionary define development, "Entwicklung," in terms of "evolution" as a "process of change" or a "development of growth involving continuity."[30] This development, however, characterizes not only "Entwicklung" but also "Bildung." In a dissertation on the modern German apprenticeship novel Berta Berger has endeavored to isolate the distinguishing features of the two processes. She draws a serviceable boundary between the psychic and the organic goals of culture, "Bildung," and development, "Entwicklung," respectively. And in support of her argument she points out that "culture is the fulfillment of a psychic challenge; development, the maturation of innate attributes."[31] But since the goals in question exist inherently in the processes of psychic fulfillment and organic maturation themselves, her distinction may prove unserviceable, even deceptive, to the author or reader whose primarily psychological interests may embrace equally the organic process of development and the psychic process of culture.

Therefore, a further distinction may be needed to clearly separate the unilateral interest in psychology of the novel of development from the psychological interest in formation of the apprenticeship novel. Susanne Howe provides the framework for such a distinction in her remark that the novel of development, although more general in scope, "does not presuppose the more or less conscious attempt on the part of the hero to integrate his powers, to cultivate himself by his experience, which is essential to the 'apprenticeship novel.'"[32] The central character of the novel of development, or psychological novel, evolves unconsciously, whereas the protagonist of the apprenticeship novel matures in full awareness of his formation. With an eye to the hero's perspective, therefore, we may agree with Stahl that the focal character in a "course of development," even though his organic goal results from the mere ripening of his inborn attributes, contrasts with the principle character in a "process of culture." The student of development does not have a conscious psychic goal to inspire its continuation, as does the apprentice to culture. In suggesting this dissimilarity Stahl argues that "the goal of culture always lies before the evolutionary process; the results of development, on the other hand, are continually present, always stages along the completed way, never however the characteristically typical goal of culture."[33] When development, "Entwicklung," assumes a typical goal, it becomes formation, "Bildung"; and accordingly, the hero becomes a form, a "Gestalt."

The conscious intent of the process found in the apprenticeship novel and the unconscious result of the process found in the novel of development, therefore, constitute a major distinction between the two types, hinging entirely on the presence or the absence of a goal in the hero. Further differentiations should serve to clarify the nature of this goal as it exists in the apprenticeship novel. Wilpert, for example, regards as psychic not only the formational process of the apprenticeship novel but also the goal itself. The novel of development, he suggests, focuses on the processes of personality and character development in the course of the hero's life. On the other hand the apprenticeship novel dwells not only on the influence of objective cultural values and personal surroundings upon the hero's psychic maturation but also on the harmonious evolution of his psychic tendencies toward a total personality, "Gesamtspersönlichkeit."[34] The goal of culture, then--in contrast to the results of development--is a multifarious personality.[35] Hans Wagner appropriately considers this distinction in his dissertation on the English apprenticeship novel when he observes, "The goal is an allround cultivation and not the alignment with a narrowly defined result."[36]

One final difference between the apprenticeship novel and the novel of development springs from the hero's capacity or incapacity to achieve his goal before death. In the former type he rarely dies;[37] not so in the latter. As Stahl describes: "In the novel of development the narrative proceeds up to an end caused by death. The apprenticeship novel, on the contrary, usually leaves off before the hero's death, because the goal of culture can be attained early in life."[38] From one perspective the reader must view the goal of culture as without end. From the hero's perspective, for instance, Wagner suggests that culture constitutes a problem because the hero, forever unable to attain the goal of the ideal, must strive as long as he lives.[39] But within the purview of the apprenticeship novel, which breaks off at a certain stage in its hero's self-formation, the novelist has indeed achieved his own goal. His hero appears, as Jost affirms, "armed for life." Judged at the novel's end as "prepared to live,"[40] as no longer an apprentice, he new prepares to serve with great caution as a master.

To summarize these many distinctions between the apprenticeship novel and its closest related types, the novels of education and of development, Christine Touaillon offers a most incisive as well as succinct definition of the apprenticeship novel in the 1925-26 edition of the German Reallexikon. Stressing the protagonist's mental, spiritual, and emotional development, she defines the apprenticeship novel as a "novel that describes the psychic development of an individual from the beginning up to the attainment of a definite life-form."[41] Centering attention on the two types most closely related to the apprenticeship novel, she then proceeds to separate the novel of education, which, she maintains, emphasizes pedagogic training rather than organic development according to inner capacity, from the novel of development, which manifests unilateral interest in psychology rather than in conscious, harmonious self-formation. Her distinctions, like those above, can be viewed as fundamentally useful both for the questions they inspire and for their help in clarifying themes within the particular types considered.

It remains for us now to examine two additional types that often share close association, if not equation, with the apprenticeship novel. Beginning with the autobiography, the "Selbstbiographie," one characteristic differentiates both it and the apprenticeship novel from the novel of development, as discussed above. Jost argues that both types exclude "death as a solution to the plot";[42] for both, he demonstrates with the intention of formulating an appropriate term, must present an "open end."[43]

The open-ended conclusion, however, comprises only one of numerous characteristics relating the apprenticeship novel to the autobiography. Wilhelm Dilthey, while acknowledging the similarities between the two types, liberates the apprenticeship form from a restriction characteristic of the autobiography. In the apprenticeship novel we witness the apprentice transcend his particular individuality to achieve universality. Dilthey observes that this type of novel, unlike the self-biography, "consciously and artistically presents the universal human in a life's course." It visualizes a regular development in an individual, whose every step has actual inherent value and simultaneously constitutes the foundation of a higher step. The apprenticeship novel as a whole, he concludes, presents the path toward personality as the final form of human existence.[44]

His distinction between the universal focus of the apprenticeship novel and the particular focus of the autobiography is reflected also in Borcherdt's argument. The quality most clearly distinguishing the former from the latter, Borcherdt asserts, "is the elevation of the path and the goal of culture to the highest awareness, the personal experience in the universally human. Thereby," he concludes, "the individual becomes a type and the event becomes a symbol."[45] This gradation of successive stages or steps in the course of a protagonist's self-formation serves basically to elevate the apprenticeship novel above the auctorial level of pure self-expression. The gradation approaches biography but of a universal type, in this case not of the author, but of the apprentice.

Often emerging as a specialized subdivision of autobiography or, more generally, biography is the artist novel, or "Künstlerroman."[46] Friederich describes the artist novel as one in which the poet is constantly preoccupied with himself: "the author analyzes his own delicate self and his attitude towards and aloofness from a crude world beyond the realm of his thoughts."[47] Seeking to achieve an aesthetic ideal, he struggles against an uncompromising and materialistic society. He must choose between withdrawal into a contemplative, artificial, uncontaminated ivory-tower existence or engagement in the social struggles within the world of his time. In either case, he generally considers himself indifferent to a reconciliation with reality, so that, as Fritz Martini maintains, his own formation or cultivation remains predominately aesthetic.[48]

Contributing to the list of many incontestable similarities between the artist novel and the apprenticeship novel, Susanne Howe views the formation of the apprentice in terms ordinarily associated with the molding of an artist. She attributes to the apprenticeship novel in particular "the idea that living is an art which may be learned" by an apprentice willing to pass through stages until he becomes a master or, analogically speaking, an accomplished artist.[49]

Such a view of life as an art, with its apprentice an artist, is an attractive analogy, but when viewed more closely, the analogy breaks down. The goals of the artist and the apprentice diverge significantly. In Borcherdt's view the artist of the artist novel may strive for "aesthetic culture," but the apprentice must thoroughly educate, not one, but all his "talents and powers." The apprentice strives initially for organic, ethical, and aesthetic development, but through a growing recognition of the discrepancy between the ideal and life he also earnestly strives to effect "a reconciliation with reality."[50] And the search for reconciliation is what distinguishes him from the artist. Both may appear to share the goal of an aesthetic development, but for the apprentice, art constitutes only a means toward the unfolding of his personality, not an end. "His goal is not art," Borcherdt asserts with reference to Wilhelm Meister's progress from the Sendung (Mission) to the Apprenticeship, "but man." From the artist develops the man: "From the artist, who views the creation of aesthetic value as a duty, emerges the man, who yearns to fashion himself into a completed personality." The artist, seeking to acquaint himself with the various forms of his art, contrasts with the apprentice, who strives for "the development of his individuality," so that art for the latter is only a means of formation, "nur Bildungsmittel," and often--as in the case of Wilhelm Meister--the wrong path to his talent, "Irrweg seiner Veranlagung."[51] This concept of art as a partial means to a comprehensive end, rather than an aesthetic and self-contained objective, suffices to divorce the apprenticeship novel from the artist novel. The comprehensive aim of culture appertains indeed to a multilateral personality.

Such a separation of the apprenticeship novel from the artist novel according to the differences in their foci avails not only to distinguish but also to clarify these two types. Jost, referring to the artist novel as the "roman d'artist," asserts that this considered type of the novel focuses on "the personality, the profession of the hero" but not, as does the apprenticeship novel, on the organization of the plot."[52] As in the contrast with autobiography, the same distinction here also applies, for a gradation of successive stages or steps characterizes the process and hence the plot of the apprenticeship novel.[53]

In concluding the present chapter, I am bound to point out that while the apprenticeship novel may differ significantly--indeed without need here of articulating the differences--from many unrelated types, such as the historical, the Gothic, or the sociological novel, it makes use of these types as well. There are historical references, Gothic scenes, proletarian themes, etc., in many of its representatives. But what it shares with any one of these unrelated or kindred types--the novel of adventure, the picaresque, sentimental, or pedagogical novel, the novel of development, autobiography, or the artist novel--is what frequently separates it and its sole companion from all the others, with the result that its existence as a synthesis of all these shared traits is what makes it unique. This unique combination, along with some traits that it claims alone, serves to identify its type, as we shall see in the next chapter concerning what in fact it does claim as its own.

3. FUNDAMENTAL PRINCIPLES

In attempting to clarify the term "apprenticeship novel" and to relate this type of novel to, as well as distinguish it from, several commonly recognized kindred types, the ultimate focus of the previous chapters has been on the present one, which will endeavor to formulate a serviceable description of the apprenticeship type in isolation. Such a description can be seen to emerge from an analysis of four basic principles that give the regulative concept its essential properties: the apprenticeship or formation itself, the nature of this apprenticeship, its pattern or phases, and its goal. The subsequent chapter may then provide a selective survey of apprenticeship novels that embody the potentialities herein described.

To begin with, an apprenticeship itself, not to a particular art, trade, or calling in a technical sense but rather to life, presupposes both "the idea that living is an art which may be learned" and the belief that a young person can become adept in the art of life by passing through its stages "until at last he becomes a 'Master.'" Susanne Howe credits these two doctrines with having inspired both the name and the story of Goethe's hero, Wilhelm Meister.[1] Indeed, the concept of "Wilhelm Lehrling" (William apprentice) ultimately presages a "Wilhelm Meister" (William master).[2] But, this final concern with mastership notwithstanding, the apprenticeship novel restricts its scope to the duration solely of the apprenticeship.

One presupposition of the type entails the key notion of choice. Directing attention to Wilhelm Meister's own words in the novel's concluding statement, François Jost argues that the *Apprenticeship* presents to the reader an individual who, "by his own choice and by his own effort" attains a happiness that he "would not change with anything in life." The notion of choice is a key concept "not only with Goethe, but it appears to a certain degree in every apprenticeship novel."[3] Even when powerful influences would seem to predetermine his choice, the apprentice nonetheless assumes the freedom to pursue his preference.

Serving as a minimal antecedent to the presumptuous notion of mastership, the apprenticeship also presupposes that its candidate must initially embody the potential for, or capability of, becoming a master. He now must incorporate the latent possibility of emerging as, if not a genius, then at the least an exceptional individual.

Hans Castorp expresses in Thomas Mann's *Magic Mountain* a clear awareness of this latent prerequisite. Ironically denying his existence as a "man of genius," he nevertheless affirms his faith in the ascending stages of transsubstantiation or "Steigerung" that characterize his theory of alchemistic-hermetic pedagogy. He reminds Clawdia Chauchat, "But of course matter that is capable of taking those ascending stages by dint of outward pressure must have a little something in itself to start with."[4]

It should be noted that the inherent qualities that render a particular individual capable of ascending these stages toward complete formation do not necessarily constitute in themselves transcendent genius.[5] The supreme goal of culture, as Hermann Weigand suggests, "finds its realization only in so far as it calls into play the totality of man's faculties in his every act of assimilating the sense data of experience."[6] Such a goal, in whatever supreme degree it may find realization, remains nevertheless a human end toward which any human being may aspire. "A man asks himself," Goethe entreats, "to what is he best suited? in order to develop this zealously in himself; he sees himself as apprentice, as journeyman, as assistant, at the latest and with utmost caution as master."[7]

The exceptional individual, in accord with Goethe's description, develops himself zealously for the life that conforms to his exceptional endowments. And occupation notwithstanding, only the individual who would claim adaptability solely to death could fail to qualify for an apprenticeship to life. Each human being carries within himself the potential for development as a unique, and hence exceptional, individual. Whether he aspires to realize his potentialities invites, of course, a vital but separate concern.[8] The apprenticeship novel presupposes only the existence of universal potentialities in its own apprentice, who, more importantly, demonstrates aspiration as well.

In such an optimistic vein I should cite Weigand's remark pertinent to the basic stance of the apprenticeship novel: "The keynote of the true 'Bildungsroman' is an affirmative attitude toward life as a whole."[9] This attitude constitutes one of the most attractive aspects of the apprenticeship, and it may also account for the essential aspiration noted above.

Turning now to the essential nature of the apprenticeship, the abstract notion of an apprenticeship in isolation can be more clearly concretized through a summary of its distinguishing qualities. Such a summary emerges from the previous chapter through its juxtaposition of the apprenticeship novel with kindred types. It should be noted and stressed, however, that salient features gleaned from an admittedly select group of contrasts cannot presume to define conclusively a particular type of novel. At the least it can and does adumbrate, with a purposeful avoidance of distinct precision, the partial and hence evocative outline of a regulative notion which may serve, with individual modifications, as an apprenticeship type.

With our intent thus qualified, an itemized checklist of several distinguishing traits should prove helpful in suggesting concrete potentialities within the apprenticeship novel, as follows:

1. a tendency toward the inner life
2. a striving for "savoir vivre," or knowledge of the world
3. a critical view of the world
4. the presentation of an individual development
5. a variegated description of life and the world
6. an individual's confrontation with his environment
7. a view of life as an evolution
8. the presupposition of a definite attainable goal
9. the presentation of an individual who profits from the

lessons of the world
10. a focus on the how and why of the process of development
11. an obligatory acknowledgment of both human and natural influences
12. a self-formation according to internal purpose
13. a consciousness in the attempt to achieve a recognizable typical goal
14. a harmonious cultivation of a multifarious personality
15. the attainment of the goal of formation prior to death
16. a recognition of the goal of formation as open ended[10]
17. an organic development according to inner capacity
18. a presentation of the universal within the process of a particular human life
19. the portrayal of a gradation of successive stages or steps in the course of a human life
20. a striving for organic, ethical, and aesthetic formation accompanied by an attempt to reconcile oneself with reality
21. the view of art solely as a partial means toward the unfolding of personality
22. an archetypal conception of Man as the ultimate goal
23. a special attention to the organization of the process and plot of the novel

To this list of concrete features can be added the five presuppositions noted at the outset of this chapter:

1. the idea that living is an art which the apprentice may learn
2. the belief that a young person can become adept in the art of life and become a master
3. the key notion of choice
4. the prerequisite of potential for development into a master
5. an affirmative attitude toward life as a whole

Several additional qualities that may be seen to augment the above checklists, if only to emphasize that no list should preclude supplementation, entail themes that frequently emerge from critical studies of the apprenticeship novel, for instance:

1. mastery of circumstances
2. self-reliance
3. earnest, purposeful activity as opposed to dilettantism
4. an insatiable yearning and striving for life's meaning
5. a deepening consciousness of human experience
6. a release from bondage to false ideals
7. self-expression
8. a continuous trial-and-error development of the natural gifts incipient in man's essence--in the

sense, for example, of Pindar's noted dictum urging, "Become the one you are."

Countless other themes apply, of course, but these few recur continually in critical studies of the type.

The recognition that these innate qualities of the apprenticeship novel often exist only in potentiality should forestall their misconstruction as normative prescriptions. But the conversion of these inherent qualities into formal existence has, in fact, set historical precedence in a variety of realized combinations subsequently qualifying as apprenticeship novels. Necessarily, the modified nature of each particular product must be acknowledged as unique, for only by virtue of its power of modification can a novel be said to preserve its individuality, even as it stands under the single and purely functional rubric, in this case, of apprenticeship novel.

If such, then, is the nature of the apprenticeship type, a focus on the phases of development within the type is of concern preliminary to arriving at a reasonably inclusive definition. Howe in "the barest possible outline" of the apprenticeship pattern delineates the path that Borcherdt chooses to call the way of cultivation, the "Bildungsweg." According to Howe, the adolescent apprentice on the path to self-formation

> sets out on his way through the world, meets with reverses usually due to his own temperament, falls in with various guides and counsellors, makes many false starts in choosing his friends, his wife, and his life work, and finally adjusts himself in some way to the demands of his time and environment by finding a sphere of action in which he may work effectively.[11]

This pattern, as Howe describes it, exists quiescently in any apprenticeship novel. But the vital issue of self-formation or self-adjustment within the pattern poses a notable problem. If indeed the formation generates itself, then the hero must be termed an active agent of his own development. On the other hand, if his development arises wholly from outer-inducement, then he falls before the charge of a dangerous passivity. Heinrich Keiter and Tony Kellen clearly imply the passivity of such a drifter's struggle within life's briny flood:

> The hero swims midway in the sea of life, frequently in danger of being swallowed up by the waves, often gently wafted by them. So powerful influences not infrequently affect him in his life, force him back, toss him, until he is no longer fully conscious of his intention, or in a totally different way, until he comes at last to a clear insight into his destiny.[12]

The hero of this pattern of apprenticeship surfaces as no hero at all but rather an auspicious recipient of good fortune. When we acknowledge the predominant role played by the sea of influences in determining his path toward cultivation, even the realized goal, as

Wilhelm Meister ultimately conceives it, appears gratuitously and adventitiously bestowed.

On the other hand, if sufficient stress is laid on the role of the swimmer in his essentially individual act of swimming, then the notion of formation extends to embrace an active, albeit passive, idea. E. L. Stahl highlights the active nature of the apprentice's role through an analogy that serves to supplant the swimmer in the ocean with the clay in a potter's hand. The apprenticeship novel "treats man as a creature, on whom the forces of the world have an effect, like the clay that lies in the potter's hand, not [and here is Stahl's essential point] like a purely passive thing allowing itself to be molded, but rather bringing with it into the world very definite active powers, upon which those external forces now act."[13] And yet on closer scrutiny the swimmer, better than the clay, would appear as the proper analogy, for it more accurately and graphically conveys the notion of an active strength contributed by the apprentice to his own progress in his apprenticeship.

The idea of definite phases or of a specific sequence of stages in a hero's development exists potentially in every pattern of apprenticeship. Wilhelm Dilthey calls these stages "Stufen" or steps. He defines the common pattern of the apprenticeship novel, supported by examples from Goethe to Hölderlin, as the representation of a young man of a definite time who

> enters life in fortunate twilight, searches for kindred souls, encounters friendship and love, . . . falls into conflict with the harsh realities of the world [Note Borcherdt's rejection of "conflict" in his treatment of the pattern below, p. 21.] and so grows to maturity through diverse experiences of life, finds himself, and becomes assured of his duty in the world.[14]

According to this delineation of the pattern, the apprentice develops in conformity with a pre-determined sequence of natural laws, that is, in definite stages: "A regular development is contemplated in the life of the individual; each of its stages has a characteristic value and is at the same time the foundation of a higher stage." The discords and conflicts of life, moreover, "appear as the indispensable gates of passage for the individual on his way toward maturity and harmony."[15]

Dilthey's conception of the individual's conflicts with harsh reality constituting indispensable phases of transition toward eventual maturity and harmony finds a fellow advocate in Jost. Jost posits an essential world-individual confrontation that effects the hero's transformation: "Always the apprenticeship novel presents a certain free play of antagonistic forces, the world and individuality, the latter, in the course of the confrontation, becoming a personality, a term that implicates a moral character." Jost adds by way of clarification that this transformation, as explained by Goethe, results from cultivation.[16]

Both Dilthey's and Jost's descriptions of the apprenticeship pattern conflict, however, with Borcherdt's. Borcherdt charges that Dilthey limits the concept of the apprenticeship novel to representatives of the

the type in the time of Goethe. The dual emphasis on "development in precise conformity [with] fixed stages of deployment" and on "direction toward a clearly outlined goal, which is presented as the ideal condition of the complete man," excludes from consideration, not only the novels of Wolfram, Grimmelshausen, and Wieland that preceded the age of Goethe, but also the works of Stifter, Keller, Raabe, Paul Ernst, Kolbenheyer, Hesse, and Mann that followed. Only in the golden age of Goethe, Borcherdt argues, did the concept of culture embrace conjointly both the goal of consummate humanitarianism, "vollendete Humanität," and the path to this goal. An enlargement of the field of vision, however, must necessarily lead to the conclusion "that Dilthey's definition and nomenclature appear too restricted." The novels of the later periods of the nineteenth century, while retaining the development of an individual as the object of fiction, have come to reveal instead "an assimilation of the individual into the community" or at least into an attitude of social consciousness. The goals of these later novels supersede the entirely too confined concept of culture in the period of Goethe as an expression of the personality's self-formation.

In his own alternative description of the apprenticeship's general pattern Borcherdt endeavors to separate the path not only from the goal but also from its artistic expression in phases. The goal or "Bildungsziel" relates to the pattern as a conclusion, an "Abschluß," only incidentally, for it changes "with the developmental phases of the history of ideas and with the particular author's worldview." In general it represents the complete unfolding of all man's natural talents. On the other hand, the path or "Bildungsweg" provides "the fixed line toward the goal and thereby the regularity of the development." It represents an apprentice's attempt to grasp the universe and thus attain a stage in his personal development. Within this concept of the path of culture as a principle of development, the world does not oppose the individual in a confrontation of I and world, "Ich und Welt," as Dilthey asserts, but rather serves as a school of life, "Schule des Lebens." The path of the individual follows a uniform pattern: "From error to truth, from confusion to clarity, from unconsciousness to consciousness."[17] Truth, clarity, and consciousness constitute the goal; error, confusion, and unawareness, the pattern or path to the goal.

The Goethe-Handbuch reinforces Borcherdt's insistence on development as social adjustment, instead of conflict, between the individual and the community. Regarding the goal of the apprenticeship novel the Handbook concludes, "It's theme is the cultivation of the self through the world; in the process of adjustment the hero becomes a microcosm."[18] Conceivably both views, the apprentice's confrontation with the world and his socialization into the world, could be said to coexist as potentialities within the general apprenticeship type. But in any case definite phases of development are seen to occur.

For instance, the artistic expression, the "künstlerische Form" of the apprenticeship pattern, as distinguished by Borcherdt from the pattern itself, normally unfolds in three phases: the years of youth, the "Jugendjahre," which from unawareness evolve toward consciousness; the years of travel, the "Wanderjahre," which comprise love, friendship, crises, and failures; and "the refinement and entrance into a terrestrial stage of paradise." The boundaries that separate the early years from the subsequent years of travel, and the travel years from the final years of refinement, generally come into focus only in retrospect "on the turning points or through reliance on memory."[19]

Borcherdt's discernment of these three phases in the apprenticeship's artistic expression closely resembles Joseph Shipley's delineation of phases in James Joyce's works. Shipley discovers epiphany in Goethe's Wilhelm Meister's Apprenticeship, which bears comparison with "stories of initiation, where the 'rite de passage' leads through the usual three stages (separation, isolation, aggregation) to a renewed communion with society on a higher and more thoroughly informed plane of living."[20]

Whether we see adjustment or conflict as the more common avenue of an apprentice's confrontation with the harsh realities of his environment, Dilthey's description of a regular development through stages, each possessing in itself intrinsic value even as it serves as the basis for a higher stage, remains a constant principle of the apprenticeship pattern. The number of stages depicted within any particular pattern varies, of course, as a matter of modified temporal choice. But the pattern itself is innately potential in the apprenticeship type.

Having established the nature and pattern of the hero's apprenticeship to life, it remains for us to characterize the end toward which that pattern is directed: its goal. Howe's general description of the apprenticeship form as the "novel of all-round development or self-culture"[21] defines the type in terms of the apprentice's objective. Self-culture or self-formation indeed permeates the apprenticeship novel as its primary recurrent theme. But just as Borcherdt has recognized the need to distinguish the path of the apprenticeship from its goal, we cannot afford to overlook two very different natures of the goal itself. A common conception frequently assumes that culture must suffice as its own end. Indeed, the history of this notion extends to the origins of Western thought. The simple Socratic maxim "Know thyself" initially proposed self-formation as a direct objective of the will. The Renaissance version of the same idea found expression in the goal of universal man, "uomo universale," requiring the development of all natural gifts to the highest level of excellence and their fusion into a work of art. The Renaissance insisted almost exclusively on the formation of the personality for its own sake.

The modern period has only altered the Renaissance objective of "uomo universale," substituting "bourgeios" for "universal." Thomas Mann depicts Goethe, himself the last universal man of modern times, as a revolutionary seeking to supplant the goal of the universal man with the modern bourgeois ideal. The bourgeois love of order, its value of personal productivity and practical achievement, and its devotion to professional duties reveal an attitude toward life that postulates as its objective: "being solidly planted in life." This goal formerly was restricted to the ranks of the nobility, who scorned not only the "universal man" with his yearning for the unattainable but also the "bourgeois" devotion to occupation. Mann, however, implies that Goethe, in replacing Renaissance "personality" by bourgeois "occupation," has sought to establish for all men, regardless of class, a new common goal, a new "uomo universale," the modern ideal: "The bourgeois, supra-bourgeois character." Characterizing this modern evolution of the universal out of the bourgeois, Mann summarizes: "the respectable, the bourgeois, as the home of the universally human; world fame as son of the bourgeois; this combination of the beginnings with the most surprising development is nowhere so much at home as with us."[22]

Mary Hatch's interpretation of the apprentice's goal as a bourgeois calling arises immediately from Mann's argument. She proposes essentially to equate "occupation and personality development."[23] Kenneth Rexroth reflects the same restricted view when he praises Goethe rather disparagingly as "the greatest poet of the business ethic," indeed "a self-made aristocrat and nobleman of the cloth, the hero of all German Burghers to come after him."[24]

All three conceptions of the goal--the Socratic "Know thyself," the Renaissance "uomo universale," and the modern bourgeois ideal--commonly assume that self-formation, whether defined as self-knowledge, development of the personality, or achievement of the occupational ideal, constitutes a willful objective of the individual.

In the apprenticeship novel, however, we would do well to forestall such an assumption. Ralph Waldo Emerson in his celebrated essay on "Self-reliance" clearly defines the nature of the proper goal. He draws the image of a ship that voyages in a zigzag line of a hundred tacks so as to establish its average tendency. For his purpose the analogy adequately depicts self-reliance, but it also clarifies the bilateral nature of the goal of an apprenticeship to life. The seemingly countless tacks that represent direct objectives of the apprentice are in retrospect subordinated to their collective drift, which can be seen to represent the indirect and ultimate objective of self-formation. "Bildung" or culture, therefore, does not comprise a self-contained end.

In this vein Max Scheler emphatically cautions, "Certain goals are reached only when one does <u>not willingly</u> intend them."[25] His insistence on the separation of volition from assured success does not preclude determination of purpose, but it does attempt to deny the possibility of self-formation as a direct objective of the will. In a discerning and penetrating address to the Lessing Institute of Berlin in 1925 Scheler forewarned his audience,

> Cultivation is <u>not</u> "desiring to make oneself a work of art," is <u>not</u> self-enamored intending of oneself, be it his beauty, his virtue, his form, or his knowledge. It is just the opposite of such intentional self-gratification, whose culmination is dandyism. Man <u>is</u> no work of art and <u>should</u> be no work of art! In the course of his life <u>in</u> the world, <u>with</u> the world; in the active conquest of its and his own passions or restraints; in love and deed, be it object related, be it brother related, be it government related; in hard work, which, yielding profits, intensifies, exalts, and expands the <u>powers and the self</u> . . . , the development of culture proceeds, occurs, behind the back of mere purpose

and of mere will. And only he who will lose himself in a noble cause or in some kind of true common interest--unafraid of what may happen to him--will reclaim himself, that is, his true self, reclaim it from within the godhead itself and the power and the purity of its breath.[26]

It can be seen, therefore, that the self cannot become the apprentice's direct goal, except as it is lost in the unexpected acquisition of a true self, an "echtes Selbst." But any objective involving the loss of self consequently negates the will, thus paradoxically denying itself as an objective. We must turn then to the indirect goal of the apprentice, which more appropriately identifies with culture or self-formation, since both it and culture represent by-products of the will turned toward something other than the self. Indeed, this something else becomes the direct goal of the apprentice.

W. H. Bruford in his article on Goethe's Wilhelm Meister further accentuates the indirect nature of an apprentice's ultimate goal: "The harmonious personality that the 'uomo universale' sought in self-cultivation is attained indirectly in work for something which is not the self, for culture, like happiness, comes to those who do not pursue it as an end in itself."[27] Goethe expresses the same idea as a loss of self in action on behalf of others;[28] and Roy Pascal follows Goethe's precedent in his own definition of the apprenticeship novel as "the story of the formation of a character up to the moment when he ceases to be self-centered and becomes society-centered, thus beginning to shape his true self."[29]

Recognizing self-formation as an indirect goal, we may turn again to the paradox of the hero's passivity. Quoting Goethe, Hermann Pongs formulates the motto of an indirectly achieved self-cultivation: "Make an agent of yourself!" Contrasting Goethe's hero with Wieland's Agathon, he notes that "Wilhelm does not actually form himself through culture; instead a kinetic adaptability develops, through which he becomes formed by life itself, owing to continual error throughout." Stumbling over endless mistakes, the apprentice confronts the elusive goal of culture less as an active contributor to his own formation than as an active recipient of his being formed by life. But, as Pongs points out, in order not to confuse this active passivity with the unaware passivity of the hero of the novel of development, we need be reminded of the apprentice's consciousness, which emerges as "the modern restriction against the encroachment of the novel of development, as the conscious process of self-cultivation through culture, until the hero arrives at a clear understanding of himself."[30] Such a process of self-formation through formation appears initially to constitute a pleonasm unless the objectives of the two separate processes are identified as the indirect and the direct goals, respectively.

Hermann Weigand designates both goals in the masterpieces of Goethe and Mann. The indirect objective in each work is a total integration of human experience, which evolves coincidentally from the apprentice's primary focus on conscious activities. Wilhelm Meister descries his direct goal as "a brilliant career on the stage," only to discover years later that he lacks the fundamental qualifications for success. Similarly, Hans Castorp sacrifices all prospects of a practical career to the direct "pursuit of a quixotic passion." Weigand concludes that "in each case, the by-product of these strivings, struggles, pursuits, and passions is something infinitely richer than the specific result coveted, altogether regardless of success or failure." He identifies this by-product or incidental yield as life-art, "Lebenskunst,"[31] otherwise known as self-formation.

Although broader in scope than all the direct goals contributing to its latent growth and eventual realization, the indirect goal of self-culture ultimately reveals its own innate limits. It is inherently restricted to the humanitarian concept of man. Arguing from the classical notion of formation, which the nineteenth century partially adopted as a philosophical humanitarian concept of culture, a "humanitätsphilosophische Bildungsidee," Berta Berger claims that in the 1700's God no longer served as the goal of culture.[32] The humanitarian idea of man as the measure of culture superseded the religious idea of culture, the "religiöse Bildungsidee," that had envisioned God or Christ as the archetype or model, as, for example, in the Christian concept of culture during the Middle Ages. "God is now no longer," Berger remarks with reference to the eighteenth century, "the archetype or model, but rather man, man who perfects all his individual talents in their totality through contact with his environment."[33] The indirect goal, as Keiter and Kellen note in their depiction of the hero of the apprenticeship novel, "is ultimately always humanitarianism." The true apprentice "has usually already become at the conclusion of his apprenticeship a man."[34]

Within the limits set by the objective of forming a man, then, the ancient dictum "Know thyself" essentially retains its relevance despite this shift in focus from direction to indirection in the individual's goal. Even though indirectly achieved, self-realization remains innately confined to the self. Not even knowledge of the world can encroach on the priority given to self as the ultimate goal. "More important than the world itself," Jost affirms in describing the realized goal of Wilhelm Meister, the apprentice "recognizes his place in the world; he begins to distinguish, to be able to define this man who is himself." To achieve the goal of culture, therefore, is to "know thyself," while "to understand the world is given to us in addition."[35] The gift of understanding the world, an unexpected bonus, accrues from a typical phenomenon that Howe describes as the apprentice's growth into "an expanding and deepening consciousness of human experience, an increased awareness of living."[36]

From one perspective the goal of self-realization represents a reach that certainly transcends the humanly limited grasp of its aspirant. Consider, for example, as Jost proposes, the analogue of Dante's Purgatorio, in which the individual who himself is destined "to become realized must pass through his childhood and his adolescence." An individual's purgatory implies in a similar sense an ascent "toward an ideal, whatever it be," which prevails upon the apprentice "to exalt himself to the stars." His ethereal aspiration represents "the very quintessence of the apprenticeship novel." However, the apprentice's purgatory must be seen as no more than "a catharsis" that restricts the goal to man himself as the optimum surrogate for God. The Eden created by the catharsis thus remains a singularly human paradise.[37]

From a strictly practical point of view the universal goal of self-cultivation must be viewed as indirect because its attainment cannot be limited to one side of an all-round formation. It entails instead a multivariety of direct goals, each of which participates only obliquely in the general tendency of the self-forming whole. Wagner characterizes such an objective as "an all-round culture and not the alignment with a narrowly defined result."[38] Considered separately from its partial contribution to the whole, any direct alignment with a narrowly circumscribed objective proves inadequate in and of itself. The hero of an apprenticeship novel, as Christine Touaillon suggests, "should not be reared unilaterally for a limited purpose, but rather formed universally, and the great life forces should contribute to this formation."[39]

Both inner and outer natures cooperate to assist the apprentice toward his all-encompassing ideal. The limited aims that attract his immediate attention often betray the composition date of the novel in which he appears. The apprenticeship novel, as Touaillon explains, "shows quite clearly in all of its stages the ideals of the era that produced it." In particular she enumerates several of these ideals:

> By turns [the apprenticeship novel] will rear its hero to become a Christian, a blithe spirit, an artist, a harmonious human being, and an inwardly autonomous individual. It is a far-reaching type, having within its limits a great deal of room . . . the incidents are inner and outer nature.[40]

Its direct aims may alter with time or even within the particular work of an era, but the indirect goal of a multifarious self-cultivation exists potentially as well as universally in the apprenticeship type as a whole.

The absolute comprehensiveness of this ultimate goal should preclude its misconception as a possible objective of the apprentice himself. As Borcherdt reminds us, the ultimate aim is "Perfection of all man's talents and powers to a complete whole, to a microcosm as mirror of the macrocosm."[41] Such a universal perfection can find its potential realization in an apprentice only as the emergent by-product of his limited perspective and active will. Hermann Weigand, as noted above, regards this goal of culture as the supreme concern of Mann's _Magic Mountain_: here the ideal "finds its realization only in so far as it calls into play the totality of man's faculties in his every act of assimilating the sense date of experience." And this "Erlebnis," this integration of experience, cannot relate directly to the process of culture except as the culminating achievement marking the completion of the process. The apprentice realizes his ultimate goal, the formation of himself, when he at last renounces all conceivable direct aims as not in themselves ultimate or self-contained.[42]

This idea of an indirectly achieved self-formation points up an all important paradox: the innate necessity for striving renders a standstill in the lifetime process of culture impossible. Wagner expressly counsels that any suspension of forward pressure can only signify retrogression in the process:

> Culture is a duty, whose ideal goal can never be attained

> unless it is constantly pursued. For a standstill here means a step back. Development, culture is a striving forward, a search for knowledge and perfection, which, for those who strive assiduously, always continues like life itself.[43]

This open-ended nature of the goal explains why the conclusions of the various apprenticeship novels considered by Howe in her survey of the type in England are "as diverse as the personalities and careers of the different authors themselves. They vary from marriage to the proper woman and settling on an ancestral estate to a career of public service as a member of Parliament, a doctor, a reformer, or a writer. But even "when the hero settles down to his vocation, we get no sense of smug completeness. None of them has solved the problem."[44] The novel, of course, must end. But though it breaks off, the apprentice persists in striving for his ideal, that is, his most recently adopted direct goal.

Heinrich Meyer attributes the open end of the apprenticeship novel to the limited perspective of the author himself. Out of this natural limitation arises one of the most obvious differences between the apprenticeship novel and the novel of education. For whereas the former "reflects the present state of an author's self-knowledge and therefore has no clear ending that must result from the antecedents," the novel of education "has" such an end.[45] Meyer tends to equate the apprenticeship novel with autobiography, but in both types he expresses awareness of the open end.

At this point we are confronted with a further but final paradox, namely, an indirectly attained goal at the conclusion of an open-ended novel. A solution, of course, exists potentially in the cyclic conception of the ending as a beginning. Within this notion the apprenticeship novel emerges not as a standard novel at all but as a forenovel. "In a sense," as Jost depicts it, "the apprenticeship novel is only a sort of pre-novel, or preamble. Indeed, at the conclusion of the work the hero appears to us armed for life, ready to live his novel."[46] He disappears from the book's view, a quiescent master in the art of forming his own life. His human existence, like the shape of the novel that represents his life, is, in M. H. Abrams' estimation, "circuitous yet open-ended." It "will go on after the novel ends, to a succeeding stage which will incorporate all that he has experienced before."[47] Irrespective of his future, however, the apprentice may estimate himself at the novel's end, even as Goethe guardedly concludes, "at the last moment and with utmost caution as master."[48]

4. CONCRETE REPRESENTATIVES

Credit for having written "the seminal instance" of the apprenticeship novel belongs to Goethe,[1] whose Wilhelm Meister's Apprenticeship has been variously designated "le prototype," "the archetype," "den Urtyp," etc., of a novel that it shaped and established, if not wholly invented.[2] But as Susanne Howe cautions, the apprenticeship novel was "in no sense a German invention, but a German reshaping of eighteenth-century ideas current in Europe . . . into a fiction form particularly congenial to German taste. Nor was it a form original with Goethe in Germany . . . , but with Goethe this idea of 'cultivation' took an especially comprehensive sweep."[3] The original form, the first German apprenticeship novel, which indeed influenced Goethe's own, was C. M. Wieland's Agathon (1766-67). François Jost suggests that Wieland's work did indeed contribute to the historical birth of the apprenticeship novel a concept of "inner form."[4] However, other than joining the novel of development with the apprenticeship novel--as Fritz Schmitt's and Gerhard Fricke's tables show[5]--Wieland's Agathon never achieved the enduring international recognition that has assured Goethe's masterpiece its unique position as archetype or model.

Taking Goethe's Wilhelm Meister, therefore, as our pivotal point of reference, a focus on several precursors as well as a multitude of direct and indirect imitators will serve to concretize the apprenticeship novel in its historical development to the present. Attempts to enumerate precursors and successors of this type of novel have often produced lists that appear either overly exclusive, omitting universally acknowledged representatives, or heavily inclusive, undermining essentially the distinctive bases for the classification itself. With this in mind, therefore, I intend to mention below an example of each extreme, prior to designating the generally acclaimed predecessors to Goethe's archetype, followed by lists of its successors in German, English, French, American, and other Western literatures. These lists draw primarily upon candidates selected by special studies of the apprenticeship novel in Germany and England, but I have sought to include acknowledgments of other foreign representatives so as to suggest the international pervasiveness of the type. I shall allude to only a few comic variations and, interestingly enough, to a dearth of representatives by women.

As early as 1820 Karl von Morgenstern in his lecture "Zur Geschichte des Bildungsromans" ("Toward a History of the Apprenticeship Novel") listed a plethora of radically differing works as examples of the type. His list is so broad, as Fritz Martini notes from the advantage of retrospect, that it argues for the inclusion of the Spanish Don Quixote; the French Télémaque and Émile; the English works of Richardson, Fielding, Sterne, Swift, Goldsmith,

Smollett, Madame d'Arblay, Henry Crabb Robinson, and Horace Smith; family novels, "Familienromane"; the German Agathon of Wieland as well as Goethe's Werther, Wahlverwandtschaften (Elective Affinities), and Dichtung und Wahrheit (Poetry and Truth), and the works of Tieck, Ernst Wagner, Novalis, Klinger, Jacobi, Heinse, Schiller, Fouqué, Jean Paul Richter, and Hoffmann.[6] Intimidated by such a comprehensive survey, the aforementioned distinctions seeking to define the apprenticeship novel, the novel of adventure, picaresque and sentimental novels, and autobiography would disintegrate entirely, as must also the boundaries between the even more closely related developmental and educational novels. Such generalities as, in this case, Morgenstern's invariably lack precision and adequate expressiveness.

An extreme opposite from the overly general, all-embracing enumeration is the ultraexclusive list. Rather than consider the view of an extreme nominalism that would restrict concrete representatives of the apprenticeship type to Wilhelm Meister alone, we might at least note one or two otherwise basically adequate compilations that nevertheless omit, for whatever reason, one or more of the major examples of the apprenticeship type.

Under the heading "Entwicklungsroman (Bildungsroman)," for example, in the index of his 1960 edition of the Handbuch der Weltliteratur (Handbook of World Literature), Hanns Eppelsheimer offers a list of sixteen works that excludes Maugham's Of Human Bondage, perhaps justifiably since he reclassifies this work as an "exotic novel"; but he omits Mann's Der Zauberberg (The Magic Mountain) without comment.[7] Werner Friederich's Outline of Comparative Literature points to fifteen examples of the Apprenticeship's precursors and successors, including Mann's Joseph und seine Brüder (Joseph and His Brothers) but also neglecting The Magic Mountain[8]--even though Friederich's own History of German Literature describes The Magic Mountain as "one of the highest achievements within the tradition of the German apprenticeship novel."[9] In his Glossary clarification of the "Novel" M. H. Abrams remarks that the vogue of the apprenticeship novel was "begun by Goethe's Wilhelm Meister's Apprenticeship (1795-1796) and includes Thomas Mann's The Magic Mountain and Somerset Maugham's Of Human Bondage."[10] Abrams lists only these three major examples, the last two of which Eppelsheimer and Friederich have omitted from their longer, albeit select, enumerations. Lists such as these, by omitting, even when justified, one or more of the principal representatives of the apprenticeship type, attest to the pitfalls of brevity.

Whatever the shortcomings of extreme selectivity, one constant holds true. Relatively few lists of the apprenticeship novel either consciously or inadvertently omit Goethe's model, hailed by Friederich as "the finest product" of the type.[11] Only those critics who view the Society of the Tower, the "Turmgesellschaft," as usurping Wilhelm's powers of self-determination[12] would choose to deny Wilhelm Meister the artistic status that it has otherwise popularly achieved. The inordinate majority of critics, however, only a few of whom are noted above, affirm this novel's unique position as the Ur-type of the apprenticeship form.

The generally acknowledged German forerunners of Goethe's

prototype include Wolfram von Eschenbach's thirteenth-century epic Parzival, Grimmelshausen's Simplizissimus (1669) and, as noted above, Wieland's Agathon (1766-67). These three works qualify only partially as apprenticeship novels. Parzival, whose pedagogic ideal reminds Jost of the novel of education, introduces a hero who develops "in a world constructed according to the order of grace and not according to the order of human experience." Simplizissimus, Jost adds, is a picaresque novel blended with the apprenticeship novel, or at least with the novel of development, since the hero does profit from the lessons of experience.[13] And Agathon, according to Gero von Wilpert, is more properly considered the first German novel of development.[14]

To these three rudimentary representatives Jost, Christine Touaillon, and Jürgen Jacobs would subjoin Karl Philipp Moritz's Anton Reiser (1785-90), whose subtitle identifies it as a psychological novel, "ein psychologischer Roman," and which Touaillon positions with Heinrich Jung-Stilling's Lebensjahre (Life), 1777-1817, as the beginning of the "autobiographical apprenticeship novel."[15] To these two Jacobs adds Johann Wezel's Hermann und Ulrike (Hermann and Ulrike), 1780, and F. H. Jacobi's Eduard Allwills Papiere (Eduard Allwill's Papers), 1775-76, as well as Wieland's Don Sylvio, 1764.[16] Initially descrying the origins of the German apprenticeship novel in Jörg Wickram's Der Jungen Knaben Spiegel (Mirror for Young Boys), 1554, Touaillon nonetheless objects that morals and adventure assume in this work too extensive a role "to permit it to be called a true apprenticeship novel." Two other candidates for classification as precursors come from the pen of Sophie von La Roche: Rosaliens Briefe (Rosalie's Letters), 1780-81, designated by Touaillon as the first apprenticeship novel by a woman, and Geschichte des Fräuleins von Sternheim (History of Lady Sophia Sternheim), 1771, a sentimental beginning of the German apprenticeship novel on a religious basis.[17]

As the earliest apprentice in English literature before the time of Wilhelm Meister, Howe selects Christian in John Bunyan's Pilgrim's Progress (1678).[18] And in a survey of French literature Jost points out Rousseau's Émile (1762) and Restif de la Bretonne's Le Paysan perverti (The Perverted Peasant), 1775, as logical forerunners of Goethe's masterpiece.

German literature certainly boasts a plurality of apprenticeship novels, as Touaillon proclaimed as early as the 1920's: "The apprenticeship novel is one of the German's especially beloved types. The other nations possess disproportionately fewer works of this kind."[19] The English novelists, however, have now gained an entirely respectable second position in the type's accumulative production. So in order to concretize the type in various literatures, several national lists drawn from special studies are provided below, with minimum critical comment, to suggest specific representatives in German, English, French, American, Danish, Dutch, Norwegian, and Russian literatures.

Touaillon's catalogue in the first edition of the German Reallexikon lists successors of Wilhelm Meister in Germany between 1793 and 1923. Supplementary to her list are candidates submitted by J. O. E. Donner, Howe, Hans Borcherdt, Friederich, Wilpert, Lothar Köhn,

Jost, Eppelsheimer, and Jacobs.[20] I have marked each of the well-known or more commonly acknowledged representatives in the consolidated list below with an asterisk to establish at least an order of priority.

*Jean Paul's Die Unsichtbare Loge (The Invisible Lodge), 1793, Hesperus, 1795, Titan, 1800-3, and Flegeljahre (Adolescence), 1804-5
Theodor Gottlieb von Hippel's novels, e.g., Lebensläufe nach aufsteigender Linie (Careers in an Ascending Line), 1778-81
Friedrich Hölderlin's Hyperion, 1797-99
*Ludwig Tieck's Franz Sternbalds Wanderungen (Wanderings of Franz Sternbald), 1798, and Der junge Tischlermeister (The Young Master Joiner), 1836
*Friedrich Schlegel's Lucinde, 1799
Dorothea Schlegel's Florentin, 1801
*Clemens Brentano's Godwi, 1801
*Novalis' Heinrich von Ofterdingen (Henry of Ofterdingen), 1802
Maximilian Klinger's cycle of nine novels taken as a whole, beginning with Fausts Leben (Faustus), 1791, and ending with Betrachtungen und Gedanken (Reflections and Thoughts), 1803-5
*Joseph von Eichendorff's Ahnung und Gegenwart (Premonition and Present), 1815
Achim von Arnim's Die Kronenwächter (The Guardians of the Crown), 1817
E. T. A. Hoffmann's Kater Murr (Tomcat Murr), 1819-21
Eduard Mörike's Maler Nolten (Nolten the Painter), 1832
*Karl Immermann's Die Epigonen (The Late Born), 1836
*Gottfried Keller's Der grüne Heinrich (Green Henry), 1854-55, 1879-80
*Gustav Freytag's Soll und Haben (Debit and Credit), 1855
*Adalbert Stifter's Der Nachsommer (The Indian Summer), 1857
Wilhelm Raabe's Der Hungerpastor (The Hunger Pastor), 1864, Die Leute aus den Walde (People from the Forest), 1863, Prinzessin Fisch (Princess Fisch), 1883, and Die Akten des Vogelsangs (The Vogelsang Documents), 1895
Friedrich Huch's Peter Michel, 1901, and Mao, 1907
Ricarda Huch's Erinnerungen von Ludolf Ursleu dem Jüngeren (Eros Invincible), 1902, and Vita somnium breve (Michael Unger), 1902
Jakob Christoph Heer's Joggeli, 1902
Emil Strauß's Freund Hein (Death the Comforter), 1902
Sophie Hoechstetter's Pfeifer (Piper), 1903
*Hermann Hesse's Peter Camenzind, 1904, Unterm Rad (Beneath the Wheel), 1906, Demian, 1919, Siddhartha, 1922, and Das Glasperlenspiel (Magister Ludi), 1943
Hermann Anders Krüger's Gottfried Kämpfer, 1904-5
Edward Stilgebauer's Götz Krafft, 1904-5
Otto Ernst's Asmus Semper, 1904-16

Paul Ernst's Der schmale Weg zum Glück (The Narrow Road to Fortune), 1904
Cäsar Flaischlen's Jost Seyfried, 1905
Gustav Frenssen's Hilligenlei (Holyland), 1905
Ludwig Finckh's Der Rosendoktor (The Rose Doctor), 1906
Robert Musil's Die Verwirrungen des Zöglings Törleß (Young Törless), 1906, and the unfinished Der Mann ohne Eigenschaften (The Man Without Qualities), 1952
Carl Hauptmann's Einhart der Lächler (Einhart the Smiler), 1907
Otto Julius Bierbaum's Prinz Kuckuck (Prince Kuckuck), 1907
Otto Anthes' Heinz Hauser, 1912
Wilhelm Schussen's Vinzenz Faulhaber, 1918[21]
Karl Bröger's Der Held im Schatten (The Hero in the Shadow), 1919
Jakob Wassermann's Christian Wahnschaffe, 1919
Alfons Petzold's Das rauhe Leben (Raw Life), 1920
Albrecht Schaeffer's Helianth, 1920-21, and Parzival, 1922
Emma Waiblinger's Die Ströme des Namenlos (The Stream of the Nameless), 1921
Ernst Frey's Güggs, 1923
*Thomas Mann's Der Zauberberg (The Magic Mountain), 1924, and the four-volume Joseph und seine Brüder (Joseph and His Brothers), 1933-42
Hans Grimm's Volk ohne Raum (A Nation Without Space), 1926
Hermann Stehr's Nathanael Maechler, 1929
Hugo von Hofmannstahl's Andreas, 1932
E. G. Kolbenheyer's trilogy Paracelsus, 1917-25[22]
Alfred Döblin's Berlin Alexanderplatz (Alexander Square, Berlin), 1929
Heimito von Doderer's Die Strudlhofstiege (The Strudlhofstiege), 1951

The above compilation may include some works that qualify also as novels of development, artist novels, or other nearly equivalent types rather than a more precisely defined apprenticeship novel. While admitting to its own shortcomings, however, it aims to provide at least the principal German language representatives of the apprenticeship type.[23]

Hans Wagner's selection of the English apprenticeship novels subsequent to Wilhelm Meister openly acknowledges the inclusion of novels of education and of development. Supplementary to his list are candidates proffered by Howe, G. B. Tennyson, Jost, and Jerome Buckley.[24] It may be useful again to distinguish the most familiar representatives with asterisks.

*Thomas Carlyle's Sartor Resartus (1833-34) and his translation of Wilhelm Meister's Apprenticeship (1824)
*Benjamin Disraeli's Vivian Grey (1826-27), Contarini Fleming (1832), and Lothair (1870)
John Sterling's Arthur Coningsby (1833)

*Bulwer-Lytton's Pelham (1828), Ernest Maltravers (1837), and Kenelm Chillingly (1873)
George Henry Lewe's Ranthorpe (1847) and Apprenticeship of Life (1850)
Geraldine Jewsbury's Zoe (1845) and The Half-Sisters (1848)
James Anthony Froude's Shadows of the Clouds (1847) and Nemesis of Faith (1849)
*Charles Dickens' David Copperfield (1849-50) and Great Expectations (1860-61)[25]
William Makepeace Thackeray's Pendennis (1848-50)
Charles Kingsley's Anton Locke (1850)
Thomas Hughes' Tom Brown's Schooldays (1857)
*George Meredith's Ordeal of Richard Feverel (1859), Evan Harrington (1861), The Adventures of Harry Richmond (1871), and Beauchamp's Career (1875)
*George Eliot's Mill on the Floss (1860)
George Gissing's Born in Exile (1892)
*Thomas Hardy's Jude the Obscure (1895)
*Samuel Butler's Way of All Flesh (1903)[26]
Henry Handel Richardson's Maurice Guest (1908)
Arnold Bennett's Clayhanger (1910)
H. G. Wells' Kipps (1905) and *Tono-Bungay (1909)
John Davys Beresford's Jacob Stahl trilogy (1911-15)[27]
Hugh Walpole's Fortitude (1913) and the Jeremy trilogy (1919-27)[28]
Compton Mackenzie's Sinister Street (1913-14)
*D. H. Lawrence's Sons and Lovers (1913)
*W. Somerset Maugham's Of Human Bondage (1915)
Dorothy Richardson's twelve-part Pilgrimage (1915-38)
James Joyce's Portrait of the Artist as a Young Man (1916)
Alec Waugh's Loom of Youth (1917)
Virginia Woolf's Jacob's Room (1922)
Frank Swinnerton's Young Felix (1923)
May Sinclair's Mary Olivier (1919) and Arnold Waterlow (1924)
Maurice Baring's C (1924)
Warwick Deeping's Sorrell and Son (1925)
Charles Morgan's Portrait in a Mirror (1929)
Howard Spring's Fame Is the Spur (1940)
Bruce Marshall's George Brown's Schooldays (1946)
William Golding's Free Fall (1959)

As noted above, this list includes examples of the educational, developmental, and artist novels, as well as autobiography, and other types closely related to the apprenticeship novel. While the two lists of representatives contain more German than English works, the English list typically reflects less precision and more mutual encroachment among its similar types.

Jost recommends as French successors to Wilhelm Meister five candidates. His list represents perhaps a practical minimum, although the apprenticeship type has never achieved in France a respectable fraction of its popular acceptance in Germany and England.[29] Jost includes the following:

*Gustave Flaubert's L'Éducation sentimentale (Sentimental Education), 1869
Paul Bourget's Le Disciple (The Disciple), 1889
Stendhal's La Vie de Henri Brulard (The Life of Henry Brulard), 1890, and Le Rouge et le Noir (The Red and the Black), 1830[30]
*Romain Rolland's ten-volume Jean-Christophe, 1904-12
André Gide's Les Faux-Monnayeurs (The Counterfeiters), 1926

To these candidates in French literature R.-M. Albérès in his Histoire du roman moderne (History of the Modern Novel) adds Balzac's Père Goriot, 1834, and Illusions perdues (Lost Illusions), 1837-43, in focusing on Rastignac and the young protagonists of the two novels, respectively; Maurice Barrès' Les Déracinés (The Uprooted), 1897; Roger Martin du Gard's seven-part Les Thibault (The World of the Thibaults), 1922-40; Jules Romains' twenty-seven part Les Hommes de bonne volonté (Men of Good Will), 1932-47; and Georges Duhamel's ten-volume Chronique des Pasquier (The Pasquier Chronicles), 1933-45, in stressing the character of Laurent Pasquier.[31]

Within Jost's list of the United States successors to Goethe's Wilhelm Meister I have starred the work that is also accepted by Friederich and Eppelsheimer as an apprenticeship novel but rejected by Buckley as a novel of youth, of adolescence:

Sinclair Lewis' Arrowsmith (1925)
*Thomas Wolfe's Look Homeward, Angel (1929)
George Santayana's The Last Puritan (1935)
William Faulkner's Go Down, Moses (1942)[32]
Saul Bellow's The Adventures of Augie March (1953)

Additionally, Friederich suggests Herman Melville's Mardi (1849) and Richard H. Fogle has offered another viable contemporaneous candidate, although properly a short story, in Nathaniel Hawthorne's "The Artist of the Beautiful" (1844).

The trend established by Wilhelm Meister has as its most appropriate representative in Denmark Martin Andersen Nexφ's four-volume Pelle Erobreren (Pelle the Conqueror), 1906-10. In Holland the type is represented by Frederik van Eeden's De kleine Johannes (Little Johannes), 1887; in Norway, Sigrid Undset's Kristin Lavransdatter, 1920-22; and in Russia, Ivan Alexandrovich Goncharov's Obyknovennaya istoriya (A Common Story), 1847. Jost concurs with Eppelsheimer in the above selections from Danish and Dutch literatures.

Two well-known German works that represent comic variations of the apprenticeship novel, as Hermann Weigand suggests, are Ludwig Tieck's Kaiser Oktavianus (The Emperor Oktavianus), 1804, in which the hero's personal history employs but one episode, and Heinrich Heine's satirical Die Bäder von Lucca (The Baths of Lucca), 1829.[33] Additionally, Thomas Mann's Die Bekenntnisse des Hochstaplers Felix Krull (Confessions of Felix Krull), 1954, undeniably a satire on "unauthentic living" in the picaresque novel, serves also as a hilarious parody of the traditional apprenticeship novel.[34]

It may prove noteworthy that of the more than one hundred authors listed above, only nine are women. Dorothea Schlegel, Sophie Hoechstetter, and Emma Waiblinger are German; Geraldine Jewsbury, George Eliot, Dorothy Richardson, Virginia Woolf, and May Sinclair, English; and Sigrid Undset, Norwegian. These lists, of course, cannot claim inclusiveness. Indeed, Christine Touaillon has added to the German representatives two more works by women--Caroline von Wolzogen's *Agnes von Lilien* (1796-97) and Sophie Mereau's *Amanda und Eduard* (1803)--while inserting an explanation for the general paucity of apprenticeship novels by women. "In general," she remarks, albeit in the late twenties, "the apprenticeship novel by a woman is somewhat rare, because it presupposes a certain command of life and a fullness of view, that does not easily develop in the narrowness of a womanly life."[35] If indeed this dearth originated from the woman's circumstantial constraints, some remarkable women, especially those noted above, have somehow transcended their limitations and have produced novels apart from, even founded on, their actual experiences. Luise von François' *Die letzte Reckenburgerin* (*The Last von Reckenburg*), 1871, and Marie von Ebner-Eschenbach's *Das Gemeindekind* (*The Child of the Parish*), 1887, for example, are two more cases in point.[36]

It should be noted and emphasized in conclusion that all the lists in this chapter, by seeking a middle ground between being too comprehensive and too selective, attempt only to concretize the apprenticeship type of novel by designating a sufficient number, if not all, of its principle representatives in several Western literatures. The existence of the type in non-Western literatures, though a worthy topic for future consideration, falls outside the purview of this book. So also does a study of Middle and South American literatures, which, for example, might provide an interesting supplement with a focus on how their particular novels in the tradition modify the values, themes, and motifs latent in the general type.

Three instances of such a particular study occupy the remainder of this book. All three choices embody potentially all the qualities, as noted in Chapter 3 above, that distinguish this regulative type. Furthermore, each of the three successfully converts a majority of its potentials into modified actual existence; that is, each book--itself a particular work of art--exemplifies the apprenticeship type of the novel.

II

THREE CLASSIC APPRENTICESHIP NOVELS

the greatest of all arts, the art of life

--Thomas Carlyle,
"Translator's Preface to the First
Edition of Meister's Apprenticeship"

Eine gesetzmäßige Entwickelung wird im Leben des Individuums angeschaut, jede ihrer Stufen hat einen Eigenwert und ist zugleich Grundlage einer höheren Stufe.

--Wilhelm Dilthey,
Das Erlebnis und die Dichtung

Introduction

Johann Wolfgang von Goethe's Wilhelm Meister's Apprenticeship stands on the threshhold of the apprenticeship tradition as the German model, the "archetype," of a special kind of novel. Thomas Mann regards it as "the greatest novel of the Germans." [1] Significantly Mann's own contribution to the type, his Magic Mountain, has been singled out as "the last important" apprenticeship novel of the modern representatives.[2] Werner Friederich considers it not only "one of the highest achievements within the tradition" but also "one of the finest masterpieces of the novelistic literature of Europe."[3] The apprenticeship novel between Goethe and Mann flourished for over a century in German literature. It was less common in English or French, but of the English representatives the best "and the closest parallel to the old apprentice tradition"[4] was W. Somerset Maugham's Of Human Bondage. Richard Cordell, in his biographical and critical study of Maugham and the allure of his works, reports that by 1961 Of Human Bondage had "outsold all other items in the popular Modern Library series."[5]

Taking these three novels, then, as the "archetype" and the "last" of the most widely acknowledged and critically acclaimed German masterpieces in the tradition and the "best" of the modern English representatives, I believe that all the potentials inherent in their portrayal of an apprenticeship can best be seen through a thematic rearrangement of their chronological order to demonstrate a three-stage hierarchy that implicitly constitutes a complete apprenticeship to life and death. In such an arrangement Of Human Bondage will present the first stage; Wilhelm Meister, the first and second; and The Magic Mountain, the first through third stages in a consummate apprenticeship to both life and death.

The arrangement itself proves revealing but should not be regarded as an attempt to "rank" the works, as if one novel possessed artistic superiority over another. I consider each work as representative of a self-contained "world" that posits its own values, and these inherent values alone should provide the criteria for its appreciation. My approach, therefore, is not from the perspective of value judgment, but rather for the purpose of value discovery. Comparisons of totalities may legitimately illuminate the values of one work most often seen only dimly and negatively within a type--such as Of Human Bondage--by justaposing the values of another work viewed more clearly and positively within the same type--such as either Goethe's Wilhelm Meister or Mann's Magic Mountain. I have taken particular care, however, to emphasize the distinction between correct and incorrect interpretations of the initial stage in this three-stage apprenticeship, that is, between holistic and incomplete recognitions of the values implicit in the first stage. The result, I trust, will be to suggest a valid perspective on Maugham's Of Human Bondage as both complete and open ended when viewed in the context of its German counterparts.

Maugham's masterpiece, particularly, has suffered from a barrage of negative criticism. Many of these unfavorable judgments, I contend, stem from misinterpretations of the first stage implicitly evident in the apprenticeship type. As a result, a central contention of this book will be that Maugham's novel stands as a positive, not a negative, work of art, especially when compared with the singular achievements of Goethe and Mann.

Critical distortions, nevertheless, are not limited to Maugham's work. Some misinterpretations have sprung from restricted perspectives on Goethe's and Mann's novels as well. From the theoretical stance that regards the apprenticeship novel as a regulative, not prescriptive, type I hope to provide a clearly corrective description of such individual themes as Maugham's view of love, Goethe's conception of guidance, and Mann's notions of morality and death. Such a stance should also set to rest recurrent charges of abstractness, egotism, and misdirection with which critics have assailed the idea of apprenticeship embodied in all three of the works under consideration.

A latent, if not readily apparent, objection to the thematic approach that I have adopted for Part Two of this book--that is, that the delineation of a fixed number of stages (in this case, three) in a complete apprenticeship is entirely arbitrary--should not invalidate the argument intended. Some critics may prefer either a different number of individual stages or a sequential progression of indistinguishable phases within the complete apprenticeship. My primary aim in the delineation has been to employ only clear and valid distinctions.

What follows, then, is an attempt to describe three significant novels as modifications of the apprenticeship type. Through a comparative focus on intrinsic analogies of plot, characterization, tone, structure, themes, motifs, images, and symbols the analyses will rely on such extrinsic concerns as sources, success, influences, and auctorial intentions solely for supplementary corroboration; shall depend on biography solely for interpretive exegesis; and shall consider matters of psychology, sociology, and philosophy only as they afford critical appreciation.

5. OF HUMAN BONDAGE

The 1898 draft of The Artistic Temperament of Stephen Carey was refused by Fisher Unwin, from whom W. Somerset Maugham, age 24, had requested one hundred pounds in payment. Thereafter it was rejected by every publisher to whom he submitted it. Maugham entitled the revised 1913 draft Beauty from Ashes.[1] Drawn from Isaiah 61:3, this phrase was employed in the subsequent edition as the epitaph for Cronshaw's pitiful death,[2] but Maugham rejected it as a title because another recent novel had used it. He finally entitled the 1915 published version Of Human Bondage, after the name of the fourth book of Spinoza's Ethic: "Of Human Bondage, or of the Strength of the Affects."[3]

The "Preface" of part IV of the Ethic points up the central theme in Of Human Bondage. "The impotence of man to govern or restrain the affects I call bondage," Spinoza argues, "for a man who is under their control is not his own master, but is mastered by fortune, in whose power he is, so that he is often forced to follow the worse, although he sees the better before him."[4] The subsequent part V of the Ethic is entitled "Of the Power of the Intellect, or of Human Liberty."

The underscoring in the above quotation is mine, for the two key phrases, which characterize both parts IV and V of the Ethic, introduce the concepts of bondage and of freedom, respectively. These two reciprocally related themes of bondage and of freedom are central not only to Of Human Bondage, as implied by its title, but also to the idea of self-formation. As an unexpected or unintended by-product of the will directed toward an objective other than self, culture evolves in this novel through the willful concentration on release from specific bonds.

Philip Carey effects his release from particular bondages to, among others, physical deformity, social restrictions, religious and moral hypocrisy, delusion of talent, passion, poverty, hope and fear. Initially bound to a physical defect, he enters life with the congenital deformity of a clubfoot. Subjected to the mimicry and ridicule of his classmates at Tercanbury, he experiences the misery of a horrible self-consciousness and introversion which influence the remainder of his life. Although he eventually gains his freedom from the clubfoot's restraining effects, he cannot at his early age overcome a bondage of such visible magnitude and must unavoidably await the end of the novel and his release from many other less obvious, though related, bonds in order to experience ultimate freedom from the physical one. His release from bondage to the ideal of the normal, which we shall consider at the end of this chapter, prepares him for freedom from his physical deformity.

Beyond the misery that his classmates inflict on him through their ridicule, Philip is bound additionally, albeit in a less physical sense, to the restrictions of King's School at Tercanbury. He suffers the terror of a shy boy abused by ill-suited, impatient, and choleric masters and the boredom of a bright mind among thick-witted companions, and he soon resents the bonds that hold him to the school. "He was tired of having to do things because he was told," Maugham informs us; "and the restrictions irked him, not because they were unreasonable, but because they were restrictions. He yearned for freedom" (20.79). The kind understanding of the headmaster, Mr. Perkins, offers only temporary refuge from his misery.

Philip leaves King's School, having chosen Germany and the study of foreign languages as far better suited to his temperament than continued study at Oxford for the ministerial career of his uncle. His exhilaration upon his arrival in Heidelberg introduces into the novel the first phrase to establish a leitmotif[5] for the vital theme of freedom: "He was his own master at last" (22.93). This phrase recurs frequently throughout the novel as a signal for the release from bondage.

Philip finds release from his third bondage--a slavery to the Christian religion, as he knows it from personal experience--in three separate stages. First is his introduction at Blackstable to the religion of his tyrannical and egocentric uncle, who causes him only misery. In the second stage at Tercanbury, when his fervent prayer that God might heal his clubfoot goes unanswered, his disillusionment precipitates a repudiation of the popular claim that this God can remove mountains for him who has faith. In the third and last stage, influenced by his discussions with Hayward and Weeks at Heidelberg, he decides to throw off this burdensome religion that outside influences have foisted on him or, as Maugham memorably narrates it, to "put off the faith of his childhood quite simply, like a cloak that he no longer needed." Almost immediately "the cloak which had fallen from his shoulders, seemed an intolerable burden of which he had been eased" (28.122). His release from religion employs again the leitmotif of freedom that was introduced upon his release from bondage to restrictions: "Freedom!" Maugham cries. "He was his own master at last" (28.123).

As proof of the permanence of this release, years later when Philip has met the Athelnys and found comfort in their home, Maugham reports that "he still looked upon Christianity as a degrading bondage that must be cast away at any cost" (88.460). The very next statement, however, establishes a link vital to a deeper understanding of his act through its motive. Maugham writes that Christianity "was connected subconsciously in his [Philip's] mind with the dreary services in the cathedral at Tercanbury, and the long hours of boredom in the cold church at Blackstable" (88.460). Here indeed the evidence admits that, not religion, but religious hypocrisy provokes his opposition.

John Brophy, in a brilliant contrast of the attitude toward religion in _Of Human Bondage_ with that in Samuel Butler's _The Way of All Flesh_, concludes that Maugham, through Philip, rejects only hypocrisy in religious conviction. Religion itself may be fantasy; but it does not signify, as it does for Butler, danger. In _Of Human_

Bondage Philip views clerical hypocrisy with distaste "but with no sense of shock, no moral indignation." He makes a decision in his own mind which seems to him logically obvious, but his standard for judgment clings to the orthodoxy of Christianity.

Butler's novel, on the other hand, denounces religion itself in a bitter and indignant satire. In The Way of All Flesh, Brophy asserts, Butler "would have the churches pulled down and sterilized; and he has already planned the temples to the Life Force which should be built in their place." With Maugham, however,

> If it is wrong to spread lies, and wrong to be a hypocrite, it is wrong only because truth and sincerity are right. If clergymen are hypocrites, it is not Christianity which has failed but clergymen; and you can judge them to have failed only if you apply to them the Christian or some other relevant standard of right and wrong.[6]

Philip, therefore, who offers no other "standard of right and wrong," actually measures hypocrites by Christian standards and, finding them wanting, properly rejects, not religion, but religious hypocrisy.

By contrast, Philip's belief in his artistic talent never really deludes him. Both Hayward and Miss Wilkinson enthusiastically encourage his study of art, and his Aunt Louisa supports his sojourn in Paris with a generous gift of a hundred pounds. But his own confidence in himself throughout the two-year trial of becoming an artist remains precariously shaky. At this point in his apprenticeship he believes in the importance of success in life; and "it was this desire," Maugham informs us, "to make a success in life which was at the bottom of Philip's uncertainty about continuing his artistic career" (50.256).

Four causes contribute to his release from this transitory delusion of talent. First of all he observes the pathetic failure of many painters and writers around him. Then he sees the meaningless life of Fanny Price--who produces only useless mediocrity in art and a futile passion for himself--violently end in an equally meaningless suicide. Third, M. Foinet in an honest appraisal of Philip's work concludes that he "will never be anything but mediocre," an indictment to which Foinet adds, "I would give all I have in the world if someone had given me that advice when I was your age and I had taken it" (51.261). The death of Philip's aunt, seen as the climax to a trend of wasted lives, serves as the fourth and final factor in his decision to abandon art.

Morality as Philip has experienced it forms a bondage closely related to that of religious hypocrisy. When he returns from Paris for the funeral of his aunt, his reaction to her "wasted life" (52.263) leads him to reassess his own life. He has thrown off the hypocrisy of religion but has retained unimpaired its concomitant morality. One year in Heidelberg, two more in Paris, and wide reading in the skeptics, however, have prepared him to question conscience as well as custom. Engrossed in Origin of Species,[7] he discovers that society opposes rather than aids the struggle of the individual. Society has created for its own preservation--with little concern for the individual--its weapons of laws, public opinion, and conscience, its kingdom ruled by the arbitrary powers of reward and punishment rather than reasoned principles of right and wrong. Laws, public opinion, and conscience therefore exist in a sphere separate from the realm of morality. The individual has no choice but to respect the external power of laws and public opinion--both of them comparatively stronger than he--though both, when necessary, "could be met by guile" (53.273). The internal power of conscience "was the traitor within the gates," a burden of deceptive "prejudice from which the free man should rid himself" (53.273).

Philip's decision to fling conscience from his breast, therefore, reflects again his rejection, not of morality itself, but of hypocrisy in moral conviction. He judges moral hypocrisy by standards of morality. Unable to formulate his own standards to replace them, he adopts instead a working philosophy of utilitarian ethics that will guarantee his survival in society until he can form from within himself a permanent "theory of conduct" (53.271). His provisional rule for conduct, which would encourage an individual to follow his inclinations "with due regard to the policeman round the corner" (53.271), it should be noted, is a temporary affair that neither encourages nor discourages morality but rather links it with an individual propensity for goodness. No one should doubt that he possesses this propensity. As in his release from religious hypocrisy, so also now in his release from moral hypocrisy, his immediate sensation reaffirms the leitmotif of freedom: with a cry of triumph "he felt himself at last absolutely free" (53.271).

His release from passion, however, proves much more difficult to achieve. At the time of his entry into the study of medicine at St. Luke's Medical School in London, his belief in the ideal has nearly faded into obscurity. He has rejected both religion and morality, or at least the hypocrisy in their practice. But he has not yet overcome the tendency toward introspection into the bitter reality of self. And for two years in Paris he has associated with Bohemian vagabonds, as symbolized by the colorless, unwashed, unhealthy image of Fanny Price. The paucity of his values has prepared him, therefore, for an anemic wanton who needs only to wound his pride in order to initiate an affair.

Here begins his infamous bondage to Mildred, a bondage foreshadowed by the Miss Wilkinson episode twenty chapters earlier and predicated by his stark recognition that the ideal of romantic love signifies only fanciful illusion. Richard Cordell highly praises Maugham's success in making this affair with Mildred entirely credible. "Maugham's skill as a story-teller," he affirms, "is never more manifest than in his making [Mildred] a living, believable woman, and in convincing us that Philip, fastidious as he is and thoroughly aware of her vulgarity, hard lack of sympathy, and appalling unfaithfulness, still loves her with all his heart."[8]

Maugham devotes the next fifty-two chapters (chs. 57-109), almost half the book, to Philip's struggle against his bondage to Mildred. The leitmotif for the theme of bondage throughout the early stages of this affair is initiated by his amazement when he discovers of a sudden, "He was in love with her" (57.294). By contrast, the leitmotif for the freedom theme--when Mildred has left him--sees him cry, "Thank God, I'm free from all that now"(67.343). The variations on these two phrases in the four episodes involving Mildred characterize his expansion from a particular to a general bondage as well as the separate stages in his release.

The first episode opens with his meeting Mildred and discovering that "he was in love with her" (57.294). But within five chapters he has realized that he is "a prisoner" and he longs for "freedom" (62.317). This freedom he achieves when she becomes engaged to Miller, for in his response, albeit delayed, he marvels that he "seemed really to be born again" (65.330). He meets Norah, with whom he preserves "his freedom" (66.337). And his last thought of Mildred provokes the cry, "Thank God, I'm free from all that now" (67.343).

However, in the second episode Mildred appeals to him for aid during her confinement with Miller's child. The phrase reestablishing the theme of bondage depicts his knowing "then that he loved her as passionately as ever" (69.349). This bond, no longer holding him particularly to Mildred, is now a general bondage to passion. Mildred departs with Griffiths on a jaunt inadvisedly financed by Philip, who now realizes that "when passion seized him he was powerless" (78.407). Even ten chapters later as he gazes at the paintings of El Greco and seems to divine a new inward freedom, he still acknowledges the power of the outward bondage of passion. "He seemed to see," Maugham writes, "that a man need not leave his life to chance, but that his will was powerful; he seemed to see that self-control might be as passionate and as active as the surrender to passion" (88.465).

The third episode opens when Philip discovers Mildred soliciting on the street. The leitmotif of the theme of bondage at this point alters significantly. When he "looked at her he knew that he no longer loved her" (90.473). Maugham assures us that "now he felt nothing for Mildred but infinite pity" (92.485). And a few chapters later Philip himself confirms, "I wore the passion out" (96.510). The episode ends with Mildred's departure in fury after she has devastated his flat and left him in abject poverty.

Mildred appears again in the final episode to seek his medical advice. Despite his diagnosis of her case as syphilis and his attempt to warn her of the inherent danger, she resumes soliciting. He responds at the beginning of this episode by despairing, "I suppose I shall never really quite get over it" (109.576). But Maugham assures us when Philip last sees Mildred on the street: "That was the end. He did not see her again" (109.579).

Maugham appears to infer much later that Philip may never extricate himself completely from this particular bondage. In the last chapter of the novel he imagines that he sees Mildred crossing Trafalgar Square. He is mistaken, but he asks himself with horror whether he will ever free himself from her. "That love," he realizes in his heart, "had caused so much suffering that he knew he would never, never quite be free of it. Only death could finally assuage his desire" (112.645). Although his passion, if not his love, finds itself subject to atrophy and death, as we shall see below, he does assure his ultimate freedom both from Mildred and from passion, if only by default. For even if she escapes succumbing early to her chronic disease--an eventual inevitability we must certainly accept--Maugham tells us most emphatically that he never sees her again.

Karl Pfeiffer, among other critics, views Philip's bondage to Mildred and later to passion as introducing the theme of the death of love. The famous passage in chapter 57, which unfolds the popular belief in romantic love only to dismiss it immediately as "old fancy" when faced with Philip's "love" for Mildred, would seem to confirm Pfeiffer's pronouncement of "the death of love."[9] Even Cordell, entirely convinced that Philip "loves [Mildred] with all his heart,"[10] recognizes Maugham's intention to dispel a popular myth and to foster a more realistic association of the word love with the exclusive attributes of passion. Almost all his critics credit Maugham with relegating love to the level of passion.

I do not believe, however, that Maugham actually intends to equate love and passion. Such an equation would certainly preclude the pure affection that Philip feels for Sally in the concluding episode of the novel. His marriage to her with the frank admission "that he did not love her" (121.640) could then be justifiably criticized as unsatisfactory. But if love can be differentiated from passion--as it is, in Maugham's novel, from affection--then we may conclude that Philip loves neither Mildred nor Sally, even though love for the latter may evolve subsequent to his marrying her.

Analogous to such an attempt to distinguish love from passion and affection, Maugham's own definitions in The Summing Up seek to define sexual love, loving-kindness, and affection.[11] "Sexual love," or earthly love, and "loving-kindness," or Platonic heavenly love, he tells us, represent two different types of love. But "affection" has no affinity with love at all. Affection, "created by habit, community of interests, convenience and the desire of companionship," lends "a comfort rather than an exhilaration."[12]

Only sexual love--which at first "depends on certain secretions of the sexual glands,"[13] then alters with the changing person, atrophies, and dies--can produce the wretchedness of Philip's bondage to Mildred. A "degrading passion" (62.317), evolving into "infinite pity" (92.485), while retaining the dregs of "a strange, desperate thirst for that vile woman" (72.645), accurately depicts the chains that shackle him to her.

On the other hand, affection--the second type of love--attracts him to Sally, a competent, self-controlled, honest, and reliable woman whom he "respected" (121.640). The "desire for a wife and a home and love" (122.646) that drives him to consider marrying her fulfills all the requirements for "a great affection that he felt for her" (121.640).

Maugham himself, who never experienced the third type of love, as he defines it, accepts loving-kindness as fantasy. Earlier in The Summing Up he admits that "though I have been in love a good many times I have never experienced the bliss of unrequited love. I know that this is the best thing that life can offer and it is a thing that almost all men, though perhaps only for a short time, have enjoyed."[14] Loving-kindness, which is neither restrictive of passion nor exclusive of affection, gleans the best traits of both types of love.

Let me summarize that although Philip asserts his complete love for Mildred, he has redefined love, as it is generally known, to signify undiluted passion. And although he denies any love for Sally, he merely discounts the presence of passion in his affection for her. Passion and affection he acknowledges as real. Love he declares as simple fantasy. Here, then, is another parallel with Brophy's conclusion that Philip rejects only hypocrisy. Rejecting hypocritical application of the term love, he does not reject love itself. He resorts to standards of love, even as he did to standards of religion and of morality. And turning his attention to hypocritical notions at face value, he repudiates their hypocrisy.

An acceptance of the novel's concluding episode, namely, Philip's marriage to Sally, depends essentially on the above distinction. Maugham himself admits that "readers on the whole have found [this marriage] the least satisfactory part of my book."[15] M. K. Naik, for instance, objects that "the ending where Philip is thrown hastily into Sally's arms is rather hard to swallow, if not disgusting." [16] Richard Ward, disbelieving that Philip has found in Sally his heart's desire, asserts that this ending "is not an ending," that it urges "a marriage in which we do not in any case believe."[17] Jerome Buckley claims it "violates the logic of the plot."[18] Referring to a "cinema-like ending" that "seems somewhat disingenuous and fabricated," Cordell explains that "many readers have found it banal and unconvincing, or at least have objected that it is 'conventional' to bring the novel to a close with Philip's supposedly happy marriage to an uncultivated, uneducated girl whom he does not even love. They cannot believe that Philip would choose a wife so commonplace."[19]

Distinctions among love, passion, and affection, however, such as those drawn above, would certainly permit a marriage based on affection, as Maugham himself admits, while not necessarily precluding the potential for love as well. From this standpoint, at least, Philip's marriage to Sally provides a proper ending. We shall see a second approach to the matter, moreover, at a point later in this chapter.[20]

In the meantime, two major types of bondage remain for brief consideration. Philip discovers himself at Mildred's third departure in a miserable bondage to poverty. Maugham notes in Of Human Bondage and reaffirms in The Summing Up that "money is like a sixth sense without which you cannot make a complete use of the other five" (51.261).[21] Mildred, having wrecked Philip's flat and rendered him at twenty-five penniless, now pushes him beyond his vaguest fears to humiliating extremes. "The situation in which he found himself was quite outside the range of his experience" (99.523). Although able to earn a meager subsistence as a shop-walker at Lynn and Sedley while residing with the Athelnys, he is possessed by a single degrading thought that "there was only one thing to free him and that was the death of his uncle" (195.551). In fact, it is his uncle's death that renews the theme of freedom. The thought "that now he could begin a new life" (112.593) characterizes his readmission to medical school guaranteed by his inheritance, and a year later he receives the diploma that enables him to practice.

The last significant bondage that restrains Philip's freedom is one that dissolves only toward the end of his apprenticeship. While he is still suffering from poverty and solitude, he discovers the answer to the riddle of the Persian rug. Sitting alone in the British Museum and meditating on Hayward's futile death in Africa, he soon realizes that

"Life" for Hayward, for Cronshaw before him, and now for himself "had no meaning" (106.558). The most obvious, perfect, and beautiful pattern in life provides a sequence in which a man is born, matures, marries, has children, works, and dies. All else in the way of elaboration has no end but that of personal satisfaction, its own reward. He perceives little need or use for a complex design in the Persian rug. He now regards the need for and use of a design in life as an illusion to be cast off like all his other previous illusions.

This realization ensures his freedom from a tenacious bondage to hope and fear. It frees him from the desire for success and happiness but also from the fear of failure and unhappiness. "It seemed to him," Maugham tells us, "that the last burden of responsibility was taken from him; and for the first time he was utterly free" (106.559). Philip must struggle to reconcile himself to such a simple view of life, for he sees his own life, if measured by any degree of happiness and success, as reduced to failure. However, he soon comes to accept the true measure of a life as neither its happiness nor its pain but the living of it, so that a life becomes its own justification.

The freedom inspired by this revelation provides the essential groundwork for the concluding episode of the novel. His release from hope and fear serves as the indispensable basis for his marriage to Sally. His renunciation of desire for worldly success and conventional happiness supports his "marriage to an uncultivated, uneducated girl," as Cordell has depicted her.[22] A significant break with the "middle-class instincts" (50.257 and 62.319) that formerly restricted him in his choice of a wife follows his release from fear of second-rate mediocrity and the overriding desire for respectability. His present conviction that the simplest pattern of life can provide adequate material for "personal satisfaction" (106.560) should justify employing the term "happiness" (122.647) to describe his surrender to "the desires of his own heart."[23]

In addition to all the constraints noted above, several minor bondages, from which Philip ultimately frees himself, confront him in his life's course. Bound at one point to an occupation for which he has no gift, he dutifully serves as an accountant's clerk at Herbert Carter & Co. in London but turns from this error within the year. Bound to an airy dream of embarking on a swashbuckling adventure in romantic Spain and then continuing to the exotic East, he finds release in his marriage to Sally.

Bound from the beginning to the end of the novel to the goal of normality, he eventually relinquishes this illusory ideal and accepts his physical deformity, viewing his clubfoot no longer as unique but as shared universally. "Everyone has some defect, of body or of mind" (121.644). Illnesses of the flesh, weak hearts, weak lungs, illnesses of the spirit, languor of the will, a craving for liquor, even the treachery of Griffiths and the selfishness of Mildred--all entail faults characteristic of the species. He recognizes "the normal" as indeed "the rarest thing in the world" (121.644). His clubfoot--an abnormality--has proved advantageous as well as common in the development of his character.[24]

Sally, freeing Philip from the obligation to marry, severs the final bond: his delusion of self-sacrifice at the novel's end. For his willful marriage to her, in accordance with "the desires of his own heart," ultimately proves no sacrifice at all.

These and other bondages from which he gains his release merely support the central theme of the novel and need not be considered in full for the purpose of this analysis. The proposition that, in chapter 7 below, will depict *Of Human Bondage* as the first stage in a three-stage apprenticeship to life and death--it may be pointed out at this juncture in the overall analysis--views Philip's marriage to Sally as the groundwork for a potential passage from one stage to the next. The cry "America was here and now" (122.647), while echoing the same cry in Goethe's *Wilhelm Meister's Apprenticeship*,[25] signals the end of the first stage in Philip's apprenticeship to life.

6. WILHELM MEISTER'S APPRENTICESHIP

Johann Wolfgang von Goethe, at age 36, entitled the 1777-85 draft of his novel Wilhelm Meisters Theatralische Sendung (Wilhelm Meister's Theatrical Mission), now called the Urmeister (Original Meister). It comprised six books (later condensed into the first four or five books[1] of the Apprenticeship of 1791-96), ending with Wilhelm's resolve to become a professional actor. Explaining the title of the published version of 1795-96, Wilhelm Meisters Lehrjahre, Inge Halpert notes that "Goethe chose the name Wilhelm only to pay homage to Shakespeare; he used the surname Meister to point to the hero's innate capabilities as well as to his ultimate role in life."[2]

Critics widely disagree concerning the unity, or lack thereof, of Wilhelm Meister. Friedrich Schlegel first called attention to books VII and VIII as the culmination of the work, as the "height, where everything is godly and calm and pure."[3] J. G. Robertson, although finding it "difficult to agree with Schlegel" in characterizing the last two books as "an artistic culmination," nevertheless distinguishes them as containing "the ethical kernel of the novel."[4]

Susanne Howe notes from a historical point of view that "as far as their message is concerned, the last three books of the Apprenticeship might as well never have been written. For Wilhelm's successors, beginning with the German romantics," heard "not at all the measured words, 'Here or nowhere is America.'"[5] Somerset Maugham in his analysis of this novel summarizes books I-V, ignores book VI, and remarks, "From now on [that is, beginning with book VII], the novel becomes more and more confused and less and less plausible."[6]

The principal disagreement of the critics, H. S. Reiss concludes, "centers on the relations between the first five and the last two books."[7] D. J. Enright, for example, comparing the Apprenticeship with Faust, argues, "The work gives the immediate impression of falling into two pieces, as cleanly as if its binding were broken."[8] He labels books I-V as a theater-novel, "Theaterroman," comparable to Faust I; book VI as a buffer between the two sections; and books VII-VIII as a life-novel, "Lebensroman," comparable to Faust II.

The incident at the end of book V that we shall consider in this study as the proper point of division is Wilhelm's departure from the theater. This act, as Joachim Müller depicts it, "initiates a new phase of life. It is a decisive turning point in his course of instruction."[9] Max Wundt agrees essentially with Müller and with Reiss, who points out, "The last part of the novel, especially the last three books, arose from an entirely new draft."[10] By resorting to this argument of composition, Roy Pascal claims that Goethe

> wrote what are roughly the first five books in the early Weimar period, between 1777 and 1785, the version that is

known as Wilhelm Meister's Theatrical Mission. He picked it up again in 1793 and finished it in 1795, rewriting the early books and adding three more. The theme was radically altered, and every reader can detect the change of style between the earlier and later sections.[11]

For the purposes of this study, therefore, books I-V will be regarded as the first stage and books VI-VIII as the second in a three-stage apprenticeship to life and death.

As will soon be made evident, books I-V of Wilhelm Meister parallel Of Human Bondage in their central theme. The uncle in book VI expresses this theme when he exclaims, "Man's highest merit always is, as much as possible to rule external circumstances, and as little as possible to let himself be ruled by them."[12] The statement reiterates Spinoza's distinction, as noted above in the previous chapter, between a man who becomes "his own master" and one who is "mastered by fortune."[13] The reciprocally related themes of bondage to fortune and freedom for self-control, although far more subtly unfolded here than in Of Human Bondage, are central to Goethe's novel as well. As in Maugham's work, they center on the idea of self-formation as a by-product of the will which directs itself toward the release from specific bonds.

Wilhelm Meister, for instance, ultimately aims for release from illusions regarding talent, fate, and guidance and from supplementary bondages to inexperience, a commercial trade, inward cultivation, etc. His initial enslavement, to the delusion that he possesses a talent for the stage, derives from a chance introduction to and fascination with the puppet theater. He identifies empathically with the heroes, first of the Biblical story of David and Goliath and then of Tasso's Gerusalemme Liberata (Jerusalem Delivered). He imagines himself the young David and memorizes his grandiloquent speech before Goliath. He becomes the ill-fated Tancred, who mortally wounds Chlorinde, lady of his heart. Years later, therefore, when chance allows him to meet the traveling actress, Mariane, he renews through her his passion for the theater. But he now attributes to fate his double passion for the stage and Mariane: "He imagined that he understood the visible beckoning of fate, reaching out its hand by Mariane" (I.ix.33/46). At the age of twenty-two, he beholds in himself "the embryo of a great actor; the future founder of a future national theater" (I.ix.33-34/46-47).

Even as late as book IV he still considers this passion of his youth a sign from the hand of fate signaling his own talent. "May it not be," he asks himself soon after his first encounter with the amazon, "that in youth as in sleep, the images of coming things hover around us and become mysteriously visible to our unobstructed eyes? May not the seeds of what is to betide us already be scattered by the hand of Fate" (IV.ix.203/58)? His belief in his talent for acting, while founded on associations of chance, has thus yielded to a vague confidence in destiny. His trust in the delusion of talent now becomes a more all-embracing bondage to fate.

His first inkling that fate provides for his future expresses itself when, proposing to Mariane, he writes with the exuberance of a love-struck youth, "Fate takes care of love" (I.xvi.58/98). He argues that practical concerns of limited funds and parental opposition will remain in the care of Heaven. Such a trust in fate heartily inspires confidence: "I have never doubted that a man may force his way through the world, if he really is in earnest about it" (I.xvi.59/99).

He calmly avows his fixed belief in a protective force when the stranger inquires about the sale of his grandfather's art collection. He confides in the stranger, "I easily content myself, and honor destiny, which knows how to bring about what is best for me, and what is best for every one" (I.xvii.63/107). But the stranger counters that protective fate is only a vague name for necessity and chance. He stresses the crucial need for man's inner reason to master outer chance. Necessity, of course, provides the basis of existence; but people often attribute to chance and accident the name of divine guidance, Providence, or fortune, accepting what they should with reason direct, guide, and employ for their own purposes. He tells Wilhelm:

> He alone is worthy of respect, who knows what is of use to himself and others, and who labors to control his self-will. Each man has his own fortune in his hands; as the artist has a piece of rude matter, which he is to fashion to a certain shape. But the art of living rightly is like all arts: the capacity alone is born with us; it must be learned, and practiced with incessant care (I.xvii.64/109).

The stranger's argument, in denying the reality of fate, gives man both the freedom and the primary responsibility for making his life a work of art. The recognition of man's need for self-direction and self-control at this point in the narrative carries the theme of mastering chance.

Wilhelm's next act, despite the stranger's advice, attests to his susceptibility to chance. As we learn in book VII, Mariane remains faithful to him until her death, so that his abandonment of her in book I depends entirely on a false appearance of infidelity. As premises for suspicion he relies entirely on two chance incidents: the imagined sighting of a dark unidentified figure leaving her room and the discovery of an anonymous letter wrapped in her kerchief. Despite his intention to wed her--indeed, he carries the proposal in his hand at the time--he concludes from these two fortuitous incidents alone that she has betrayed him. He immediately abandons her without doubting even momentarily his grounds for mistrusting her. Unaware of his actual vulnerability to chance, he characteristically persuades himself in book II that his disappointment over her represents a test "ordained by fate for the best" (II.ii.70/124). Therefore, he finds himself bound, not to fate itself, but to the illusion of fate.

His bondage to this illusion recurs as a motif throughout books I-V. As proof of the notion that fate is, in fact, an illusion, chance becomes so inextricably interwoven with destiny that by the end of book III the distinction between the two has dissolved into ambiguity. Wilhelm's silent avowal of love to the Countess and sudden parting from her at the end of book III parallel his loss of Mariane at the close of book I. But in the incident with the Countess the evidence even more conclusively points to the probability of chance although still masquerading as an admonishment from fate. The author, suggesting the ambiguity of his theme in the last line of book III, asks: "What singular warning of chance or of destiny tore them asunder" (III.xii.174/326)? The question, as Goethe's use of the term warning implies, is weighted in the balance toward fate, but chance is now vying for equal footing.

Goethe returns to this ambiguity at the outset of book IV. Wilhelm imagines the harper as one who "by chance or destiny" (IV.i.180/12) has erred in commiting some serious crime. The harper has asserted, however, that he belongs to "an inexorable Destiny" (IV.i.179/11). As Eric Blackall observes, "At this point in the novel Wilhelm is caught in the ambiguity, whereas the Harper accepts only external Fate."[14]

In each incident of Wilhelm's experiences chance eventually proves victorious over fate. Even in the above incident between Wilhelm and the Countess, as illustrated in book V, his departure results actually from the chance pressure of her locket against her breast: the physical pain prompts her cry. And although she considers herself judged by fate and subsequently withdraws from the active world, Goethe reveals her decision as similarly motivated by chance. On the other hand, Wilhelm, still trusting in a protective fate, has felt his confidence measurably shaken by this incident with the Countess.

Chance eventually bears the blame also for the episode in book IV in which bandits attack the theatrical troupe. Led by Wilhelm and arriving before the noble and rich company against whom the marauders have planned their attack, the troupe undergoes "the fate which was provided for the others" (IV.xi.206/65). Wilhelm at first blames himself rather than his protective fate, whose clarity has nonetheless diminished in his eyes. "The threads of his destiny," we are told, "had become so strangely entangled, he wished to see its curious knots unravelled or cut in two" (IV.xii.208/68). His dreamy longing for an assurance that will reestablish his confidence, an outward sign of certainty--"even though it were by chance"--well accords with the wish in the song: "Only he who knows yearning," sung by Mignon and the harper, who both reflect his perplexity.

He reads into his interpretation of the role of Hamlet much of the trouble and bitterness that he himself experiences. Therefore, he, rather than Hamlet, best embodies the character of those celebrated lines: "The time is out of joint: O cursed spite,/That ever I was born to set it right" (IV.xiii.211/75)! William Diamond, arguing against the "many critics and interpreters of Hamlet" who read Wilhelm's own interpretation out of context, emphatically cautions that "in Wilhelm Meister's picture of Hamlet we have not an impartial critical analysis of Shakespeare's Hamlet, but a creation that resembles more strikingly Wilhelm Meister himself than Shakespeare's Prince of Denmark."[15] Similarly, Blackall reminds us that in his revision of Hamlet, in book V, "Wilhelm agrees to the cuts, not because he comes round to Serlo's point of view, but in order to preserve the parallel between himself and Hamlet."[16] His search to identify with Hamlet, even a Hamlet whom he distorts, reflects an attempt to free himself from the burden of responsibility for the theatrical troupe's losses. He desperately attempts to shift the blame to fate.

At the close of book IV he has reached the moment of decision whether or not to commit himself to acting on the stage. Whereas in book I it was Mariane who inspired him superficially to act in the theater, in book IV it is the actress Aurelie who inspires him truly. Through his sympathy for her suffering he has discovered in her a fellow victim of infidelity whose fate in love compares with his own loss, as he sees it, of Mariane.

Moreover, he has also found in her a kindred enthusiast for a national theater. Serlo extends him a contract to act professionally and at last fulfill his early dream. Although he still wishes for "some preponderancy from without" (IV.xix.237/125) as a sign of certainty, he praises fate for having apparently led him through the vicissitudes of chance toward achieving his goal. "And ought I not to honor Fate, which, without furtherance of mine, has led me hither to the goal of all my wishes?" he muses. "Has not all that I, in old times, meditated and forecast, now happened accidentally, and without my co-operation" (IV.xix.238/125)? Fate and chance remain bewilderingly balanced in his expectation of a sign.

The arrival of Werner's letter, at the outset of book V, therefore--the letter bearing news of the death of Wilhelm's father--sets free the apprentice at a moment when he still hesitates crucially in his choice. He certainly cannot regard the letter as the sign sought from fate, and he makes no mention of fate in his celebrated reply. Thus Goethe relegates to mere chance the connection between Werner's letter and the progress of Wilhelm's own life. The commercial views of civic life and happiness expressed by the letter decisively repel the youth, who then opts for the theater: "Who would have thought," observes the author, "that a letter of Werner's, written with quite different views, should have forced him on resolving" (V.i.246/141)? Even as he binds himself by contract to act on the stage, he severs his chains to any consciousness of fate: "He wrote his name mechanically only, not knowing what he did" (V.iii.252/154). He has convinced himself in lieu of an incontestable sign from fate that inclination and the aim "to cultivate my individual self, here as I am" (V.iii.250/154) have guided his progress, although imperceptibly, since youth.

Even this belief in self-formation, as Pascal ascertains, "is to be shown to be an illusion."[17] But the passage itself is pivotal, shifting the stress from fate as the active agent to Wilhelm himself. His belief in a protective destiny has now succumbed to the recognition of a labyrinth of accidental incidents that confuse the unity of his own purpose. For the sake of clarity he must cut asunder the threads binding the incidents. He must therefore cast out all external relations in his revision of Hamlet, reducing them to one. He no longer identifies with Hamlet, having determined that this hero posseses "only sentiments." Hamlet seems to lack the strength of character that he believes himself to possess, as evidenced in his letter to Werner. Although for Hamlet fate has "drawn the plan," for himself he no longer experiences self-assurance. Fate--which in drama never protects but must "always be terrible"--is "tragic in the highest sense." Fate "admits of no other than a tragic end" (V.vii.265/178-79). In drama, as in life, destiny has lost for Wilhelm its protective character, and he has grown indifferent to its signs.

The ghost in the opening performance of Hamlet, according to

Blackall, "is the decision from outside" that Wilhelm has sought as a sign of certainty since "before the Hamlet analysis." Blackall claims that "it points him away from the theater."[18] If we consider the actual intention of the ghost and the warning on the veil as clues, such a claim on the surface rings true. But Wilhelm's reluctance to abandon the theater until long after the specter's appearance, indeed not until Aurelie's death, as well as Goethe's disinclination to attribute Wilhelm's departure to the incident certainly suggest that the ghost does not serve as "the turning-point"[19]--as Blackall would have it--directing him to reenter life. Although struck with horror at the specter's countenance, he does not regard its appearance as a sign of fate. Aware of inconsistencies, he tends to link it with Serlo, who appears "to be deep in the secrets of the Ghost" (V.xiii.283/213). It nearly slips from memory as Boisterous takes on the role. The next mention of the ghost involves Mignon's placing its veil in Wilhelm's traveling bag after Aurelie's death. He virtually ignores the veil, remarking significantly to Mignon "that it could not be of any service to him" (V.xvi.306/255). He thus avoids acknowledging any link between the ghost and fate.

Wilhelm cannot conclusively resolve the ambiguity between chance and fate until his admission into the Society of the Tower, the "Turmgesellschaft," at the conclusion of the seventh book. But what transpires during this second meeting between him and the stranger merely explicates what the close of book V has sufficiently implied. The stranger in the seventh book suggests, as he did in his first discussion with Wilhelm, that character controls destiny. And in open confirmation of an awareness acquired as early as book V, Wilhelm simply responds, "Is what we call Destiny but Chance" (VII.ix.60/122)? We may conclude, therefore, that his illusory trust in fate, which he subconsciously abandoned before the end of book V, has awaited book VII for its renunciation in full consciousness and acknowledgment of chance alone.

In any adequate discussion of Wilhelm Meister, apart from consideration of the issues of fate and chance, the question of guidance must inevitably provoke concern. The country clergyman in book II alludes to the force which, as Wilhelm belatedly discovers, significantly triggers his release from most, if not all, of his bonds. The clergyman, as did the stranger before him, questions him about art while suggesting the need for direction. But at this stage in his development Wilhelm still solidly trusts in the guidance of fate. "Happy then are those," he replies, "whom fate takes charge of, and educates according to their several natures" (II.ix.105/192)! The clergyman has argued, however, that education far surpasses fate as a trustworthy schoolmaster. "Let no one think that he can conquer the first impressions of his youth," he assures Wilhelm. If a youth has grown to maturity surrounded by worthy teachers who have guided the force of his efforts toward habits of excellence, he will undeniably lead "a purer, more perfect and happier life" than one who has wasted his energies in opposition and error. "Fate," he asserts, "is an excellent, but most expensive schoolmaster" (II.ix.105/191-2); for chance frequently corrupts and misdirects its decrees. On the other hand, educational guidance proves more trustworthy than fate for the management and direction of chance.[20]

Wilhelm, however, characteristically ignores the country clergyman's message. He subsequently meets and befriends the harper. He retains his friendship with Laertes and his attachment to Philine, who is admittedly "dangerous"; but Philine, genuine and warm-hearted though obviously amoral, embodies delight. He foolishly considers himself safe from her wiles, for he believes his experience with Mariane has prepared him to guard "against the encircling arms of woman" (II.x.108/197). But no sooner does he find himself "encircled with [her] soft arms" (V.xii.282/210) than his surrender to her insistence strikes a violent note of jealousy in Mignon and hastens the day of her death. He cannot escape Philine's wiles so easily as he imagines; nor can he evade his bonds to Mignon, the harper, and Laertes and continue with his proper business. The stroller Meline, cajoling him into purchasing all the sets and costumes of the theatrical company, forges the last link in his complete bondage to the troupe.

Unworthy guiding forces indeed enslave him and misdirect his life, so that toward the end of book II he begins to sense his bonds to the ill-directed decrees of fate. "He now clearly saw," Goethe affirms,

> that of late he had fallen into a broken, wandering path, where, if he tasted, it was but in drops what he once quaffed in unrestricted measure. But he could not clearly see what insatiable want it was that nature had made the law of his being; and how this want had been only set on edge, half satisfied, and misdirected by the circumstances of his life (II.xiv.122-23/226).

Although persuaded within himself that he possesses "force enough" (II.xiv.123/227) to leave his surroundings without delay, he yields at the end of book II to Mignon's filial entreaties to stay.

Book III introduces the first inkling that guidance is a substitute for fate. The inkling appears initially in the advice of Jarno, who warns him caustically and bluntly that the theater will squander his time and energy. "It is pity," Jarno tells him, "you should play with hollow nuts, for a stake of hollow nuts" (III.viii.151/283). With overtones allusive to the puppet theater and the troupe of acrobats, he links Wilhelm's present fascination with acting to his past interest in an art without soul: "It is sinful of you to waste your hours in dressing out these apes to look more human, and teaching dogs to dance" (III.viii.155/290). He then introduces Wilhelm to the extraordinary art of Shakespeare, an art that manifests soul.

Jarno, as Jürgen Rausch observes, seeks to encourage Wilhelm to glean from his reading of a literary master his own "artistic futility."[21] Such a recognition, he believes, will incite Wilhelm to renounce his mediocre future in the theater and embark on the promising development of his inherent talents "in active life" (III.xi.166/311). Although both the stranger in book I and the country clergyman in book II have sought to guide him imperceptibly, in conformity with the Abbé's precepts, Jarno contradicts the Abbé's intent by resorting to precaution. He fears misfortune, illustrated in book III by a "traveller, who, at but a short distance from the inn, falls into the water" (III.viii.156/290-91) and in book VIII by "a nightwalker going straight to break his neck" (VIII.v.106/214). He feels constrained, as a prudent friend, to deliver Wilhelm from such dangers. Wholeheartedly he believes in the efficacy of immediate aid and preservation from error.

Wilhelm appreciates this strange but distinguished man's interest in him as he begins to perceive vaguely "that things went forward in the world differently from what he had supposed" (III.viii.156/291). Moreover, the officer who embraces him in the Count's park strengthens the hint of a force in effect other than fate and advises him to follow Jarno's counsel, adding sufficiently that he will thereby fulfill the wish "of an unknown man, who takes a genuine interest in you" (III.xi.167/313).

Goethe, however, exposes Jarno's guidance as no more effective than fate, a failure clearly evidenced when the original intention in advising Wilhelm to study Shakespeare leads him astray. Wilhelm at first finds in Shakespeare "a thousand feelings and capacities" about which he "formerly had neither notion nor anticipation" (III.ix.160/299). But later, as he informs Jarno, he discovers "all the anticipations that I have ever had regarding man and his destiny, which have accompanied me from youth upwards, often unobserved by myself" (III.xi.165/310). He has found in Shakespeare, not a master whose talent overwhelms him--although this celestial "Genius" (III.xi.168/310) profoundly astonishes him--but rather a confirmation of his own belief in the reality of fate, a belief from which Jarno has sought to dissuade him. Similarly, the officer accompanying Jarno attempts fruitlessly to correct this adventitious effect of his friend's advice on Wilhelm.

In the end, Jarno unwisely condemns Wilhelm's attachment to the harper and Mignon, singling them out specifically as "a wandering ballad-monger" and "a silly mongrel" (III.xi.166/312); and Wilhelm properly dismisses both advisers for Jarno's unfeeling callousness. He rejects his guidance entirely and as a result plunges more deeply into error, until Jarno frankly admits to him in book VIII, "I myself have been of less service to the cause of our Society, and of my fellow-men, than any other members. I am but a bad schoolmaster" (VIII.v.106/214).

After the failure of both Jarno and the officer to rescue Wilhelm from his illusions, the Abbé contrives to guide him more directly than did the stranger and the country clergyman but more subtly than Jarno. He provides the ghost for the production of Hamlet. His belief, as Jarno later informs Wilhelm, is "that it was the only way of curing you, if you were curable" (VIII.v.107/215). The Abbé hopes that Wilhelm's portrayal of Hamlet will satisfy his thirst for the theater and rechannel his interest toward other non-theatrical undertakings. For a younger Wilhelm had once similarly embraced extended plans for his puppet theater, had made "mighty preparations, then a few trials" and then abruptly abandoned his dream. "My greatest pleasure lay in the inventive part, and the employment of my fancy" (I.vi.24/29), he had told Mariane. The Abbé doubtlessly infers from his insight into Wilhelm's nature, therefore, that the apprentice, having achieved his goal of acting in the theater, will predictably abandon it. And to Jarno he maintains that Wilhelm will "never go upon the stage again" (VIII.v.107/215).

The Abbé's plan, however, like Jarno's before it, cannot succeed in turning Wilhelm from his error. "I believed the contrary," Jarno says regarding the Abbé's design, "and I was right" (VIII.v.107/215). The ghost appears as planned at the appointed time, but its similarity to an actual specter fills Wilhelm with horror and profoundly impresses him with its cry: "I am thy father's spirit" (V.xi.277/201). The catharsis of the scare inspires the entire performance. For Wilhelm and the other actors it results in a magnificent success. Returning to his room both drunk and elated with the evening's results, he overlooks the words of warning on the ghost's veil, which he has now acquired. And Philine's arms, drawing him back into bed, thwart his attempt to question the ghost as it appears in a vision. The unabated enthusiasm of the following night, including the interruption of the fire, further distracts him. Not even the threat of Philine's departure with the disguised Friedrich can impair the continued success and unity of the company. He remains naïvely sidetracked. The Abbé's plan has failed to avert him. He becomes hopelessly confirmed in the error of his illusion.

Rausch calls the Abbé's basic philosophy of guidance "Werden lassen" (let be) or "Irren-lassen" (allow error),[22] as is illustrated in book VIII by the abbot's maxim: "error can never be cured, except by erring" (VIII.v.107/214). The country clergyman, who, though disguised, resembles the Abbé and indeed may be the Abbé himself, expounds part of this philosophy to Wilhelm in the tower:

> To guard from error is not the instructor's duty, but to lead the erring pupil; nay, to let him quaff his error in deep satiating draughts, this is the instructor's wisdom. He who tastes his error, will long dwell with it, will take delight in it as in a singular felicity: while he who drains it to the dregs will, if he be not crazy, find it out (VII.ix.61/122. The underscoring is mine).

Wilhelm immediately and significantly responds to the clergyman's inference. "What error can he mean?" he asks himself, "but the error which has clung to me through my whole life; that I sought for cultivation where it was not to be found; that I fancied I could form a talent in me, while without the smallest gift for it" (VII.ix.61/123. Again the underscoring is mine)?

The philosophy of guidance in its entirety as it applies to Wilhelm's cultivation--from his first meeting with the stranger in book I to his encounter with the ghost in book V--is contained above in the country clergyman's statement and Wilhelm's reply. Describing in book VIII the final step in his cure (by now simply a matter of time), Jarno quotes the Abbé's dictum: "A man is never happy till his vague striving has itself marked out its proper limitation" (VIII.v.108/218. My underscoring).

The key concepts of guidance within these three quotations emerge as (1) fancy, "Einbildung," which subsumes the notions of vague striving and of fancying oneself able to form a talent from within, while without the smallest gift for it; (2) salvation, "Bewahrung," or guarding from error; (3) guidance, "Leitung," or leading into error; (4) self-limitation, "Selbstbegrenzung," including the notions of satiation in error and of marking out one's own proper limitation; and finally (5) cultivation, "Ausbildung," which, as noted above in chapter 3, forms an unexpected consequence of the will directing itself toward a goal other than self, as characterized by the phrase, "sought for cultivation where it was not to be found."

Wilhelm centrally errs, at the outset of the novel, in linking fancy, "Einbildung," with fate, "Schicksal." The stranger in book I suggests reason, "Vernunft," as a substitute for fate. The country clergyman in book II supplements reason by introducing the human tutor, "Menschenerzieher." And Jarno in book III attempts salvation, "Bewahrung." (Note that although in his own opinion Jarno fails, he does not fail within the Abbé's broader perspective. Wilhelm initially feels drawn by him, then repelled even more deeply into error--which is how the Abbé originally envisioned the pattern that he must follow.) The ghost of book V represents the culminating effect of guidance, "Leitung," for the specter too lures Wilhelm more abysmally into error.

The last step in the total process, however--the step which the Abbé, after each act of guidance, has patiently anticipated--is self-limitation, "Selbstbegrenzung," the deciding factor in Wilhelm's cure. Although this final step properly occurs at the end of book V, the death of Aurelie in the same time frame more appropriately represents the "turning-point" that Blackall seeks in the earlier incident involving the ghost (See p. 55 above). Aurelie's death, prompting Wilhelm's mission to Lothario, serves as the ostensible excuse for his departure from the theater. But self-limitation is the more legitimate underlying motive for this abandonment of his error.

Having decided to separate himself from the theater by the end of book V, Wilhelm does not return to the stage. Indeed, his "formal leave" (VII.viii.57/114), taken of the theater in book VII, appears solely as an afterthought. As Wundt notes, "Wilhelm's temporary return to his theater companions and the departure from them appears [in book VII] only as an episode."[23] The initial incident of book VII, which occurs immediately and chronologically after his departure two books earlier, depicts his informing the country clergyman that he has indeed renounced his error: "On looking back upon the period which I passed in their [the theatrical company's] society, it seems as if I looked into an endless void; nothing of it has remained with me." The cleric replies, however, "Here you are mistaken; everything that happens to us leaves some trace behind it, everything contributes imperceptibly to form us" (VII.i.2/4).

With its concomitant illusions of talent and fate, the fancy, "Einbildung," which bound Wilhelm in books I through V has thus led indirectly to cultivation, "Ausbildung," as a more substantial by-product. Although the Abbé and his aids have guided him deep into his illusions of talent and fate, self-limitation, "Selbstbegrenzung," releases him from his bondage to error. He drains error to the dregs, and satiation dissolves error's bonds. The voice of the ghost in the Tower cries, "Thou are saved, thou art on the way to the goal. None of thy follies wilt thou repent; none wilt thou wish to repeat"; and adding, no doubt with a knowing smile: "no luckier destiny can be allotted to a man" (VII.ix.61/123).

Guidance, as I have attempted to show, has abetted but not

entirely wrought Wilhelm's cure. Halpert misinterprets the basic philosophy of the Society of the Tower when she disparages his "purely receptive and dependent relationship," pointing to his frustration in book VIII at having been "observed, nay, guided" (VIII.i.70/143) in countless actions of his life. She describes the Wilhelm of the early part of the Apprenticeship as "independent and energetic" and intimidated only by "a fate which he recognizes as being beyond man's will." The Wilhelm of the second part, however, she considers "helpless in making judgments and decisions" and dependent "completely on the intervention of his friends of the 'Tower,'" concluding that "Wilhelm does not know what he wants and must be led."[24]

Other critics, sharing Wilhelm's immediate frustration, quote his complaint to Natalie, accusing the Abbé of "having joined with others, as it were, to make game of me" (VIII.iii.82/168). They note his demand that Jarno tell him, "how, and in what manner you intend to sacrifice me" (VIII.v.108/218). Like Halpert, these critics share his resentment and charge the Society of the Tower with usurping an individual's powers of self-determination.[25] Indeed, such an indictment, if true, would invalidate an essential feature of the apprenticeship novel by depriving self-formation of its dependence, be it direct or indirect, on the will of the individual.

But the Society does not represent the dominant force in the Apprenticeship, even though its function as guide, admittedly, supersedes the role of fate. Wundt remarks that the Society:

> plays fate, but only to subjugate it to the authority of reason. So many apparently fortuitous and yet significant connections in Wilhelm's life, in which he wished to discover the rule of fate, are traced back to the secret willful arrangement of these men.[26]

The line most often lifted from context and hence overemphasized --that is, Jarno's lighthearted jest regarding the Abbé--states that "in general he likes to act the part of Destiny a little" (VIII.v.109/219-20). But we cannot thereby accuse the Society of having dominated an individual's "powers of self-determination."[27]

Pascal points out, with insight as vital as it is perceptive, that "the 'Society of the Tower' symbolizes the world [or, as R. B. Farrell characterizes it: "life"[28]]. And like the world its members apply different educative methods . . . . All are right in their way, together they make up the total process of education."[29] Note that Jarno, quoting the Abbé in book VIII, reflects just such a worldview: "It is all men that make up mankind; all powers taken together that make up the world" (VIII.v.108/216).

The Society as "world" holds no more power over Wilhelm than does nature itself. It guides only as nature guides. Further, its educators "guide," as Irvin Stock observes, "so delicately, often so imperceptibly" because "they aspire to teach as nature herself teaches."[30] The Abbé can lead Wilhelm deeper into error, but Wilhelm alone can and must call a halt and choose another path. When he has transcended the guidance of nature and accepted personal responsibility for that which he had previously attributed to fate, when he has admitted paternal accountability for Felix's welfare, then he has outgrown the guidance of the Society and achieved his freedom, fully deserving these liberating lines: "Hail to thee, young man! Thy Apprenticeship is done; Nature has pronounced thee free"(VII.ix.63/127).

The Society of the Tower does not dominate the Apprenticeship. It replaces fate only as education replaces illusion. It does not choose for Wilhelm; it only aids him in his choice just as inclination aids endeavor. Jarno, in full accordance with the Abbé's principle of encouraging every tendency of nature, reassures Wilhelm, "It is your affair to try and choose; it is ours to aid you" (VIII.v.108/218). Indeed, the Society supports his direct objective, but it is his decision alone that can impose a limit. In this way self-limitation decisively releases him from his bondage to an unlimited and vain striving, for guidance can only encourage the striving. The Abbé and his Society subordinate their role as guide to the individual power of self-determination.

In restricting the particular Society to a limited role in the Apprenticeship, the above analysis can be equally applied to the more general "higher hand" of the author's famous declaration to Eckermann. Goethe suggests, in referring to Wilhelm Meister, "that man, despite all his follies and errors, led by a higher hand, reaches some worthy goal at last."[31] But even a belief in that priceless good, or "unschätzbarem Guten," as Howe calls it--even faith in "that beneficent if mysterious guidance that shall somehow make all right in the end"[32] ultimately subordinates itself to the individual act of self-limitation.

This act depends so crucially upon the self and its capacities that the moment of decision must vary among individual selves. Again quoting the Abbé, Jarno reassures Wilhelm, "He in whom there is much to be developed will be later in acquiring true perceptions of himself and of the world. There are few who at once have thought and the capacity of action"(VIII.v.106/213). The limited nature of man restricts the effectiveness of guidance, whether human or divine, to the role of assistance. And although guidance, necessarily, cannot embrace everyone as it embraces Wilhelm, neither can it prove dominant when manifesting itself. "For Goethe it is not crucial," Müller declares, "whether actually a higher hand, a divine providence, orders life's way; rather what is important is that a man does not hold himself passive, is not satisfied with a determination, and does not submit to an ever so questionable result as God-willed."[33]

Wilhelm's bonds to the illusions of talent, fate, and guidance all burst when his own powers transcend theirs. It is interesting to note in retrospect that his enslavement to the delusion of talent and his trust in the illusion of fate are both reflected in his attachment to Mignon and the harper. Philine, in book II, describes Mignon as "the enigma" (II.iv.85/153), a creature without name--except that which people call her--and of uncertain age. Her name and the clothes she wears contradict her sex.[34] Her history and parentage remain unknown until book VIII. And she possesses a single talent: an egg dance performed while blindfolded. The harper, whom Wilhelm also meets in book II, proves to be even more of an enigma. He is Mignon's father, as revealed in book VIII, by an incestuous union with his sister. The obscure force of unmastered fate binds both

Mignon and the harper.

The physician in book VIII diagnoses Mignon as betraying through her songs the anguish of a "double longing" (VIII.iii.86/174), which so dramatically undermines her being that it ultimately precipitates her death. The double nature of her longing--"the desire of revisiting her native land, and the desire for you [that is, Wilhelm]" (VIII.iii.83/169)--provides two equally unattainable objectives. At the time of her kidnaping she had vented an oath to the Holy Virgin never to trust a human being with the history of her origin, swearing instead that she would "live and die in hope of immediate aid from Heaven" (VIII.iii.84/170). So from that moment until her death her self-imposed bondage to fate restricts her life. Her song at the end of book V seeks to express the key to her suppressed emotions:

> O, ask me not to speak, I pray thee!
> It must not be revealed, but hid;
> How gladly would my tongue obey thee,
> Did not the voice of Fate forbid!

And her final couplet completes the pathetic portrait of fate's victim:

> My lips an oath forever closes,
> My sorrows God alone can know!
> (V.xvi.306/256)

Like Mignon, the harper betrays through his songs the oppression of a "double *idée fixe*."[35] The same physician who has treated Mignon now diagnoses his insanity with marked insight:

> His chief delusion is a fancy that he brings misfortune everywhere along with him; and that death, to be unwittingly occasioned by a boy, is constantly impending over him. At first he was afraid of Mignon, not knowing that she was a girl; then Felix frightened him; and, as with all his misery, he has a boundless love of life, this may perhaps have been the origin of his aversion to the child (VII.iv.14/31).

Therefore, the harper's double fixed idea, like Mignon's dual longing, insidiously weakens his being and hastens his death.

His fear, as Robert Clark suggests, proves justified; for "he does meet his death because of Felix, who is completely innocent of any action that might bring it about."[36] When he erroneously assumes his laudanum has poisoned Felix, he cuts his own throat in remorse. Treated immediately by the physician, he then discovers in the Abbé's manuscript the horrible crime of his youth. He loosens the bandages and bleeds to death. He, like Mignon, belongs not to himself. "I belong to an inexorable Destiny" (IV.i.179/11), he has told Wilhelm. He represents, in Blackall's interpretation, "the extreme standpoint of recognizing only outer force"; he "accepts only external Fate."[37] The famous lay characterizing his slavery to fate laments:

> Who never ate his bread in sorrow,

Who never spent the darksome hours,
Weeping and watching for the morrow,
He knows ye not, ye gloomy powers.

To earth, this weary earth, ye bring us,
To guilt ye let us heedless go,
Then leave repentance fierce to wring us:
A moment's guilt, an age of woe!
(II.xiii.118/217-18)

Wilhelm's adoption of Mignon and the harper as his "strange family" (III.ix.161/301), therefore, welds an intimate link between himself and two slaves to the illusion of fate. The two scarred individuals share with him a passive dependence on fate as well as the dreamy longing, "Sehnsucht," and inexpressible anguish that alternately accompany such a debilitating submission. In the latter respect Mignon and the harper symbolize, as Eugen Wolff remarks, "Wilhelm's dreamy yearning, in which he [the harper] with Mignon as an irregular duet sing the song: 'Only he who knows yearning.'"[38] The "two sufferers" are characterized by Edward Dowden as "wasted by deep but vain longing, an endless sehnsucht [sic], and who must needs descend to the tomb as the victims or martyrs of desire."[39]

Wilhelm's release in book V from his unrestrained striving for talent in the theater and from his bondage to the illusion of fate ensures his release from Mignon and the harper. Thereafter his reason, rather than his heart, determines his relationship with them. He begins to see them as Goethe reveals them, in terms that Pascal describes as "ineffectual, dangerous." Mignon, although loved for the poetry of her existence, more realistically embodies "the beauty of immaturity, even of disease." Thus in book VIII we should feel no surprise, as Pascal concludes, "to find that Mignon's death passes almost without comment. Wilhelm, conscious that all his efforts to help Mignon have resulted in her destruction, dismisses the problem from his mind; a pompous funeral-ceremony is a substitute for personal feeling."[40] Both Mignon and the harper recede into obscurity led by the illusions that dominate and kill them.

There are other minor bondages, apart from those noted above, from which Wilhelm gains his release. Initially he is bound to an occupation for which he has no gift, wherein he serves three years in his father's trade and then, sporadically, gathers commercial data for the journal of his travels. There is also the bondage to inexperience, as characterized by his trust in all men until the officer in the Society of the Tower prepares his release through an appeal to his matured understanding: "Learn to know the men who may be trusted" (VII.ix.61/123)! Of more consequence is the bondage entailing inward cultivation to the neglect of outward circumstances, which is severed only when he abandons the stage. Through his inquiries into the affairs of his property he discovers that he must also consider outward means for effective work. These and other bonds may be targeted for consideration, but they merely supplement the central theme of self-culture as a release from bondage and need not lend themselves to full discussion for the goal of this preliminary analysis.

7. THE FIRST STAGE

Of Human Bondage and books I-V of Wilhelm Meister's Apprenticeship depict the first stage in an apprenticeship to life. As two similar expressions of the same stage, they can be compared and viewed as a unit. The parallels between their plots, their central characters, their structure, tone, motifs, and central themes are legion within the type of novel they both represent.

The parallels in plot alone reveal their basic commonality as apprenticeship novels even while pointing up their individual modifications of the type. Although a century and a nation apart, Philip and Wilhelm mature into manhood within similar patterns. Philip is sired by a successful middle-class surgeon; Wilhelm, by a thriving middle-class merchant. Only Wilhelm benefits from the companionship of both parents, yet his father intends him for the calling of commerce, exactly as Philip's uncle directs him toward the ministry. Furthermore, each youth has a real or adoptive father who misunderstands him and a real or adoptive mother who solicitously cares for him.

Philip learns the delightful joys of reading at the same early age that Wilhelm embraces the puppet theater. As Maugham says of Philip:

> Insensibly he formed the most delightful habit in the world, the habit of reading: he did not know that thus he was providing himself with a refuge from all the distress of life; he did not know either that he was creating for himself an unreal world which would make the real world of every day a source of bitter disappointment (9.32).

Similarly, Goethe has Wilhelm relate:

> I surrendered myself to my imagination; I rehearsed and prepared forever; built a thousand castles in the air, and saw not that I was at the same time undermining the foundations of these little edifices (I.vi.25/29).

Both youths love foreign romance, as their selection of books confirms. Philip devours E. W. Lane's translation of The Thousand and One Nights; Wilhelm memorizes copious sections of J. F. Koppe's translation of Jerusalem Delivered. Both the pleasures and the perils of fancy fill their young minds.

Philip childishly depends on religion because it offers refuge from sorrow and pain, while the more practical Wilhelm uses religious plots and heroes in his puppet shows. Religion provides Philip's first serious disillusionment; love initially disenchants Wilhelm. Both apprentices act without sufficient cause, for Philip's rejection of religion--as indeed Maugham admits of himself in The Summing Up--can be justified no more realistically than can Wilhelm's desertion of Mariane. "I have no doubt," Maugham acknowledges, "that my reasons for coming to the conclusion I came to were inadequate. They were the reasons of an ignorant boy. They were of the heart rather than of the head."[1]

Embarking on their artistic careers early in life, both Philip and Wilhelm awake to the reality of their middle-class instincts. As W. H. Bruford describes Wilhelm: "The carefully nurtured son of a respectable family is presented with a first alternative to his middle-class ideals in the Bohemianism of the actors."[2] Comparably, Philip, confronted with the unconventional mode of artists' and writers' lives--clearly recognizes his own "instincts of the middle class" on two separate occasions: on examining the sordid Bohemian existence (50.257) and in considering marriage to a common waitress (62.319).

Both apprentices oscillate constantly in their choice of life style. When he leaves King's School, Philip declines a career coincident with his uncle's plan as he renounces the ministry, electing instead the study of language. After the episode with Miss Wilkinson, however, he dedicates himself for a brief span to the commercial life before relinquishing it forever in favor of art. In a similar pattern Wilhelm declines a career in his father's firm, turning first to the theater. After his affair with Mariane, however, he reapplies himself to commercial life, then enthusiastically relinquishes it for the lasting allure of the stage.

Both youths acquire confidence in their assumed genius for the imitative arts through the vital reassurance of a woman. Miss Wilkinson originally encourages Philip's interest in painting, beseeching him dramatically to believe in himself: "Who would be a clerk when he might be a great artist" (38.177)? Comparably, Mariane inspires Wilhelm, who beholds "in himself the embryo of a great actor" (I.ix.33-34/46). Ultimately both Philip and Wilhelm become aware that they will never transcend the level of mediocrity in their chosen fields, wisely conceding the futility of their hopes. Philip renounces art, Wilhelm forsakes the theater.

Even the antagonists of the two novels compare remarkably in their adamant prejudices against change. In Of Human Bondage the Vicar believes in completing whatever one has begun: "Like all weak men he laid an exaggerated stress on not changing one's mind" (39.180). And he will not consider Philip's discontinuing his role as an accountant. Philip reacts violently to his rigid attitude. Similarly, in Wilhelm Meister Werner adheres uncompromisingly to the notion of carrying a task to its conclusion, whereas Wilhelm, confronted by Werner's rigidity, retorts:

> And still the question might be asked: Is there not good hope of a youth who, on commencing some unsuitable affair, soon discovers its unsuitableness, and discontinues his exertions, not choosing to spend toil and time on what never can be of any value (I.x.34/49)?

With Of Human Bondage and Wilhelm Meister nearing their conclusions, the Vicar and Werner reappear as revealing foils to Philip and Wilhelm, whose mature outlooks expose the narrow lives that their antagonists have led in the interim and the superficial values that have enslaved them.

In Of Human Bondage the death of Philip's uncle, bringing therewith an inheritance, frees Philip from poverty, whereas in Wilhelm Meister the death of his father releases Wilhelm from a commercial career. Both apprentices, as imprudent spendthrifts, have either trusted too naïvely in the integrity of their debtors or fallen victim to the impulsive whims of the heart. Philip expends his generosity on Mildred, Wilhelm secures stock in the theater: two ultimately unwise investments. And yet both Philip, who was penniless at twenty-five, and Wilhelm eventually receive inheritances, which they employ wisely.

The search for a transcendent order in life provides a further parallel between the two apprentices. The recurrent motif of Cronshaw's Persian rug sumbolizes the principal mystery confronting Philip, namely, life's meaning. Whereas life's force, as presented by the stranger, the country clergyman, Jarno, the officer, and others, poses the enigma commanding Wilhelm's attention. Significantly, the acknowledgment of chance in each case resolves the problem. Philip rejects "meaning" in life, conceding, "It seemed pure chance. The rain fell alike upon the just and upon the unjust, and for nothing was there a why and a wherefore" (106.558). And Wilhelm rejects meaning's equivalent, "fate" in life, discovering the answer even before questioning himself in the Tower: "Is what we call destiny but Chance" (VII.ix.60/122)? Both meaning and fate are dismissed upon the awareness and acknowledgment of chance.

Philip, like Wilhelm, matures at the expense of his own errors. He discovers that "one profits more by the mistakes one makes off one's own bat than by doing the right thing on somebody else's advice" (52.268). In essence his conclusion parallels the Abbé's description of Wilhelm, when he informs Natalie:

> I augur better of a child, a youth who is wandering astray on a path of his own, than of many who are walking aright upon paths which are not theirs. If the former, either by themselves or by the guidance of others, ever find the right path, that is to say, the path which suits their nature, they will never leave it (VIII.iii.82/167).

Further similarities abound. Introducing the motif of self-reliance, Philip discerns "that all his life he had followed the ideals that other people, by their words or their writings, had instilled into him" (122.647). Wilhelm correspondingly realizes, "that experience was sadly wanting to him; and hence, on the experience of others, and on the results which they deduced from it, he put a value far beyond its real one; and thus led himself still deeper into error." Wilhelm, too, "frequently took foreign lights for his loadstars" (V.i.245/139-40).

The development of a conscious self-formation proceeds in each novel as a gradual, somewhat obscure evolution into awareness. At the moment of Philip's decision to abandon rather than remain involved in art, Maugham narrates:

> Of late Philip had been captivated by an idea that since one had only one life it was important to make a success of it, but he did not count success by the acquiring of money or the achieving of fame; he did not quite know yet what he meant by it, perhaps variety of experience and the making the most of his abilities (50.256).

And in an essentially comparable moment of resolution Wilhelm writes to Werner:

> To speak it in a word; the cultivation of my individual self, here as I am, has from my youth upwards been constantly though dimly my wish and my purpose (V.iii.250/149).

On the surface two parallels appear to link the conclusion in *Of Human Bondage* with books VI-VIII of *Wilhelm Meister's Apprenticeship*, but the differences here prove more significant. Philip and Wilhelm both stumble unwittingly into marriages with women they prefer. And both eventually practice medicine, for later in the *Travels* Wilhelm also becomes a surgeon. In effect, both heroes, as Howe summarizes, deliberately accept "the commonplace instead of the romantic destiny."[3]

But two differences sharply isolate Maugham's protagonist from Goethe's. The cry "America was here and now" in *Of Human Bondage* precedes by many incidents the "Here or nowhere is America" of book VII in *Wilhelm Meister*. And Philip, who accepts a marriage of affection without passion, proves to be the antithesis of Wilhelm, who, by setting aside the respect and admiration he feels for Therese, achieves with Natalie a union of love that meets all the demands of his romantic dream. These differences between the two loves, which are as significant and as vital as the dependence of a second stage in an apprenticeship to life is on the first, will be treated in more detail in the analysis of that second stage in chapter 8 below.

Suffice it to state at this point that, books VI-VIII of *Wilhelm Meister* notwithstanding, the first five books and the entire *Of Human Bondage*, through the distinct parallels in their common theme and separate plots, constitute a unit, that is, two remarkably similar expressions of the first stage in an apprenticeship to life. Goethe and Maugham each represent this initial stage in self-formation, involving the release from bondages to self-delusion, illusion, and external circumstances, as crucial and worth the effort required in its attainment.

To doubt the intrinsic worth of this first stage in an apprenticeship, with its unmasking and abandonment, is to risk viewing it as negative in intent. Such a view, shared by critics who attack the negativism in *Of Human Bondage*, can be seen to reflect not necessarily the intrinsic value of the initial stage itself but the extrinsic vantage point of the critic. A critic, for example, whose perspective ignores or overlooks the prerequisite nature of a first stage in an open-ended process of self-cultivation, will judge the stage achieved by Philip Carey as negative. And critical judgments of this type are frequent in the literature on Maugham.

The critics of Maugham almost unanimously disapprove of "the negative quality of Of Human Bondage."[4] Richard Ward argues that "Of Human Bondage is not, for some reason, a satisfying book." He attacks the novel's concentration on "realism," that is, materialism, as having produced "a good book but an unillumined book," a work that "produces in (at least some of) its readers a sense of dissatisfaction due to its negativeness."[5] M. K. Naik complains, "The negativeness of Of Human Bondage lies mainly in the solution which Maugham ultimately has his protagonist find to the question: 'What is the meaning of life?'" Naik argues that "the total lack of positive values in Philip's creed is self-evident."[6]

Maugham and his novel are only mentioned in passing in Lovett's and Hughes' The History of the Novel in England.[7] Perhaps the most clearly characteristic devaluation of the work is expressed in Diana Neill's cursory summation of its plot as follows: "Life from his [Philip's] schooldays onwards is a dismal succession of defeats and fresh starts, all of them embittered by his acute sense of deformity. . . . Of Human Bondage is a sad grim book in which the working of fate has a menacing inevitability; its sincerity cannot be questioned, but the total effect is undeniably depressing."[8] Theodore Spencer, however, noting the popular disagreement with the critics, suggests that "the problem for anyone trying to judge Maugham's permanent value is to decide whether the critics or the public are right."[9]

In a matter significant for the question of positive or negative intent in Of Human Bondage, I should point out that I know of no published critic who considers books I-V of Wilhelm Meister as negative. Yet these books progress, like Maugham's novel, toward an unmasking or abandonment. Whatever positive value dominates Wilhelm's enthusiastic optimism toward the world and toward himself, the author intrepidly undermines all false idealism and vain fancy, so that books I-V become esentially, even as Maugham interprets them, "realistic."[10] They progress, H. S. Reiss argues, "from illusion to reality" and from vagueness toward precision, enabling Wilhelm to abandon a "false and unrealizable romanticism."[11] Indeed, as Max Wundt concludes, Wilhelm "experiences the collapse of ideals," which must be viewed as a process toward a recognition of reality, "Wirklichkeit," that is, as a positive step toward life, "Leben."[12]

Admittedly, a select few critics have discerned this positive note in Maugham's work. Against the plethora of negative criticism, Richard Aldington issued his W. Somerset Maugham, An Appreciation, which praises Maugham's attitude toward life as "the not especially popular one of truth-seeker and truth-teller" and his method of composition as "the exacting one of unadorned and uncompromising precision and clarity." Through both his attitude and his narrative style Maugham's positive, conscious attempt to avoid "comforting half-truths" and "pretentious vagueness"[13] reflects his emergence, in Leslie Marchand's depiction, from an adolescence of honest introspection, clinical skepticism, and cynicism tempered with compassion into "a critical and a positive philosophy which have been the constant guides of his serious attempts in literature."[14]

In his own defense Maugham has argued, "I have been called cynical. I have been accused of making men out worse than they are. I do not think I have done this. All I have done is to bring into prominence certain traits that many writers shut their eyes to." And indeed he rebuts, "I am not a pessimist."[15] With particular reference to this his greatest novel Spencer reasons along the same lines that "Of Human Bondage is not one of those novels which press us urgently into new areas of awareness; it merely fills out, in its moving, efficient, and vivid way, those areas of awareness which we already possess."[16]

Maugham's most ardent and competent supporter, Richard Cordell, refutes nearly every argument mentioned above that depicts the book as a negative work of art. As if in reply to Neill, he claims that "the book is not actually depressing, any more than Antigone, Hamlet, or Anna Karenina, for in art only stupidity and banality are depressing." Rebutting Ward's argument, he remarks, "For all the loneliness, suffering, and unhappiness, the book is not negative in essence, for it traces the hero's evolution from painful uncertainty and bewilderment to maturity and spiritual freedom. Eventually he achieves adjustment and a reasonably satisfying philosophy of life." And in anticipation of Naik, he asserts that "although Philip's (and Maugham's) exultant discovery that life has no meaning may seem grimly existential, it is for Philip a positive and liberating discovery that enables him to come to terms with life." Indeed, he characterizes the central theme of the book as "Philip's quest for a philosophy that will free him from intellectual and emotional bondage."[17]

In partial agreement with Cordell against Ward and all other readers who complain of the "negativeness" of Maugham's philosophy, Karl Pfeiffer contends "that the majority of readers enjoy the novel while rejecting its philosophy."[18] For my own part I consider its philosophy indispensable within the purview of the initial stage of the apprenticeship.

Paul Dottin in discussing this novel hints at the permanent nature of this first stage in an apprenticeship to life. Remarking on Philip's present and future plans and then his past, Dottin notes an irreversible alteration in his attitude and situation. The Philip of the present and future has abandoned the Philip of the past:

> He has found moreover great happiness in the practice of his profession: he has for the first time the sensation of doing something useful. He accounts for the happiness not in love, nor in art, but in tranquility and the possibility of serving. [Concerning particularly this last conclusion, cf. Wilhelm Meister.] And this is why, without strong passion, he marries Sally: he knows that this vigorous and healthy woman brings peace into his troubled soul. And when he abandons his plan to travel in Spain in order to establish himself as a doctor, the former Philip is indeed dead: he has crossed stormy regions and he has finally reached a haven, without a broad horizon, but tranquil, which wisdom and experience will never induce him to leave.[19]

Dottin's conclusion concerning Philip is remarkably reminiscent of the Abbé's judgment, quoted in part above, concerning any youth, namely Wilhelm, astray on a path of his own. The abbot claims that when young men astray on their own paths, "either by themselves or by the guidance of others, ever find the right path, that is to say, the path which suits their nature, they will never leave it" (VIII.iii.82/167). The wish to repeat or return to the follies that have plagued the initial stage of the apprenticeship will never arise again, because Philip, like Wilhelm, has located the path that satisfies "his nature and his business," as Maugham defines it,[20] and will never more fall prey to the temptation to leave it.

I should acknowledge at this point that to imagine a subsequent stage in Philip's apprenticeship, beyond that achieved in Of Human Bondage, is to risk critical censure for inferring authorial intent where none is warranted by the text. The caution, so stated, is valid. Three extrinsic considerations, however, might serve to suggest such intent preliminary to an intrinsic focus on what actually constitutes a second stage and how the first stage can be viewed either prior to or, in and of itself, apart from consideration of a subsequent higher stage.

From the autobiographical perspective, for example, Maugham claims that in writing the novel he intended primarily to relieve his mind of certain obsessions. "The book did for me what I wanted," he writes, "and when it was issued to the world . . . I found myself free forever from the pains and unhappy recollections that had tormented me."[21] He adds in The Summing Up, "I put into it everything I then knew and having at last finished it prepared to make a fresh start."[22] His recognition of a "fresh start," as it were, establishes a threshhold of a second stage of self-cultivation on a level entirely free of, though derived from the first. Released from intellectual and emotional bondage, Maugham, like Philip, possesses the groundwork for a subsequent stage, which, barring death, can develop naturally.

From a second perspective, involving the novel's psychological impact, the average reader in concluding the book, as is usually the case, will find himself a pace behind. For Maugham, who has dismissed the intolerable torment from his own mind, has in fact transferred it unequivocally to the mind of his reader. Granted that some may reject the novel's philosophy[23]--for, as Cordell admits, it "answers few or no questions"--Of Human Bondage nevertheless "leads the reader to ask himself questions about good and evil, justice and injustice, fact and superstition, the good life and the wasted life."[24] If our answers to our own questions release us from intellectual and emotional bondage, then we, like Philip, have completed the groundwork for a second stage.

Finally, from a purely logical perspective, the essential function of the initial stage of an apprenticeship as preparation implies its being inclined toward a "fresh start" or second stage. The critic who overlooks the mutual dependence of the two steps, who overlooks the embryo of a second step nourished entirely by the first, often neglects as a direct result to discern the positive intrinsic worth of the preparatory action considered alone. Much criticism therefore judges Of Human Bondage adversely. But a proper overall perspective on the novel's type should avert such unwarranted negativism.

William Dilthey, in order to clarify his definition of the apprenticeship novel and to encourage an appreciation of each separate stage, emphasizes, "A regular development is contemplated in the life of the individual; each of its stages has a characteristic value and is at the same time the foundation of a higher stage."[25] Like books I-V of Wilhelm Meister's Apprenticeship, Of Human Bondage ventures a provisional step in an apprenticeship to life that has positive value in and of itself even while serving as the foundation for a new beginning, that is, for a passage to a second and higher level of existence.

8. THE SECOND STAGE

While composing the first books of Wilhelm Meister in February of 1778, Goethe recorded in his diary: "Definite feeling of limitation, and thereby genuine expansion."[1] Such is the transition from the first to the second stage of an apprenticeship to life. The key to this phenomenon, which links Of Human Bondage and books I-V of Wilhelm Meister's Apprenticeship with a second stage as depicted in books VI-VIII of the Apprenticeship, is contained in the phrase expansion through limitation, "Ausbreitung durch Einschränkung." Limitation, "Einschränkung," primarily characterizes the first level; expansion, "Ausbreitung," the second. Both stages contribute to the process of cultivation, "Bildung." Philip's cry, "America was here and now," at the conclusion of Maugham's novel recognizes that the first phase in Of Human Bondage, the gradual limitation of vain fancy and false idealism, has attained its climactic goal of release from various bonds. Self-limitation, the decisive act at the conclusion of book V of the Apprenticeship, similarly marks the culmination of this phase in Wilhelm's formation.

The second phase in the apprenticeship does not develop in Of Human Bondage but evolves beginning with book VI of Wilhelm Meister. At the end of book V, Wilhelm, like Philip, has recognized his delusive values, discarded them, but not yet adopted valid alternatives. Unlike Philip, who satisfies himself with the positive worth of the first phase alone, Wilhelm in book VI enters a second phase by virtue of an expansion toward a more profound and genuine condition that Max Wundt characterizes as "consciousness of inherent worth."[2] This stage, by comparison, appears unquestionably positive.

Of Human Bondage hints that Philip vaguely intuits the higher nature of a second level, but the novel ends before he can actually move forward. When Athelny introduces him to the paintings of El Greco, he seems to sense in them the meaning of life that he seeks, and he reassesses his "disdain for idealism" (88.464). In El Greco

> he seemed to divine something new. . . . He felt vaguely that here was something better than the realism which he had adored; but certainly it was not the bloodless idealism which stepped aside from life in weakness; it was too strong; it was virile; . . . it was realism still; but it was realism carried to some higher pitch. . . . He seemed to see that a man need not leave his life to chance, but that his will was powerful; he seemed to see that self-control might be as passionate and as active as the surrender to passion (88.464-65).

The underscoring is my own, for the ideas suggested by Maugham point to a beginning, middle, and end in the process of culture. Bloodless idealism depicts Philip's condition at the outset of the novel; passionate realism, his intermediate stage, that is, at the close of the novel; and active idealism, Wilhelm's stage of preparedness by the conclusion of the Apprenticeship. These three descriptive concepts portray a progressive trend in culture: from art, to life, to a fusion of art and life; from withdrawal, to acceptance, to an engagement in activity; from pure thought, to practical action, to a union of thought and deed.

Applied to stage two, as portrayed in the Apprenticeship, the expansion into an active idealism results from a more thorough consciousness of both life, "Leben," and culture, "Bildung." Schiller expresses his appreciation of this active idealism in his celebrated assessment of Wilhelm Meister when he remarks, "he stepped from an empty and indefinite ideal into a definite, active life, but without thereby losing the idealized force."[3] Active idealism also reflects the notion formulated by Wundt, who concludes that Wilhelm "experiences the collapse of ideals, but the higher spirit of life allows him to see reality more clearly and to risk attempting to recapture the ideal from himself, not to force it upon himself from outside."[4] Finally, H. S. Reiss too depicts an active idealism when, forestalling potential objections to Wilhelm Meister's philosophy, he cautions, "Clearly thus Wilhelm Meister does not exchange the imaginative poetic world for a drab humdrum existence, but rather abandons a false and unrealizable romanticism for a realizable, but not unimaginative, activity which allows the growth of his spiritual, social, and personal powers."[5]

Wundt argues that Wilhelm's growth results directly from his acquaintance with the embodiments of four separate phases of the "ideal of personality."[6] From each of these confrontations he acquires a more perceptive cognizance of both life and culture. In book VI he experiences a profound religious enlightenment through the "beautiful soul," the "schöne Seele."[7] He develops his aesthetic acumen through her uncle. In book VII he gains practical awareness through Lothario, Therese, Jarno, and the Abbé--all exponents of "the deed." And in book VIII, he acquires ethical consciousness through Natalie, whom he then marries.

The "beautiful soul" of book VI gravely affects his religious consciousness. In one sense she represents an apprenticeship gone astray. A noble lady, she acts as her heart and conscience direct and learns to value God above her bridegroom Narziss. Because of a hemorrhage in her eighth year she has benefited from the early development of her soul--reading Christian works but also romances, learning to cook, dance, and draw, and mastering French. Through her father she then meets Narziss, an ambitious young diplomat whose influence provides her with an opportunity to further cultivate her mind. When Narziss is wounded in an unfortunate dispute, he finds himself nursed in her care to restored health, proposes marriage in his gratitude, and she accepts. But he pursues her with a passionate intent that she cannot accept, and his constant preoccupation with the amusements, the prejudices, and the misfortunes of the world cannot satisfy her need for the loftier emotions of the soul.

After two years of anxious spiritual struggle she seeks to focus her mind directly on the bond that holds her to Narziss, finds it too weak to endure, and determines at last to sever it and deliver herself from the mask of appearances. "No sooner thought than tried," she remarks. "I drew off the mask, and on all occasions acted as my heart directed" (VI.324/292). Turning from the world of homeland, parents, and friends, she adheres openly and exclusively to the dictates of her conscience. Her relationship with Narziss wanes. He finds himself another beloved, and she becomes for Germany--at a time when a pious undercurrent prevailed--the maiden "who had valued God above her bridegroom" (VI.327/298-99). Her faith fears neither Hell nor Satan, nor death. She has no consciousness of sin, remaining cheerful and contented under the guidance of her invisible mentor, God.

Then she meets Philo, a new neighbor, who inspires within her a love that awakens a revolutionary thought: she cannot be better than he. Hence sin may exist even within her own heart. In her growing fear of evil she turns to the Biblical story of David and Bathsheba, reconsidering its familiar queries. And in an instant she stands on the threshhold of revelation. Jarred by an unexpected force that draws her soul upward as if propelled toward a long-absent loved one, she suddenly comprehends the essence of faith. This "necessary force" (VI.337/318) of faith injects into a former but less immediate knowledge of God an enduring strength of personal revelation. She has penetrated the shell of organized religion to enjoy the kernel of Christian morality, and through Philo's affinity with the "Herrnhuther Community" she joins the only society that appears familiar with her particular experience. Ultimately, however, she feels pressured by contention and contradiction within the group to renounce it and worship alone. So she becomes preoccupied exclusively with inward religious perfection.

The uncle of book VI influences her only nominally, even less than he indirectly affects Wilhelm. When he arranges a marriage for her sister and hosts the wedding festivities at his castle, he admittedly impresses her with his valuable objects of art and, realizing his advantage, uses the opportunity to instruct her. Appearing to admire her ethereal goals and extolling the virtues of decision and perseverance, he proceeds to suggest a flaw in her development. He compares man, who ideally molds his own life, to the architect, who from a fortuitous mass produces a most economical, fit, and durable form according to the pattern his spirit dictates. By analogy, then, like the architect's greatest work, "Man's highest merit always is, as much as possible to rule external circumstances, and as little as possible to let himself be ruled by them" (VI.345/332).[8] Man in his maturation, however, cannot afford to slight either his moral or his sentient power but must strive to effect an active harmony among all his forces. The "beautiful soul," her uncle tactfully implies, may indeed have chosen to develop the more virtuous part of her nature, but she has erred by cultivating her moral power exclusively. She desperately needs to improve also her "sentient power" (VI.348/338) as a defense against the glittering lures of tasteless trifles that could morally diminish her integrity. To this end he sends her his best "works of art," which he expounds in all his letters to her (VI.350/342).

Disregarding her uncle's wisdom, she continues in her pious mood and ignores also her physician's advice until her preference for the spirit neglects her body and undermines her total being. Her health disintegrates. When her sister's death produces four homeless orphans, she hopes to influence their future. But at this point her uncle intervenes. He withholds them from her, considering her religious piety dangerous for them. So now, ironically disavowing the stubborn pride that indeed constitutes her salient fault, she gradually weakens and dies.

These two influences of book VI, the "beautiful soul" and her uncle, significantly broaden Wilhelm's religious and aesthetic consciousness of life. In book VII Lothario affects his practical consciousness. In his youth Lothario had misapplied his energy to an abstract idea, for which he had contracted debts, quarreled with his uncle, and abandoned his sisters. Subsequently in America he had hoped to appear useful while preoccupying himself with any insignificant and easily available duty. But he has now unwittingly stumbled upon a major truth, for he writes to Jarno from America, "I will return, and in my house, amid my fields, among my people, I will say: Here or nowhere is America" (VII.iii.10/20)! Unlike his brother-in-law the Count, who, mistaking Wilhelm for his double during his last night at the castle, had relinquished his entire fortune to the Moravian Community, Lothario devises a more active sacrifice that will not necessitate abandoning his property. He will administer his wealth and influence for himself and for those who labor with and for him. Indeed, by the beginning of book VIII, he is prepared to enact his plan. His practical influence on Wilhelm proves to be considerable. His "quick and comprehensive vision," as Jarno points out, is "inseparably united with activity" (VIII.v.109/218). His focus on "tangible existing objects" as opposed to "some idea" (VII.iii.9/20), even his sacrifice of external architectural beauty to internal efficient convenience in the construction of his own home (VII.i.2/6), show a practical turn of mind in an aggressive, influential, animating leader, a man of few words and considerable business acumen.

Even more influential on Wilhelm is Lothario's strong, practical counterpart: the handsome, alert, and purposeful Therese, who manages her own property and superintends a neighbor's estate as well. "Decided inclination, early opportunity, external impulse, and continued occupation in a useful business" (VII.v.20/42) are focal issues in her disciplined worldview. Like Lothario, she shows skill in efficiency. She maximizes the use of space in her garden and keeps her firewood precisely stacked in her courtyard, her tools immaculate and available for immediate use. She is constantly active, intent on wasting nothing, a "household" person (VII.vi.28/56), she claims. She converses intelligently with Lothario about "general finance and political economy" (VII.vi.29/59). Religion, when free of hypocrisy, she regards as a year-round diet, requiring constant practice, rather than use only in times of dire need (VII.vi.32/66). Lothario encapsulates in her character "this clearness of view, this expertness in all emergencies, this sureness in details" (VII.vii.39/78), to which Jarno adds penetration, steadfastness, and trust. She herself discerns in her nature "clearness and prudence" when, in writing Natalie, she cogently distills her own essence: "Skill, order, discipline, direction, that is my affair" (VIII.iv.91/185).

Ultimately, however, Natalie unites all these separate concepts of books VI-VIII into one perfectly harmonious "humanitarian ideal."[9] She combines the pure thought of book VI with the practical activity of book VII, embodying both thought and action in the last book of the novel. By birth she inherits the spiritual leaning of her aunt, the "beautiful soul," and the sentient propensity of her granduncle, as expressed in book VI, and shares the practical tendency of her brother Lothario, as portrayed in book VII. Always observing people's wants, for example, she regards money as a practical "means of satisfying wants" (VIII.iii.87/177). Indeed her practical, as well as ethical, notions of education spring from this need she has to help people in need of help. Opposing the Abbé's basic tenet of allowing error, she reckons it vital that a teacher "lay down and continually impress on children certain laws, to operate as a kind of hold in life" (VIII.iii.88/178). There exists a hunger in human nature that only fixed rules of conduct can satisfy, and if these taught laws be wrong, they remain far preferable nonetheless to the state of anarchy that must result in a youth devoid of any governing laws at all.

Jürgen Rausch, contrasting Natalie with Therese and the "beautiful soul," adroitly characterizes her as relating the art of book VI to the nature of book VII. "Her view," he notes concerning Natalie, "includes all the earth, but her viewpoint is above the earth. Therese has her view and her viewpoint on the earth. The beautiful soul has her viewpoint on the earth, but her view in heaven."[10] For Wilhelm, Natalie embodies no illusion of nobility, as did Mariane. She emerges instead as "genuinely noble,"[11] as a "Realist."[12] She functions, however, in her relationship with Wilhelm, not as a realist but as "a purely aesthetic being."[13] Lothario's and Therese's practical, active realism in book VII has seriously challenged Wilhelm's initial sympathy with the idealism of the "beautiful soul," that is, with what he later calls "the purity of being" and the "self-dependence of nature" (VIII.iii.80/163). Through his respect for Lothario as a valued friend and his reverence for Therese as a potential wife, he has disposed himself to become a realist too. In this tendency he risks the same fate that threatens Philip as Of Human Bondage draws to a close--unless, of course, Philip should espouse an active idealism replacing the bloodless philosophy that he has properly renounced.

But in book VIII Natalie assures Wilhelm's salvation by offering a third alternative to the two extremes now confronting him. She delivers him from the excessive realism that can neither tolerate nor indulge the excessive idealism of a pure and self-dependent "beautiful soul." As he recoils from renouncing one extreme, she also dissuades him from endorsing its opposite by offering a union of the two, that is, a realistic idealism. Rausch describes her reconciliatory function as follows:

> Wilhelm incurs the risk of falling from reality-blind idealism into ideal-blind realism; Natalie saves him from both, since she unites the two and renders each for the first time in this union genuinely valuable.

Singling out Natalie, Rausch concludes, "Through her the ideal of a harmonious cultivation of the human being achieves for the first time its middle point."[14] I have underscored the progression from bloodless idealism, to idealless realism, to at last a reconciling realistic idealism, which extends beyond the first stage in the apprenticeship.

Critics have consistently assailed books VI-VIII of the Apprenticeship for seeming, as Roy Pascal asserts, "pale and abstract, the lessons and experiences are theoretical, and they do not strike home to our imagination." Pascal distinguishes Natalie herself as "a completely ideal character"[15] who dwells apart from actual experience. On the other hand, Joachim Müller draws a vital distinction between the "Vorbilder" and "Leitbilder"[16] of books VI-VIII. Natalie as an inspiration, a guiding principle, a "Leitbild," is of course ideal, but a practical, attainable ideal rather than the inaccessible vision, the complete model, the "Vorbild," against which Pascal argues above.

Natalie herself reinforces this distinction in that she regards her noble aunt, the "beautiful soul," as an ideal both unattainable and inadvisable. The "beautiful soul" reacts too purely, too conscientiously. She has overcultivated herself. She has become for the exterior world an ideal of perfection but for the interior mind a model, "not for being imitated, but for being aimed at" (VIII.iii.80/164). Müller legitimately argues for the difference between ideal models, to be striven for but never attained, and the more practical guiding principles, to be adopted as aids in the striving.[17] His distinction justifiably emphasizes the dangers inherent in equating the two.

The "beautiful soul," the uncle, Lothario, Therese, Jarno, and the Abbé of books VI-VIII all exemplify models, "Vorbilder," deserving reverence for their own particular talents and advantages. But Natalie as a guiding principle, a "Leitbild," invites imitation.[18] Still idealized, she is not yet fact; but unlike the more singularly abstract, even allegorical figures, she can become fact. "She represents," as Eric Blackall discerns, "a potentiality rather than a fact."[19] In contrast to the characters that surround her, both she and Wilhelm, uniquely unrealized but realizable, possess, in Therese's judgment, "that noble searching and striving for the Better" (VIII.iv.91/184). Together they represent "a perpetual seeking without finding; not empty seeking, but wondrous, generous seeking" (VIII.iv.92/185). They project into the world their inherent goodness, which they ingenuously attribute to the world itself.

Wilhelm's impending marriage to Natalie at the end of the Apprenticeship parallels only superficially Philip's imminent marriage to Sally at the close of Maugham's novel. Indeed, if Wilhelm had been permitted to marry Mariane or if he had married Therese at the culmination of the first stage in his apprenticeship, critics would no doubt have objected strenuously to Wilhelm Meister on the same grounds that they reject the last episode in Of Human Bondage. Ostensibly a marriage such as Philip's debars an apprentice from an expansion into stage two. Indeed, before Philip could marry a Natalie, assuring his marriage the mutual love and respect that would satisfy his disgruntled critics, he would have to submit himself, like Wilhelm, to a second-stage expansion into a more intense awareness of a genuine religious, aesthetic, practical, and ethical idealism. As Of

Human Bondage ends, he is not prepared in his cultivation for a wife of Natalie's worth and needs. I should acknowledge in passing, however, that he need not marry a Natalie, for an expansion into a more profound consciousness of the ideal remains entirely viable within his marriage to Sally. In Wilhelm's case, however, marriage to Natalie appropriately concludes stage two in his apprenticeship to life.

A component part of Wilhelm's expanded consciousness of life entails his recognition of the true nature of self-culture. In the first five books of Wilhelm Meister and in Of Human Bondage both he and Philip direct their attention and energies toward releases from specific bonds, amounting to goals other than the self. Consequently, their particular selves evolve unnoticed as a result of their conscious efforts to limit certain tendencies and fancies that have proven either false or vain. Although each apprentice divines at the close of the first stage of his apprenticeship that he has obscurely but constantly desired from youth the formation of his individual self, neither yet realizes that self-culture is only indirectly attained.

The hidden principle of indirection that characterizes the first stage describes also the nature of the second. In books VI-VIII of the Apprenticeship, for example, Wilhelm completes the second stage by further expending his thoughts and talents on direct objectives other than the self. Goals variously designated as "the task that lies nearest to us" (VII.i.2/4), "well-directed practical activity" (VII.vi.34/68), and "action" (VIII.v.106/213) supersede the vague and obscure bonds that usurped his attention in stage one, so that his on-going formation remains contingent upon his conscious focus on external concerns.

Therefore, the essential difference between the Philip and Wilhelm of the first phase and the Wilhelm of the second resides much less in their indirect attainment of self-culture--for both stages depict culture as a by-product--than in the recognition or consciousness of the obscure nature of their own formation. Philip and Wilhelm as they appear in phase one escape this recognition, but Wilhelm in phase two acquires it. His expanded consciousness of life leads him to realize that self-formation as a direct objective of the will--even beyond the limited sense of a vain hope for talent in the theater--can only be sought in vain. Concerning the Apprenticeship as a whole, Goethe affirms, "It sprang from an obscure feeling of great truth: that man often wishes to attempt something, for which talent is denied him by Nature, wishes to undertake and practice what he cannot complete."[20] Goethe does not restrict his remark to the vain and limited cultivation of an imperfect talent, for such a restriction would apply only to books I-V. On the contrary, the entire novel, universally applied and including books VI-VIII, symbolizes, as George Henry Lewes observes, "the erroneous striving of youth towards culture."[21]

Cultivation of any kind, when intentionally directed toward molding oneself into a work of art--as an egocentric self-planning, whether of one's own beauty, virtue, form, or knowledge--springs from false idealism and encourages some crippling results. The uncle in book VI--who first inquires of any individual he encounters, "With what does he employ himself, and how, and with what degree of perseverance?" (VI.347/336)--feels an affinity for the person whose objective, "Gegenstand," exists, not as the illusion of a concrete self, but as an actual object outside the self. The uncle therefore considers his niece, whose "beautiful soul" ironically corresponds to the treacherous lure of a siren, as "dangerous for the little ones" (VI.357/355). Her illusory objective is herself.

Similarly, in book VII the Abbé, who shares the uncle's respect for decision and perseverance in a man's character, perceives the peril of directing two such noble qualities toward self-culture as a specific goal. The abbot warns, "For either we grow proud and negligent, or downcast and dispirited; and both are equally injurious in their consequences. The safe plan is always simply to do the task that lies nearest to us" (VII.i.2/4).

Wilhelm's recognition of the true nature of self-cultivation occurs in the Society of the Tower when at last he assesses his error. Throughout his life he has held primarily to the general intent "that I sought for cultivation where it was not to be found" (VII.ix.61/123). The speech in which Jarno prepares him for his introduction both to the Society and to a less superficial consciousness of life expresses most accurately this essential recognition of the self as by-product. Jarno declares, in one of the novel's most comprehensive statements:

> It is right that a man, when he first enters upon life, should think highly of himself, should determine to attain many eminent distinctions, should endeavor to make all things possible: but when his education has proceeded to a <u>certain pitch</u>, it is advantageous for him that he learn to <u>lose himself</u> among a mass of men, that he learn to live for the sake of others, and to forget himself <u>in an activity prescribed by duty</u>. It is then that he <u>first</u> becomes acquainted with <u>himself</u>; for it is conduct alone that compares us with others (VII.ix.59/119-20. The underscoring is mine).

Wilhelm has attained the "certain pitch" from which he can view his past and see through his superficial understanding of culture. He knows now that the loss of self "in an activity prescribed by duty" and in the service of others constitutes a nobler objective than the solipsistic search for self.

In the last chapter of the <u>Apprenticeship</u> he adopts a viewpoint which--instead of confirming any "characteristic" weakness, irresolution, or lack of initiative within himself, as William Diamond would interpret it[22]--merely attests to this vital modification in his matured perspective on culture. When Therese advises him to accept an invitation to visit Italy, he responds compliantly:

> I leave myself entirely to the guidance of my friends and you . . . ; it is vain to think, in this world, of adhering to our individual will. What I proposed to hold fast, I must let go; and benefits which I have not deserved descend upon me of their own accord (VIII.x.142/286).

He does not revert here to his former belief in fate's sovereignty. He does not surrender his powers of self-determination. On the contrary, he has recognized both fate and self to be illusion; and illusions dispelled can claim no further sovereignty nor compel surrender. He "ceases to be self-centered and becomes society-centered, thus beginning to shape his own true self," as Pascal argues in his definition of the "moment" vital to the apprenticeship novel.[23]

The controversial last line of the Apprenticeship analogously reassures us of Wilhelm's state of maturity. It also reaffirms the positive nature of both stages in his apprenticeship. Irvin Stock, in playing on the logic of this last line, subordinates the achievement of culture to the process when he observes, "If Saul had not gone to seek asses, he would not have found a kingdom."[24] Wilhelm has found something far more valuable than what he was seeking. His happiness is assured duration, for he now recognizes irreversibly that neither the "kingdom" of self-formation nor "happiness" can survive as a self-contained goal. The focus at this point then, at the end of the second stage, is on neither the process nor the achievement of culture but on Wilhelm's consciousness of both.[25]

To consider only the first phase in his apprenticeship to life, therefore, is to risk overlooking the more intense consciousness of life and culture that characterizes the second. Somerset Maugham, for example, argues regarding the later books of the Apprenticeship that "the novel becomes more and more confused and less and less plausible."[26] Since Maugham concerns himself only with the faults of the plot, many other literary judges share his opinion.[27] However, he appears to misinterpret--both in Points of View and in further isolated comments about the Apprenticeship--many themes in books VI-VIII that he subsequently rejects.

In The Summing Up, for instance, he interprets Goethe's notion of "self-realization" to mean man's active attempt to experience all of life, his "bringing to the highest perfection every faculty of which [he is] possessed, so that [he draws] from life all the pleasure, beauty, emotion and interest [he] can wring from it" while not allowing "the claims of other people" to limit his activity. Maugham concludes that "if you aim at self-realization only in so far as it interferes with no one else's attempts at the same thing you will not get very far. Such an aim demands a good deal of ruthlessness and an absorption in oneself which is offensive to others and thus often stultifies itself."[28]

Stage two, however, tries to avert this egoism by consciously redirecting the "aim" of realization toward some attainable goal other than the unattainable self. Such a distinction between an attainable and an unattainable self, between the process and the goal of self-formation, lies beneath the consciousness of stage one in Maugham's apprenticeship novel.

In a similar vein Maugham misinterprets "self-limitation," noting that "Goethe asked for survival after death so that he might realize those sides of himself which he felt that in his life he had not had time to develop." Maugham then wonders:

> But did he [Goethe] not say that he who would accomplish anything must learn to limit himself? When you read his life you cannot but be struck by the way in which he wasted time in trivial pursuits. Perhaps if he had limited himself more carefully he would have developed everything that

properly belonged to his special individuality and so found no need of a future life.[29]

Here Maugham has forgotten or ruefully ignored the Abbé's reminder: "Everything that happens to us leaves some trace behind it, everything contributes imperceptibly to form us" (VII.i.2/4). Ironically indeed he has lost sight of his own Philip, who in Of Human Bondage defends himself against his uncle's accusation that he has "wasted time" during his two years in Paris. Implying that time cannot be wasted, Philip retorts, "I learned to look at hands, which I'd never looked at before. And instead of just looking at houses and trees I learned to look at houses and trees against the sky. And I learned also that shadows are not black but coloured" (52.269).

At the end of Maugham's novel Philip, though poised on the threshhold of a potential second stage in his apprenticeship, does not strive beyond the "passionate realism" that crowns the first stage. He does not acknowledge a more substantial and passionate development of active idealism. Maugham's criticisms of books VI-VIII of Wilhelm Meister, therefore, may reflect his own reluctance, if not outright refusal, to recognize in these books the validity of a positive development beyond that achieved in his own Of Human Bondage. He assails the final books of the Apprenticeship, ironically enough, as fundamentally negative.

Admittedly, he fluctuates in his opinion of Goethe's apprenticeship novel. In Cakes and Ale (1930) he notes in dialogue, "I could not read Goethe's Wilhelm Meister; now I think it his masterpiece."[30] The Summing Up (1938) refers to Goethe's work as "that wonderful and neglected book."[31] But in Points of View (1958) he judges it "on the whole . . . a failure,"[32] a pronouncement primarily reflecting his unenthusiastic opinion of the last books. Regarding the extent of his preparation to critique Wilhelm Meister, Richard Cordell affirms that "in his eighties [Maugham] reread all of Goethe's prose before writing his excellent essay in Points of View."[33] Yet even with unquestioned maturity and intelligent preparation Maugham still dismisses the confused and implausible last books of the Apprenticeship, explaining that "Goethe was unable to finish his novel on the lines on which he had begun it."[34]

It is interesting to speculate without necessarily endorsing the conclusions that, if a youthful Maugham or Philip had welcomed the second stage at its threshhold as did Wilhelm, Of Human Bondage might have rivaled or even surpassed Wilhelm Meister's Apprenticeship--if not in depth of understanding and intellectual genius, then at least in unity of plot and realistic characterization. Accurately assessing the regrettable weakness of books VI-VIII of the Apprenticeship, Maugham himself passed by an auspicious opportunity to inspirit stage two with the substantiality of experience and the sensuous reality that are sadly lacking in Goethe's treatment of the same. Certainly, a higher step ventured by Philip would have allayed some or much of the criticism that vehemently labels Of Human Bondage negative; and England's critically acknowledged "best" and "closest parallel"[35] to the Wilhelm Meister tradition might very well have earned in the opinions of critics and populace alike a permanent and indisputable position of favorable comparison.

9. THE THIRD STAGE: THE MAGIC MOUNTAIN

In 1924 Thomas Mann published Der Zauberberg in two volumes, dividing the book almost exactly in half. The five chapters of the first volume progress through seven months of Hans Castorp's apprenticeship, achieving an emotional climax in the famous "Walpurgis Night" scene. The two chapters of the second volume extend his sojourn to seven years and rise to intellectual or spiritual culminations in the "Snow" and the "Thunderbolt" scenes. Henry Hatfield designates in the novel, at the minimum, four outstanding climaxes or "set pieces": the Walpurgis Night carnival, the snowstorm, Peeperkorn's "last supper," and the spiritualistic séance.[1] Hermann Weigand adds a fifth, the thunderbolt, as a major crisis.[2]

We may recognize at least three distinct phases in Hans Castorp's apprenticeship, for critics generally agree that the "Walpurgis Night" and the "Snow" scenes represent the two most visibly prominent peaks, dividing The Magic Mountain into thirds. Like Weigand, however, I prefer Mann's own division, since indeed "the most conspicuous line of cleavage coincides with the end of the first volume."[3] Such a recognition of two phases of the novel, however, can still acknowledge several major turning points in the action.

Rather than treat in exhaustive detail the myriad particular bonds from which Hans Castorp gains his freedom in the first stage of his apprenticeship, it should suffice to focus instead on his enslavement to three salient illusions as they appear in volume I of the novel, that is, his middle-class instincts for work, order, and time. The first illusion, to which he is intimately bound, is the Protestant work ethic. Chapter 2 of the novel poses a significant paradox: for try as he might, he cannot love the work he respects. In his latent dissatisfaction with a business career he resembles Philip Carey, a former accountant's clerk, and Wilhelm Meister, a merchant's apprentice. But he differs significantly from them both in his unquestioning esteem for a solid vocation regardless of personal distaste for a technician's exacting responsibilities. For him, work is "the most estimable attribute of life; when you came down to it, there was nothing else that was estimable."[4] As the absolute principle of life, work justifies itself. Whether he can love it--and he cannot--remains of little concern.

On the other hand, he lavishes unqualified affection on his Maria Mancini cigar. His enjoyment of porter breakfasts, the finger bowl and a Russian cigarette after a meal, and even his reverence for music betray a middle-class desire for comfort in life that often conflicts with his positive regard for work. In his instinctual appreciation of leisure and his fastidious concern for personal appearance and hygiene, he reminds us again of Wilhelm Meister, whose taste for cleanliness and finery is that of another bourgeois advocate of good living.[5] Unlike Goethe, however, Mann employs these bourgeois habits of leisure as leitmotifs, emphasizing and developing the theme of Hans Castorp's release from a spiritually stifling bondage to the middle-class work ethic.

As primary leitmotif the Maria Mancini cigar attracts central attention, but the breakfast porter reinforces its role. Both the porter and the cigar, like music, represent eminent pleasures that lure Hans Castorp from his work even before his departure for Davos-Platz.[6] After his arrival on the mountain and before the end of the first day, his dependence on the porter, which the Sanatorium cannot provide, finds a ready substitute in "Kulmbacher beer" (iii.68/98), while he satisties his need for a cigar with the Maria Mancini that he has brought with him.

Ironically his cigar has already introduced the first threat to his instinct for convenience. "Maria," he marvels, "tastes like paper mâché" (iii.52/76). Joachim's explanation--"it isn't so easy to accustom oneself to life up here"--defines the change in Hans Castorp's sentiments. He believes himself to have reconciled his respect for occupation with this newfound desire for leisure at the Sanatorium, for he has only temporarily relinquished the opportunity to work. But to his surprise, he feels a definite disappointment in his now unopposed and thus diminished love of ease. Previously he could not accustom himself to work. Now he cannot abide the chief instrument of his leisure. Unable to reconcile himself to the loss, and seeking in desperation to regain the inexpressible pleasure, he lights another Maria Mancini before lunch, but this one tastes of leather (iii.71/102), so he flings it away.

His newly acquired disaffection for his favorite cigar crystalizes the difficulty of familiarizing oneself with a foreign manner of life. Joachim's assertion that "it isn't so easy to accustom oneself to life up here" introduces the idea of habituation, which Mann then discusses in his "Excursus on the Sense of Time." Variously employing the terms: accustoming oneself, "Sicheinleben" (iv.104/147), and habituation, "Gewöhnung" (iv.104/148), Mann characterizes the process whereby Hans Castorp will ultimately sever his bondage to the bourgeois veneration of work. Even if habituation to a life of total leisure consists only in becoming accustomed to not becoming accustomed to life on the mountain (v.252/351-52)--as we perceive toward the end of the first volume--in the final analysis we must come to regard his adjustment to leisure as complete.

The proof of the completed process stems from the continuing function of the Maria cigar as leitmotif. The leathery flavor of the cigar persists, his taste for it languishes, and in chapter 3 he discards it as detestable. At the end of chapter 4, even as Kulmbacher beer has proven a welcome replacement for the porter, so "the glass cigar" (iv.175/246) supersedes Maria. This thermometer, costing him five francs, signals an important stage in his retrogression from work. Measuring a temperature of 37.6° C as his three-week stay approaches its conclusion, he readily accepts the enthusiastic welcome of Hofrat Behrens and Dr. Krokowski to join the artistocracy of "horizontallers," as Settembrini has dubbed these relaxed squatters on the mountain.

Midway through chapter 5 his habituation to life "up here" still consists mainly of mental endurance. But his physical faculties have fully adjusted. He has regained an organic satisfaction in the Maria Mancini cigar. "He rejoiced," Mann remarks, "in a faculty regained" (v.252/352). And to ensure a lasting supply he orders five hundred of the Bremen brand in addition to the two hundred he has brought to the Sanatorium. He even discusses cigars with the Hofrat, a fellow connoisseur. Nine or ten weeks on the mountain have thus effectively restored his love of leisure.

Therefore, when the Austrian aristocrat's widow inquires as to his chosen profession, his reply provokes in us no surprise. If she had posed this question on the day of his arrival, he would have answered just as he informed Dr. Krokowski, "I am an engineer" (i.16/30). But he now tells her he "had been" an engineer (v.293/408). Joachim alone betrays alarm at his implying a major change in his life after only six months of leisurely living; for Joachim remains a soldier, still seriously aspiring to a military officer's career. He cannot comprehend a fundamental alteration in his cousin's priorities that now value, even esteem, relaxation more prominently than work.

With the onset of volume 2 Hans Castorp has fully discarded his respect for work, indulging an unclouded enjoyment of leisure, so that Mann can now declare his acclimatization, after only eleven months on the mountain, consummate. Except for the hot blush in his cheeks, which he has accustomed himself to endure, he no longer experiences such discomforts as nosebleeds or visions embodying Pribislav Hippe here in his favorite location near the waterfall: "The progress of acclimatization was over" (vi.389/540). Maria Mancini has recovered her former relish; indeed, she constitutes the one remaining "bond between him, the exile, and his home in the 'flat-land'" (vi.389/538)--a bond reminiscent only of leisurely enjoyment, with no reference to work or even to a respect for work.

If the end of volume I has witnessed the completion of his habituation, then the culmination of volume II simply confirms an established fact. After seven years he is settled, indeed is experiencing "an orgiastic kind of freedom" (vii.706/981). He has long ago abandoned any intention of returning to the flatland. The death of his great-uncle, his foster-father, who had predetermined him for a technical career, has sundered "yet another bond" (vii.708/983), effectively ratifying his "freedom" from work. And finally Maria Mancini has succumbed to a more compact and milder brand of cigar called "Light of Asia." It replaces his watch as well, if not also his thermometer, as a more appropriate hourglass for measuring immeasurable time.

His release from any esteem for work does not imply, however, an abject retreat from active life. Settembrini's intimate farewell to him after the "Thunderbolt" heralds the departure of a young man both intellectually and emotionally committed to voluntary action: "I hoped to discharge you to go down to your work," Settembrini marvels, "and now you go to fight among your kindred" (vii.712/989). The implications of the novel's final thoughts will be the focus at the end of this chapter, for the conclusion of The Magic Mountain may appear "inconclusive,"[7] but for the purpose of the present discussion Hans Castorp effectually severs the bond to his technical career as a bourgeois specialist. As Fritz Kaufmann proposes: resembling Wilhelm Meister in his dissatisfaction with a middle-class vocation, he emerges "into a richer and wider realm, trying, like Meister . . . , to assimilate within himself what is assigned to all mankind."[8] He merely surrenders esteem for an occupation that he cannot love, rejecting the superficial values, as Brennan argues, "not of 'capitalism,' but of the normal humdrum workaday world,"[9] just as his forebear Wilhelm Meister repudiates the "stagnant, weary, drudging life, out of which he had so often wished for deliverance" (I.ix.33/46). At the end of The Magic Mountain Hans Castorp, as Hinton Thomas contends, returns to the bourgeois world as a burgher, revering no longer the narrow industry of a particular calling but rather the broader "practical business life."[10]

Hans Castorp's initial enslavement, a bondage to the middle-class work ethic from which he wins his freedom, constitutes a subclass of his more general bondage to the bourgeois notion of morality. Individuals born in the flatland inhabit a sphere of morality whose values include tradition, order, decorum, honor, respect, and responsibility. Precluding sin, self-abandonment, and experiment in forbidden realms, this bourgeois norm binds him to a superficially credible ethos that sets the stage for Armageddon in the dual emancipation of his body and soul.

Clawdia Chauchat becomes the principal agent affecting his release from middle-class morality. His angry reaction to her ill-bred entry into the dining hall, foreshadowed by his alarm at the offensive Russian couple early in chapter 3, discloses an innate and inviolable sense of etiquette that proves intolerant of reckless impropriety. Although content to dismiss the erotic couple at the "'bad' Russian table" (iii.42/63) as barbarians, he cannot ignore the woman at the "'good' Russian table" (iii.76/110) who has heedlessly slammed the glass door behind herself three times in a single morning. Her laggard appearance and negligent behavior at first shock his bourgeois sensibility, even as Mildred's green pallor and slovenly manners repel Maugham's Philip Carey. At his own table Frau Stöhr further offends his middle-class breeding with her vulgar allusion to Dr. Blumenkohl's conference "with his 'Blue Peter'" (iii.78/112). The self-abandon surrounding him during his first complete day on the mountain injects a melange of horror and hysteria into his inviolate respect for responsible self-control.

Herr Albin unwittingly serves as the first test of his vulnerability to self-abandonment. Indistinctly reminded by Albin's reckless actions of his own shameful failure in his early school years, he shudders in recalling the juvenile pleasure he experienced at feeling totally lost to disgrace. He envies Albin's apparent ability to slough off the burden of an honorable existence and function freely within the limitless advantages of shame. Reliving his own past, he provides a striking parallel to Maugham's Philip Carey, for Philip, willfully discarding the intolerable burden of a naïve faith in religious hypocrisy, physically relishes the sweet gusto of freedom (28.140) that Hans Castorp twice more will savor but in dreams. In his reverie Hans Castorp kisses the roughened hand of Madame Chauchat, vividly imagining himself shirking the heavy obligation of honor and freely relishing "the boundless joys of shame" (iii.92/131).

In chapter 4 Mann again mentions the crashing of the glass door but significantly refrains from commenting on the young bourgeois' reaction. Apparently Hans Castorp's discomfort no longer warrants special notice. In the next incident involving the door, shortly after his dream that links his onetime secret attachment to Pribislav Hippe with his current enchantment with Madame Chauchat, her misconduct still annoys but no longer angers him. In fact, unable to relax until she arrives, he now anticipates the event as if he must share in her disgrace. His secret relationship with her has entered "into a higher phase" (iv.135/191), as the old spinster at his table quickly discerns.

He recognizes the impropriety of cultivating a social attachment to this foreigner of a questionable ethos. Attributing the throbbing of his heart to the emotion he now feels for "Clawdia," by the end of his second week on the mountain he still cannot imagine himself, the grandson of Hans Lorenz Castorp, even mildly affected by a slovenly woman who not only chews her fingers and slams doors but also frequents resorts without wearing her wedding ring. His instinctual reservations reflect his bourgeois bondage to caste and tradition, a tie--considering her questionable morality--that he still cannot sever lightly, nor does he desire to (iv.144/203).

Nevertheless, he has relaxed his demand for middle-class virtue. His interest in Clawdia as "a holiday adventure" (iv.144/203) prompts aggressive action, for twice he consciously arranges to cross her path to the dining hall so that "he and she might meet on the way" (iv.145/204). At this point we are offered a contrast. For while Hans Castorp resolutely indulges his whims in uneasy self-abandon, his cousin struggles for self-control by eschewing the charms of the light-hearted Russian girl Marusja. Significantly, the same irresistible attraction that lures Hans Castorp toward Clawdia repels Joachim from Marusja. Joachim serves as a foil to his development--even as the Vicar and Werner contrast with Philip Carey and Wilhelm Meister, respectively--for Joachim's dutiful devotion to moral order represents the bourgeois norm. On the other hand, Clawdia's creed of self-gratification embodies "the appeal," as Thomas suggests, "of values and experiences beyond the bourgeois norm."[11]

Other than Joachim, it is Settembrini who presents a serious challenge to Clawdia's evolving hypnotic influence on Hans Castorp. This garrulous pedagogue characterizes his young protégé's susceptibility to self-indulgence as "placet experiri," that is, making experiments with a variety of points of view. He feels compelled to redirect his young friend by enlightening him.[12] His philosophy of self-control, while differing in the main from Joachim's bourgeois standard through its progressive appeal to reason, primarily opposes Clawdia's ethos of self-abandonment. Thus by chapter 4's conclusion Hans Castorp finds himself suspended between two antithetical moralities: one binding, the other liberating. But Clawdia's alluring influence proves the more tenacious. He agrees to a two-week extension of his visit. He becomes, in effect, a febrile patient.

In chapter 5 his "honour and good sense" (v.207/290), which he shares with Joachim, still rule out any overtures to Clawdia. However, his temperature rising, he relaxes his customary rigidity, even chooses to imitate her "slackness" (v.228/320). He slumps at the table and permits a door to slam behind him: "In brief, our traveller was now over head and ears in love with Clawdia Chauchat" (v.229/321). Oscillating between the extremes of joy and anguish, his love affords him emotional involvement in both passion and fantasy. Crying out in his boundless exaltation, "Oh, unbelievable adventure!" (v.230/322), he parallels Philip Carey in love with Mildred, exclaiming, "It was incredible" (57.294). But even as Philip in his passion denies the dream, so also Hans Castorp retains the subconscious awareness that Clawdia's "slackness" constitutes "in good part, if not entirely" (v.228/319) a moral illness. This was just as Settembrini had diagnosed it. Both Clawdia and Mildred appear physically diseased.

Settembrini's warning against "too much Asia" in the air (v.242/339), although ostensibly directed against the Asian lavishness with time, alludes obliquely but pointedly to Hans Castorp's obvious infatuation with Clawdia. It embarrasses the youth with its insistence. Settembrini argues from the culture premise, "that man's profoundest natural impulse is in the direction of self-realization" (v.244/341). He severely admonishes, "Flee from this sink of iniquity, this island of Circe" (v.247/345)! Like Jarno in Wilhelm Meister, he feels constrained to ward off the apprentice's error, to protect him from the unknown, to avert an impending plunge into the forbidden realm of sin.

However, finding himself suspended once again between two moralities--"Here was a schoolmaster--but yonder was a woman with narrow eyes" (v.248/346)--Hans Castorp confidently asserts the role of self in his own cultivation. He quickly resolves the duel, the "Gefecht," between the influences of Settembrini and Clawdia by siding against his self-annointed mentor. He dismisses the Italian's influence from his life. When Settembrini next appears, he examines only briefly Hans Castorp's exposed nature as "life's delicate child" (v.308/429). And his final appearance in volume I during the magic madness of the "Walpurgis Night" constitutes little more than a prefigured "parting" (v.329/459). His equating Clawdia with Lilith neither impresses nor concerns the inebriated youth, who, since the "duel," has beheld the organ-grinder with detached amusement. Defying Settembrini in his ardent passion for Clawdia, Hans Castorp declares himself--as in retrospect he later admits--for the "principle of unreason" (vii.610/848). And as he pursues Clawdia, Settembrini is heard to exclaim: This boy is crazy! "Ma è matto questo ragazzo" (v.332/462)! No term in the pedagogue's native tongue serves to characterize his protégé's reckless irrationality more precisely than crazy, "matto."

The "Walpurgis Night" stands as the moment of Hans Castorp's supreme self-abandonment, the achievement of his emancipation from the bourgeois notion of morality. Although Clawdia still perceives in him "a little bourgeois" loving "order more than liberty" (v.334/466), his actual thoughts during the past seven months have dwelt on liberty, on freedom from the middle-class respect for order. The practical result is that he now relies on French as the foreign verbal medium that serves to release him from his native respect for bourgeois "responsabilité" (v.336/469), as he himself acknowledges.

Since Clawdia's ethos of "self-abandonment to danger" locates ethics only "in transgression" (v.340/473), she persists in defining her admirer as a bourgeois "gentleman" whose virtues of reason, discipline, caste, manners, and custom circumscribe his restrictive morality. But she overlooks the essential alteration that he recognizes in his own development: his "fever" (v.341/475), his love for her, which constitutes in his own perspective a self-abandonment to perdition, indeed an "adventure in evil" that identifies with her and her Dostoevskian revolt against the middle-class norm. Intensely affected by his awkward confession of love, she concedes that this "delicate bourgeois" has indeed acquired an anti-middle-class blemish, a "moist spot" (v.342/476), signifying a breach in his bourgeois morality. His plunge into the forbidden realm of sin later the same evening signals his unrestrained freedom from working-class ethics.

More relevant to a clear understanding of his freedom, however, than the bourgeois judgment of his act as sin is a way of educational thinking in the apprenticeship novel which more profoundly concerns itself with all-round cultivation. This is the argument which The Magic Mountain has modified to portray as the morality of sin. During the "Walpurgis Night" Hans Castorp adopts Clawdia's ethical standards, variously designated by critics as "true morality," "the higher morality," "the morality of the artist or, speaking more generally, of genius."[13] Her ethos, as she formulates it, discovers "morality not in virtue, that is to say, in reason, discipline, good manners, honesty--but rather in the opposite, that is, in sin, in self-abandonment to danger, to what is harmful, to what consumes us" (v.340/473). The great moralists, she insists, were not self-disciplined paragons of righteousness but rather heedless adventurers in forbidden realms, great sinners: "des grands pécheurs."

Such an ethos presupposes self-abandonment to sin. In one respect it opposes bourgeois morality, paralleling Philip Carey's rejection of middle-class moral hypocrisy. Remarkably similar to Goethe's essential ethos of error, this new standard further reinforces the Abbé's principle that only through erring can error find its cure. It presupposes, of course, that the youth who entirely exhausts his potential for error must, if he be not a fool, find it out and forever renounce it.

The morality of genius, as espoused by Clawdia, serves to supplement the Abbé's philosophy. Founded on "the principle of the interdependence of morality and sin," to use Hinton Thomas' terminology, this new ethic further presupposes that only through the "interpenetration of opposites"[14] can a native bourgeois achieve his release from the superficially binding ethos into which he is born. Hans Castorp's ethos of experiment, previously derived in theory from Settembrini's "placet experiri," now finds its justification in the practice of Clawdia's ethos of sin. It unavoidably necessitates an adventure into the forbidden realm, as opposed to the domain of virtue, in order to escape the latter's stifling bonds. Consequently, Hans Castorp's affair with Clawdia on the night of the Mardi gras, irrespective of any or all objections to the unconsidered perils, does in fact deliver him through evil from his bondage to bourgeois morality.

His emancipation, achieved at the end of volume I, permits him to marvel at the confining life and superficial values that still enslave his Great-uncle Tienappel. The visiting Consul provides in chapter 6 a foil to his great-nephew, a striking resemblance to the contrasts that distinguish the Vicar from Philip Carey and Werner from Wilhelm Meister. As a coldly practical businessman the Consul reacts to the indolent life "up here" in a manner certainly suggesting Hans Castorp's experiences a year earlier. But unlike his great-nephew, while very much like Joachim, he gladly saves himself by flight: not only from the feminine charms of Frau Redisch but also from the rife enticements of living at one's ease. Defeated in his campaign to return his truant relative to the flatland, he actually grants to Hans Castorp "the consummation of freedom" (vi.440/608) because the apprentice now possesses "no contact with the flat-land" (vii.593/823) and is at last "wholly lost to life down below, and dead in the eyes of my friends" (vii.611/848).[15]

Joachim's death at the conclusion of chapter 6 dissolves only a material bond between his cousin and the morality of the flatland, for "the honour" that kills Joachim (vi.539/744) is the same honor that Hans Castorp has already abandoned in his Walpurgis-Night affair with Clawdia. Similarly, the Consul's death at the end of the novel, although minimally affecting the now triply orphaned youth, does sever "yet another bond" with the bourgeois flatland (vii.708/983), rendering physically complete that which he "rightly called his freedom" (vii.708/984). But this too he has psychically enjoyed since the night of his unfettered abandon at the conclusion of volume I.

In addition to the bourgeois notion of morality, which has bound him to inviolable values of propriety, order, honor, and responsibility, and from which he gains release, Hans Castorp's initial esteem for work, with its scorn of unproductive indolence as a waste of valuable time, introduces at the novel's outset an entirely independent bond, the most persistent illusion from which he must eventually achieve his emancipation. This is the bourgeois notion of time. Constituting a central theme in Mann's perspective, time not only warrants several long digressions but also prompts extensive use of the leitmotif, creating for the reader the intended illusion of simultaneity at each moment in the narrative.[16]

It should not be necessary to point out the manifold chronometric categories that distinguish every level of Mann's "time-novel."[17] Let it suffice for the particular purpose of this discussion merely to trace the hero's gradually diminishing consciousness of time in all its forms until the moment when, experiencing timelessness, he gains complete freedom from its illusive enslavement.

At the outset of the novel his bondage to the bourgeois idea of time seems securely established. Joachim and Settembrini, seeking on three separate occasions to advise him of time's irrelevance to life on the mountain, cannot penetrate his naïve self-assurance. Joachim administers the first rebuff to his strictly "human idea of time." Easily equating three weeks, the proposed length of the visit, with one day, he adds, "One's ideas get changed" (i.7/16). On the next day, again minimizing the seriousness of time, he characterizes the cheerful pneumatic members of the "Half-Lung Club" as entirely "free" from time's bond: "time is nothing to them" (iii.51/76). Settembrini upon his arrival disavows even the existence of the week as a unit of time on the mountain: "Our smallest unit is the month" (iii.58/85). In all three instances Hans Castorp decorously defers to the authority of an enigmatic experience that poses no serious challenge to his own.

In his earliest attempt to resolve the enigma, he draws an awkward Bergsonian distinction between objective and subjective time. Endeavoring to excuse his cousin's depreciatory notion of time as phenomenologically based on apparent rather than actual qualities in the world, he analyzes Joachim's experience of measuring his temperature. He concludes that the "seven minutes" that Joachim's thermometer "actually" remains in his mouth "seem" to him only as long or as brief as his psychological experience of them (iii.66/95). But this philosophical analysis, impulsively begun and seeking to impress Joachim, abruptly ends in an inconclusive quandary over what human organ permits the perception of time, and Joachim remains notably unimpressed.

Hans Castorp's first actual experience of Joachim's timeless world occurs in the afternoon. His shock at the apparent passage of the hours constitutes genuine surprise: "Good Lord, is it still only the first day? It seems to me I've been up here a long time--ages" (iii.82/118). Not only has he forgotten, he claims, his philosophical discussion with Joachim; he has even lost sight of his age. "In my twenty-fourth year, of course" (iii.86/122), the twenty-two-year-old youth informs Settembrini. Furthermore, by the end of chapter 3 in his night of dreaming he has experienced as many additional adventures as in his waking day, doubling or tripling his impression of the apparent passage of time. Ostensibly his staid bourgeois awareness of chronology has weakened under the strain of fatigue and excessive novelty.

But in one dream he betrays the dogged pertinacity characteristic of his middle-class instinct for time. Gaining a sudden insight into the quality he now believes actually constitutes time's essence, he imagines time as simply a "silent sister" (iii.92/131), an unmarked column of mercury designed to expose a trickster. Since he remains a proper bourgeois, incapable of exculpating a swindler, his dream of time's imperviousness to cheating merely reinforces his fixed allegiance to a working-class respect for the sanctity of time. And he confidently resolves to inform Joachim in the morning of his conclusive discovery. Thus at the end of chapter 3 he retains his faith in the importance of measured time, despite his incipiently distorted experience of it on the mountain.

In chapter 4 his diminishing perception induces him to appreciate a change. Experiencing within two days both a brilliant summer and a furious winter, he learns from Joachim that such common extremes in the weather oblige the Berghof patients to regard not only the clock's hours but also the seasons as indistinguishable. Days of winter, summer, spring, and autumn intermingle. Joachim admits, "The seasons here are not so distinct from each other; they run in together" (iv.94/134). By the third day Hans Castorp's preoccupation with the deliberate passage of time prompts him to marvel, "I feel I have been up here two months" (iv.105/149). His remark occasions Mann's excursus on habituation as a weakening of the discernment of time, for Hans Castorp has begun suffering from a long daily routine free of change and novelty, which, according to Mann, afford the only means of refreshing his sense of time and his consciousness of life. Mann emphasizes the bond between consciousness of life, "Lebensgefühl," and perception of time, "Zeitsinn"--two states of mind so intimately related, "that the one may not be weakened without the other suffering a sensible impairment" (iv.104/147). Gradually losing his awareness of both time and life, Hans Castorp senses that "an eternity" (iv.105/149) has elapsed since his arrival only three days earlier.

During the second week of his visit he comes to regard time as a veritable enigma. Each day passes more slowly than its predecessor, but the days already spent have expired more precipitately than he has realized: "Time did not hang heavy on his hands--rather he began to feel the end of his stay approach all too near" (iv.141/199). Time's elusive essence now bewilders his attempt to apprehend it. It invades his own experience as "a riddling thing." Toward the end of the third week neither Joachim nor Settembrini need instruct him concerning the enigma, for he himself lucidly understands in retrospect that three weeks up here are "as good as nothing at all" (iv.162/228). And he expresses his regret that during these weeks he has allowed time to escape his attention (iv.162/229). In order to savor time's duration discriminately, he laments, he should have heeded it as closely as would a patient during the seven minutes of measuring his temperature.

The desire to measure time, aside from the cold that he contracts, prompts him to purchase a thermometer. The results of his first calculation prove alarming. Although assured that he can trust himself implicitly, that he requires no "silent sister" (iv.168/237) as a guard against cheating, he discovers that his ability to calculate a length of time as definite as seven minutes has suffered unmistakable impairment. He overestimates the measuring time: "when he looked again, the eighth minute was already past its first quarter" (iv.169/238). Inclined to discount the gravity of his error, he weakens further in his respect for the seriousness of time and, by chapter 4's conclusion, offers no resistance at all to a two-week extension of his retreat from the flatland. Indeed, the Hofrat welcomes him as "a better patient" (iv.182/256) than Joachim, whose desire to forsake life on the mountain fills him with an impatience that Hans Castorp cannot share.

In chapter 5 he achieves his final break with time. Confined to his bed as patient rather than guest, he exists for ten or twelve days "in a state of vacant suspense" (v.190/267) while both time and life languish. He courts the eminent danger of losing both consciousness of life and perception of time, as Mann has earlier noted and as Settembrini now admonishes, endeavoring to describe his pupil by employing the solemn phrase: "being lost to life" (v.198/278). Thus, adroitly characterized in only his second month on the mountain, Hans Castorp already finds himself not always "sure of the date" (v.202/284). He has no calendar, and Joachim can offer no help.

In a letter to his Great-uncle Tienappel he espouses the same notions that Joachim and Settembrini had expressed at his arrival, for he writes, "Ideas about time were different up here from those held about the length of stay at the baths, or at an ordinary cure" (v.224/314).[18] He adds that "the smallest unit of time, so to speak, was the month, and a single month was almost no time at all" (v.224/314).[19] Mann has entitled this subchapter "Freedom," which is what Hans Castorp expresses as he substitutes for the flatland conception of time the prevailing notion on the mountain. This letter, Mann informs us, "asserted Hans Castorp's freedom" (v.225/314). His emancipation from time has taught him the complete meaning of liberty, not--in Settembrini's sense--responsibility, but rather a withdrawal from bourgeois life. He no longer equates time as a natural phenomenon--seeming at once both unnaturally long and unnaturally short--with the conception of actuality. "Time has no divisions to mark its passage" (v.225/315). It now flows for him divorced from hours, days, or months. Even the seasons of the year lack the indicative signs of a normal landscape; "the whole region held no deciduous trees" (v.226/316). Only evergreen firs and pines and dead oaks clothe the mountain.

His emancipation from the bourgeois conception of time severely curtails Settembrini's influence as his mentor. This pedagogue's urgent warning against excess "Asia" in the air (v.242/339), while alluding to his friend's singular attraction to Clawdia Chauchat, directly assaults his fragile consciousness of time. Already suffused with freedom from time, Hans Castorp cannot appreciate Settembrini's denigration of the Asiatic "barbaric lavishness with time." His eloquent plea--"Time is a gift of God, given to man that he might use it" (v.243/340)--can excite only disregard; for Hans Castorp, whose adopted philosophy of "Carpe diem" Settembrini now execrates, awards no value to the costliness of time.

In Hans Castorp's fifth month at the Berghof, Mann casually remarks that he can now regard with any seriousness only the smallest unit of time: only "those seven times sixty seconds during which one held the thermometer between one's lips and continued one's curve" (v.288/401). For him those seven minutes alone can expand into a "little eternity" within time's indistinct general course. Conversely, any time-unit greater than this briefest segment holds for him neither worth nor meaning.

During the "Walpurgis Night" festivities at the end of his seventh month, therefore, he does not regard it as strange when, addressing Clawdia, he refers to an incident of six months earlier as if it happened only yesterday: "six months ago, when I left the table for my first examination--you looked round after me--do you remember" (v.338/471)? Clawdia's astounded reply--"What a question! Six months!"--reveals not only her disregard for the incident as insignificant but also her inability to share his contracted view of time. The Hans Castorp that on his arrival at the novel's outset had expressed astonished indignation at his cousin's free use of the term "half a year" (i.7/16) has developed by the end of chapter 5 an even freer acceptance of "half a year" (v.323/450) as a term barely sufficient to describe a definite unit of his own stay. Thus in volume I he has experienced the release from the illusory bondage of bourgeois time.

Volume II both confirms and crystallizes his freedom from time. Mann's answer to his own opening question, "What is time?" suggests that time measured by conceptions of distance, movement, change, or even existence must ultimately confront the notions of eternity and infinity (vi.344/479). Thus are eliminated all limits in both time and space. Volume II at its outset serves to introduce the inchoate theme of timelessness as a surrogate for volume I's defunct regard for bourgeois time.

Describing the midsummer solstice as his first year comes to a close, Hans Castorp attempts to characterize for Joachim his sense of infinite duration experienced on the mountain. He depicts eternity as a circle, "not 'straight ahead' but 'merry-go-round'" (vi.371/515), thereby suggesting not only now but also in a later discussion that the idea of recurrence explains the experience of timelessness.[20] He argues that in addition to the intermingling of summer and winter days on the mountain, "the new winter, when it comes, isn't new, but the same old winter all the time" (vi.415/574). Recurrence, as Joachim rightly observes, appears to satisfy Hans Castorp, whose consciousness of bourgeois life has languished. But Joachim, still suffering from an enslavement to military life, has become cloyed with excessive recurrence and timelessness. His subsequent departure for the flatland signals an antinomy between his own bondage to and his cousin's freedom from the preciousness of time.

Mann defers until chapter 7 his open suggestion to the reader that, each conforming to his own attitude toward time, Hans Castorp acquires strength while Joachim weakens and dies. A year has elapsed since Joachim's departure. Hermetically secured like a buried miner who lacks an inner "time-organ" (vii.543/751), Hans Castorp has economized on time by disposing of it altogether. By habit he now confuses "a year ago" with "yesterday," and "tomorrow" with "next year" (vii.546/755). But Joachim, associating time with life, has lived his time and died. Mann asks rhetorically whether Hans Castorp has gained his strength in trifling "with eternity" by perceiving the excessive zeal that has hastened Joachim's fate (vii.548/757).

Irrespective of a judgment against Joachim, as the deluded victim of urgency, his surviving cousin by the end of chapter 7 readily characterizes himself as hermetically "free" from time: "he no longer carried a timepiece." Furthermore, he has long ago abandoned "using a calendar" (vii.708/984). His "freedom," achieved at the end of the first volume, serves to establish and explain in the concluding pages of volume II the final cause of his indifference. He has transcended time, "escaping its bondage," as Philo Buck suggests, by recognizing that "behind the illusion of time lies the only significant reality": eternity, as a positive alternative to death's annihilation of time.[21]

As we have thus far seen, the first stage of Hans Castorp's apprenticeship, being the individual's release from bondage to illusion, involves an effective process of analysis. "Analysis," Settembrini counsels in volume I, "as an instrument of enlightenment and civilization is good, in so far as it shatters absurd convictions, acts as a solvent upon natural prejudices, and undermines authority; good, in other words, in that it sets free, refines, humanizes, makes slaves ripe for freedom" (v.222/311). As such, analysis serves to deracinate the fruitful garden of excessive growth, preparing for a new stage in its cultivation.

As a result, the second stage in Hans Castorp's apprenticeship advances unfettered by stifling illusive thought. Free in volume II to realize himself, he does not acquire any new or better qualities, but the characteristic values inherent in his being attain unincumbered their realization. Settembrini, insisting in volume I that "man's profoundest natural impulse is in the direction of self-realization" (v.244/341), evokes the salient principle underlying Hans Castorp's transubstantiation from "mediocre" (ii.32/50) to genius, "homme de génie" (vii.596/827). Self-realization, involving a process of intensification, heightening, or "Steigerung," depicts in volume II his deepening consciousness of life and culture.[22]

Settembrini, Naphta, and Peeperkorn represent the primary influences on his intellectual, emotional, political, moral, philosophical, and human faculties. In discussing these three principal characters in the order of their appearance, I shall defer until the end of their consideration a discussion of the subservience of their roles to the apprentice's final act of self-limitation. Such a discussion should provide a perspective on the practical implications of the "Thunderbolt" scene on Hans Castorp's complete development.[23]

In the "Walpurgis Night" episode ending volume I, Settembrini's rational influence on Hans Castorp, as noted above,[24] meets only frustration and defeat. Ostensibly he represents humanitarian ideals gleaned from five centuries of modern European intellectual thought. As "homo humanus," a man of mankind, he embodies ideas from the Renaissance, the Age of Enlightenment, the French Revolution, and nineteenth-century progressive science. Although epitomizing rational humanism, he paradoxically betrays to Hans Castorp an inhumanity in his abstract idealism and moralism. As Pascal observes, his attempts "to ignore certain aspects of reality" and his fear of "certain experiences" induce Hans Castorp to reject him in favor of Clawdia.[25] For example, in chapter 5 his plea for "conscious activity" (v.246/343)--while echoing superficially the "well-directed practical activity" (VII.vi.34/68) of Goethe's Wilhelm Meister--concludes with his admonishing Hans Castorp to flee "from this sink of iniquity, this island of Circe" (v.247/345). It thus reveals more profoundly his restrictions on activity and his fear of the unknown. Hans Castorp in volume I discredits his influence along with the illusions that unjustly stifle individual thought and action, and Settembrini departs.

Only after Clawdia's departure in volume II does he return, but not without her surrogate. Replacing Clawdia as his "antagonist" (vi.408/564), as indeed "a voluptuary" (vi.411/569) who has yielded to the power of death even as Clawdia has abandoned herself to the supremacy of sin, Herr Naphta counterbalances Settembrini's rational humanism with irrational mysticism. As "homo dei," a man of God, he embodies precepts of the Middle Ages. His influence on Hans Castorp, despite Settembrini's attempt to discredit its essence as "confusion" (vi.407/564), seeks to supplant reason by intuition. Furthermore, in his uncompromising devotion to duty he usurps the role of Joachim, offering fanaticism as preferable to humanism.[26]

In their clash of democratic and theocratic presuppositions Settembrini and Naphta represent a form of guidance far less clear and united than the members of the Society of the Tower, who influenced Wilhelm Meister; yet the function of these two mentors bears a striking resemblance to that of the Society. The Settembrini-Naphta debates involve Hans Castorp in a process of mental development referred to as "taking stock" (vi.390/541), which has permitted him, by the end of chapter 6, to regard each influence as qualified by its opposite, suggesting a mean between two extremes. Transcending the polarities of rhetorical "humanism" and illiterate "barbarism," he formulates an intermediate alternative to both views of life, affirming thereby "the human" (vi.523/722).[27] In the subchapter "Snow," although acknowledging his preference for Settembrini's benevolent intentions over Naphta's motives of terrorism (vi.478/660), he repudiates the confused teachings of both pedagogues. Defining man's proper role as master of antinomies, "lord of counterpositions" (vi.496/685), he relegates their antagonistic positions and counterpositions to the status of "just a guazzabuglio . . . , and a confused noise of battle, which need trouble nobody who keeps a little clear in his head and pious in his heart" (vi.496/685). Having developed his own inherent faculties of reason and intuition through the influences of these two mentors, he has transcended the limitations of each.

But at this crucial point in his apprenticeship a third force arrives to delay his independence of external authority. Peeperkorn, with his commanding "personality," unquestionably supplants Settembrini and Naphta, whose attenuated influences have paved the way for his arrival. Peeperkorn embodies human feeling.[28] He represents "the human," which Hans Castorp has endorsed as the medial alternative to reason on the one hand and recklessness on the other. Although he arrives accompanied by Clawdia, he eclipses her role. Her entrance into the dining hall is noiseless, "for Mynherr Peeperkorn closed the door behind her" (vii.554/767). Indeed, Hans Castorp eventually addresses him with the familiar form previously reserved for her alone (vii.612/850).

In chapter 5 Hans Castorp had been the object of a struggle between the antithetical influences of Clawdia and Settembrini, which he resolved independently by dismissing his mentor, but in chapter 7 his alliance with Peeperkorn makes a struggle entirely unnecessary, for he accords the Dutchman full and uncontested ascendancy over his Asian consort. Peeperkorn replaces Clawdia, Settembrini, Naphta, Joachim, Hofrat Behrens, and Krokowski, for his "blurred personality" (vii.553/765) actually subsumes all their apparent incompatibilities. He is "not the man to be the bearer of logical confusion" (vii.548/759), yet he affects his audience as "incoherent" (vii.553/765). He conveys the impression of faultless omnipotence and life while carrying within him the flaws of impotence and death. Oskar Seidlin summarizes his mysterious influence over Hans Castorp as "not only an 'educational experience' but perhaps the most momentous that [Hans Castorp] undergoes on the magic mountain."[29]

Representing "life itself,"[30] Peeperkorn appears initially to embody a "Lebenswert," designated by Seidlin as the "absolutely positive" value in Hans Castorp's overawed perspective.[31] The three subchapters specifically devoted to him as a beginning, middle, and end in his influence over Hans Castorp closely parallel in Wilhelm Meister the digression in book VI concerning the "beautiful soul." Although his elemental vitality may appear attractive, he too cultivates one force exclusively. Like the "beautiful soul," he may indeed have developed the more obviously vital segment of his nature, but he cannot afford to slight either his rational or intuitive powers.

He has neglected to strive for an active harmony among all his forces. Erich Heller suggests that he differs from Naphta in the same way that "Life without Mind" differs from "Mind without Life." This explains why their "suicides may be Thomas Mann's way of killing his oldest pair of irreconcilable opposites. Neither Life nor Mind can exist the one without the other."[32]

Despite Peeperkorn's death, his influence over Hans Castorp persists, as Brennan points out,[33] within the two realms of inquiry that assure his posthumous effect: music and the occult. Filled with a fresh "passion" (vii.639/888) for the joys that his new Gramophone provides and soon thereafter with an unqualified "curiosity" (vii.657/914) that countermands his aversion to the supernatural world, Hans Castorp ventures into kingdoms that lie far from Settembrini's stress on the articulate Word yet well within Peeperkorn's embodiment of the inarticulate "mystery of personality" (vii.658/914). Thus the mysteries of music and the occult coalesce within the séance. They culminate in a world of human feeling, which is entirely congruent with this posthumous extension of Peeperkorn's effect on Hans Castorp.

But in the séance even Peeperkorn's influence abruptly terminates with the spiritual reappearance of Joachim. Whispering "Forgive me" through his tears, Hans Castorp here marks decisively the boundary of human feeling. He transcends Peeperkorn's example by interposing the lesson of Settembrini, whose role he has come to emulate when "with one quick movement [he] turned on the white light" (vii.681/947). The sudden illumination of reason, which Settembrini had introduced in chapter 5 when he flooded Hans Castorp's sickroom with light (v.192/270) and which Hans Castorp later described to Peeperkorn as the pedagogue's weakness (vii.612/850), now springs from within Hans Castorp himself as the necessary strength to limit the scope of human feeling. Reason, intuition, and human sensitivity coalesce into an active harmony of all his heightened forces, signaling his attainment of a phase in self-limitation that exceeds, even while incorporating, each of the individual influences contributed by Settembrini, Naphta, and Peeperkorn.

For instance, there should be no surprise at the end of _The Magic Mountain_ when Mann relates the manner in which Hans Castorp, now reversing the roles of pupil and teacher, restores "sudden illumination" (vii.709/985) to the sickroom of Settembrini. Likewise, in the duel between Settembrini and Naphta,[34] which erupts over himself, the now-matured youth can be expected to adopt only the role of the "neutral party" (vii.700/972). Naphta's suicide would appear to confirm Settembrini's position in the intellectual dialectic, but more profoundly it proves irrelevant. For Hans Castorp has outgrown both positions. He has effectively limited himself.

With the proper cultivation and limitation of reason, intuition, and human feeling now completed in his apprenticeship, there remains for him--and it couldn't come at a more appropriate time--his practical awakening to life. Characterizing his apprentice's existence on the mountain throughout the full seven years of his sojourn, Mann informs us that each value inherent in his being has attained the zenith of its potential development. Hans Castorp's hermetic enchantment emerges as "the fundamental adventure of his life, in which all the alchemistical processes of his simple substance had found full play" (vii.708/984).

One latent value in this young "Seven-Sleeper," however, still awaits its vital awakening. The restricted technical competency of which he had boasted at the outset of the novel, an illusory bourgeois practicality that he has discarded in stage one of his apprenticeship, now gives way to a more profoundly practical consciousness inspired by the "Thunderbolt." Characterized by Weigand as a philosopher rather than a pragmatist, as a contemplator who instinctively "regards the world of ideas as a higher reality than the world of sense," Hans Castorp certainly appears inclined toward "the theoretical as contrasted with the practical sphere."[35] But with the declaration of war, that unexpected flash of illumination, he emerges from the enchanted realm of contemplation into the domain of action. Originally an engineer, he now volunteers to enter a war--not to be confused with its great successor--to end all wars. He answers the call, motivated not solely by his own choice but also "by the operation of exterior powers, of whose activities his own liberation was a minor incident indeed" (vii.711/988). Thus he returns to the flatland and practical life, amazing his friend and former teacher Settembrini, who marvels, "Quite otherwise had I thought to see thee go. . . . I hoped to discharge you to go down to your work, and now you go to fight among your kindred" (vii.712/988). Hans Castorp completes the second stage in his apprenticeship to life, achieving the full awakening of all his inherent values, including reason, intuition, human sensitivity, and a practical awareness of reality.

The first and second stages of his apprenticeship to life involve, respectively, a release from bondage to various illusions and a heightening of values inherent in his nature. Mann's portrayal of stage one in volume I of The Magic Mountain parallels, as noted above, similar portrayals in Maugham's Of Human Bondage and Goethe's Wilhelm Meister, books I-V. The delineations of the second stage in Mann's novel, volume II, and in Goethe's novel, books VI-VIII, as also demonstrated above, reveal further similarities. However, Mann's work progresses a stage beyond Wilhelm Meister in its reflection on the metaphysical problem of death. I do not mean to imply, as Friedrich Schlegel argues, that Goethe's novel is thus "incomplete, because it isn't entirely mystical."[36] On the contrary, although Mann's novel surpasses Goethe's in its final consideration even as Goethe's adds a stage to Maugham's, each of the three works possesses intrinsic value exactly as each stage of the apprenticeship provides, in its turn, the foundation for a higher stage. Thus the second phase, like the first, constitutes a self-sufficient prerequisite to a higher or third phase, as we shall see below.

Because of its concern with disease and death The Magic Mountain has been assailed by various critics as "An Epic of Illness," "The Epic of Decay," a "romance of hypochondria," or an "Odyssey of disease";[37] and such epithets do characterize volume I. In fact, the themes of disease and death climaxing the process of organic dissolution permeate Mann's entire novel. However, volume II introduces a change in the protagonist's attitude. Overshadowing his former sympathy with death is a growing fascination with life. Stage three in Hans Castorp's apprenticeship to life and death--that is, the stage that prepares the apprentice for death--unfolds in two parts. Volume I portrays his progressive enslavement to a death-fascination concomitant with his release from the bondages to life's illusions. Volume II then depicts his gradual disenchantment with death in concert with the development of values inherent within himself. In other words, the first and second stages of the apprenticeship to life in The Magic Mountain coincide, respectively, with the two divisions of the third stage in the apprenticeship to death.

The first part of stage three unfolds in volume I. At the novel's outset, although the Austrian aristocrat's ghastly cough introduces Hans Castorp to an entirely new experience (i.12/24), he comes from a previous acquaintance with sickness and death that dates from his earliest childhood. His "sympathy with death," his "reverence of" or "fascination by death," as characterized by Lydia Baer,[38] arises from the successive losses of his mother, father, and grandfather even though Mann describes only the last bereavement in detail. He is doubly affected by his grandfather's demise. The "spiritual side" appears to him sacred, holy; the "physical side," profane, almost improper, especially when a fly settles on the old patriarch's waxen brow (ii.27/43-44). In childhood Hans Castorp's senses, more than his spirit, had experienced the physical impact of death. But fourteen years later the spiritual aspect now prevails: "after all," he informs Joachim, "a dying man has something in a way--sacred about him. . . . sort of holy, I should think" (iii.55/81)!

His surrender to "the spirit of sickness and death," as J. M. Lindsay observes,[39] proceeds unimpeded until the third day of his visit on the mountain. Only then does it meet its first serious challenge. Settembrini, speaking of his own deceased father, cogently attacks Hans Castorp's respect for the refining dignity of illness: "Disease has nothing refined about it, nothing dignified" (iv.98/139).[40] Characterizing an homage to disease as an aberration of the intellect, he denigrates such "spiritual backsliding" as in itself a disease (iv.99/140).

Although struck by Settembrini's rhetoric, Hans Castorp nevertheless preserves his esteem for illness and death. At his first actual sight of a dying man--"This was the first dying man Hans Castorp had ever seen; for his father and mother, and his grandfather too had died, so to speak, behind his back" (iv.107/151)--he marvels at the moribund's waxen profile: "How full of dignity the young man's head . . . !" He considers the sight of a coffin "positively sublime" and funerals "very edifying" (iv.109/155). Dignity, sublimity, and edification typify his attitude toward death and disease.

Only once, in chapter 4, does he momentarily sense the degrading physical aspect of mortal illness. As he studies Joachim's powerful form during the physical examination, his own evanescent thought startles him: "Disease makes men more physical, it leaves them nothing but body" (iv.178/251). But the impression vanishes even as it occurs, for after his own physical examination he willingly accepts the Hofrat's "early diagnosis" (iv.181/254) of a disease within himself. He enters the "aristocracy" of illness (v.204/286) no longer as a guest but as "a better patient . . . with more talent for illness" than his veteran cousin (iv.182/256).

In vain Settembrini exhorts him again to abandon his reverence for ill health and death: "For death, as an independent power, is a lustful power" (v.200/280). Death, when revered as a mighty and dreadful force apart from living, haunts the aberrated mind as a specter viciously distorting life, of which it actually constitutes no more than a component part. Despite Settembrini's valiant effort Hans Castorp plunges deeper into the attraction of death. Just as Jarno strives in vain to protect Wilhelm Meister,[41] so too Settembrini fails to guard his pupil from error. Indeed, his advice hopelessly confirms the youth in illusion. Permitted to view his own hand through the screen of the Hofrat's X-ray machine, Hans Castorp with supreme pleasure peers into "his own grave" (v.218/306). He understands for the first time "that he would die" and responds with a dull, sleepy expression of piety akin to the effect produced on him by music, which he has now come to associate with death.

His thriving fascination with death spawns related interests in anatomy, physiology, and biology--sciences substantiating the Hofrat's definition of "living" as "dying," of life as "organic destruction" (v.266/371). From his research he bolsters his conception of life as "a fever of matter" (v.275/384), as "only an infection, a sickening of matter" (v.285-86/398), as indeed "the Fall" of inorganic matter into organic life, awaiting its death. Even as he has associated music with death, he now combines in a dream the attractive image of death with "the image of life," embodied in the diseased Clawdia.

His "sympathy with death" culminates near volume I's conclusion in a "Dance of Death." The Austrian aristocrat dies, awakening in him a profound interest, "partly because the signs of life he had heard from the gentleman rider were among the earliest impressions of his stay up here" (v.291/405) but in part also because the Austrian's death provides him with an opportunity of viewing the corpse "to show his contempt for the prevailing system of secrecy" (v.292/406). Endeavoring henceforward to concern himself openly with death, he further resolves, because of a "spiritual craving," to visit without constraint or concealment the "suffering and dying" (v.296/412). He and Joachim acquire reputations as "good Samaritans and Brothers of Charity" (v.308/429), but more memorably he earns from Settembrini the epithet "life's delicate child." This phrase, although purporting to warn a gifted individual exposed to peril, is misinterpreted. For in his reverence for death he accepts the epithet as an appreciation of his Samaritan role in its care for the "children of death" (v.308/429). Indeed, within his romantic conception that sets up death as an independent, life-opposing, spiritual force, a delicate child of life is of special concern only through his solicitous concern for a child of death.

The "Walpurgis Night" scene sets the stage for his ultimate capitulation to his erotic fascination with death. Combining "death," "the body," and "love" (v.342/476-77) as three aspects of a single phenomenon, he abandons himself to his dream-image of death in the affair with Clawdia. The cry "I love you" addresses itself to death and disease as passionately as it does to Clawdia. It thus establishes the relevance of his concluding plea in an otherwise grossly technical confession of love. For he implores her, "Let me feel the exhalation of thy pores and taste thy down, the human image of water and of albumine, destined for the anatomy of the tomb, and let me perish, my lips on thine" (v.343/477)! Volume I closes with his hopeless ensnarement in a bondage to the twin-allure of illness and death.

"Sympathy with death," as Thomas argues concerning The Magic Mountain, must properly be "regarded as vicious romanticism when death is opposed to life as an independent spiritual force instead of being absorbed into it, sanctifying it and itself being sanctified."[42] To support this disavowal of death's magnetic power over life, Thomas quotes an excerpt from Mann's address on "The German Republic," where the author of the as-yet-unpublished Magic Mountain proposes a possible theme for an apprenticeship novel, which could demonstrate "that the experience of death in the end is an experience of life, that it leads toward 'mankind.'"[43] Indeed, volume II of The Magic Mountain translates Hans Castorp's concern with disease and death throughout the previous volume into an emerging appreciation of health and life. Love of life eclipses love of death, from whose bondage he gradually achieves deliverance.

Even at the outset of the second volume we discern in him a significant transformation. Weigand claims that "after Clavdia's departure, the course of his life has been somehow altered. The change may be imperceptible at first, but it becomes increasingly clear that in a peculiar way the fascination of death has become subordinated to the fascination of life."[44] His modified perspective brings humanity into focus. Immediately after the subchapter appropriately entitled "Changes" his interest in the biological sciences shifts to a specialization in botany and the excitement of astronomy. Although classed as a physical science, astronomy, through its relation to Chaldean astrology and soothsaying, inspires in him awe before the magnificence of "humanity" (vi.370/514). Already he sympathizes with Settembrini's esteem for life and humankind. He listens attentively when Settembrini disparages Naphta, whose arrival "under the aegis of death" (vi.412/570) concretely embodies the abstract principle of death, now decried by Settembrini as "the power opposed to life," as a power hostile to humanity and "life" if accorded sovereignty over the mind of man.

Each of Settembrini's efforts to affirm life and defame death, each of his attempts "to exalt health and cry down and belittle illness" (vi.453/627), Naphta parries with a trenchant reply. Settembrini contends that the sick man should feel only shame for his illness and consequently merits no pity. Furthermore, death must be judged a natural part of life rather than a mysterious terror: "No, death was neither spectre nor mystery. It was a simple, acceptable, and physiologically necessary phenomenon; to dwell upon it longer than decency required was to rob life of its due" (vi.458/633). Naphta counters with arguments defending "Disease and death as nobility, life and health as vulgarity" (vi.466/643). Hans Castorp retires from the exacerbating controversy vastly confused. He feels suspended above the contradictions, not just those between the disputants but those also within each contention itself.

In the subchapter that Weigand designates "the spiritual climax of the whole novel"[45] Hans Castorp ventures into the perilous "Snow," as yet unaware that he has deliberately "set out to lose his way" (vi.481/664). Already numbed by the mental debate between life and death, he repudiates all caution, accepting the "challenge" (vi.481/665) of the elements, and loses himself in an analogous struggle between life and death in the physical world. His vivid dream-poem follows upon the heels of the realization that in his wandering he has strayed "in a circle" (vi.487/673). In a precarious balance, experienced only once before at birth, the forces of life and death hover about him, competing for dominance in his mental perspective of the world.

Jürgen Scharfschwerdt analyzes his reverie in the snow as a twofold "dream of images," succeeded by a "dream of thoughts."[46] Hans Castorp imagines "in pictures" (vi.495/683) a lovely apparition of life, immediately followed by a nightmarish vision of death. The latter scene makes him "sick, sick as never before" (vi.494/683) so that he dreams "in thoughts" (vi.495/683) of a compromise between the contrary extremes of Settembrini and Naphta. Knowledge of life, he discovers, is at the same time knowledge of death. Fascination with disease and death is fascination with health and life. He now recognizes "life's delicate child," the one alone that merits all sympathy, as "the human being" (vi.495/684). Both accepting and rejecting Settembrini's and Naphta's dogmas, he acknowledges death's role as "a great power" while denying it any "mastery over [his] thoughts" (vi.496/685)! Determined to withhold his love from death as from an enemy, he has come to regard love itself as the only power intense enough to achieve a victory: "Love stands opposed to death. It is love, not reason, that is stronger than death" (vi.496/686). Then in the only italicized sentence of Mann's novel[47] he resolves conclusively that every man "for the sake of goodness and love" should permit death "no sovereignty over his thoughts" (vi.496-97/686).

Frank Hirschbach questions the enduring validity of this revelation concerning death. Events subsequent to the "Snow" episode, he argues, patently demonstrate death's persistent power over the apprentice: "Between 'Snow' and 'The Thunderbolt' lie almost five years of continued lethargy. . . . years of 'dullness,' infertile periods during which Hans Castorp merely vegetates." He insists that the "Snow" scene constitutes merely "a glorious episode without consequences," an ignis fatuus inserted into "a novel in which death triumphs over life."[48] He opposes critics who regard Hans Castorp's revelation as a turning point in the novel or indeed a legitimate revelation at all. His focus on the unproductive events that succeed the "Snow" subchapter champions vigorously, although superficially, death's undiminished role in the novel's conclusion. Certainly any reader who restricts his argument to a consideration of incidents will focus on the growing number of dying and dead characters. Joachim succumbs to his illness; Peeperkorn appears and within the same chapter commits suicide; the séance tolls the approach of war, which, after Naphta's suicide, brings the novel to a cataclysmic end. Admittedly death does function as a persistent reality in Hans Castorp's experience.

But such a restricted approach to death, with a view to its footprints in the novel, overlooks a significant change in the hero's attitude toward the events that surround him. Pascal properly reminds us that Hans Castorp's revelation in the "Snow" crisis fosters "a new attitude; but only an attitude."[49] According to Seidlin, the

"Snow" scene portrays first and foremost death's diminishing authority over Hans Castorp's thought without reference to his action: "the spell of death is broken, and with it the enchanting magic of the magic mountain."[50] After his dream Hans Castorp regards death no longer as a power, tantamount and antithetical to life, but rather as a value, subordinate to and innate in life: "The recklessness of death is in life, it would not be life without it" (vi.496/685). His "consciousness" of death's inherence in life, as Baer insists, "robs death of its terrors," infusing the novel with a synthetic view of death as "A Positive Value" in exchange for the illusory view, now dispelled, that would consider it the "Negation of Life."[51]

Therefore, the "Snow" crisis stands as a conversion in the hero's attitude, an expanded awareness. It retains validity, in Weigand's sense of its worth, as the spiritual climax of the novel. Mann himself in his address on "The German Republic" describes a metamorphosis in attitude which can establish a permanent change in consciousness: "No metamorphosis of the spirit is for us better trusted than one that begins with sympathy toward death and ends with the decision to serve life."[52]

I believe Mann purposes that we view Hans Castorp as a dynamic partisan of life. In Munich on his fiftieth birthday he voiced his most intense wish that posterity should regard all his work as kindly disposed toward life, "lebensfreundlich," although acquainted with death, "obwohl es vom Tode weiß." Concern with death, not as a spiritual objective but as a component part of a full and more nearly complete knowledge of life, prompted him to suggest two ways in which a person can wax enthusiastic toward life: "one that knows nothing of death, is quite simple and healthy; and another that knows of it, and only this one, I believe, has complete spiritual worth."[53]

He repeats the idea almost verbatim in the subchapter introducing Peeperkorn. Here Hans Castorp, for Clawdia's enlightenment, characterizes the second path that leads through death as "the <u>spiritual</u> way" (vii.596/827)! As noted above, one cannot and should not dismiss death from his thoughts, but neither should he permit its dominion over his thinking. Indeed, this newly affirmative attitude emerges from the "Snow" enlightenment as an optimistic view of life. For the knowledge afforded Hans Castorp in his dream, Joseph Stern argues, "is that the untrammeled dominion of death over men is as corrupting to their minds and hearts as is the frivolous avoidance of all thought of death." Life must be "informed but not paralyzed by the apprehension of disease and the expectation of death."[54]

Within one perspective, death's role in <u>The Magic Mountain</u> parallels that of the theatrical stage in Goethe's view. "Death," as Baer suggests, "is the great educator in the 'Magic Mountain' just as the theatre is in 'Wilhelm Meister.'" Indeed, death provides "the medium by which [Mann] attained to his synthetic outlook of life, just as the theater was Goethe's medium."[55] In viewing death as the way of error we are then in the position of regarding Hans Castorp as heir apparent to Wilhelm Meister. He quaffs the intoxicating brew of death to its astringent dregs, indeed until satiation dissolves error's bonds, and self-limitation emerges as a new control.

At the end of chapter 6 he has transcended his initiation into the mysterious "cult of the sarcophagus" (vi.511/707). He has emerged from the well-guarded "crystal retort" (vi.511/706) of his hermetic experience with death. "The grave, the sepulchre," he learns from Naphta, initially served as "the emblem of initiation into the society." It therefore predated Settembrini's association with Freemasonry and its modernized philosophy of reason and progress. It also preceded Hans Castorp's deeper and more aware association with life. The sepulchre has thus symbolized his initiation into the mysteries of a higher state of existence.

By chapter 7 he has clearly recognized death's transitory character in its relation to life. Describing death as "the spiritual principle," as pedagogically prerequisite to a spiritual understanding of life, he instructs Clawdia that "love of [death] leads to love of life and love of humanity" (vii.596/827). Reducing death to the status of a vehicle on the path toward the ultimate goal of living, he no longer esteems the spectacle of a dead man. Even as early as the previous chapter, when Joachim dies, he cannot ignore "the seeds of corruption" in the corpse's corrosive smile: "It was good that the coffin was now to be closed, the lid screwed on; that the hour for removal was at hand" (vi.540/746). And when Joachim is buried, he discerns nothing exalted in "Ziemssen's root-pierced grave" (vi.540/747).

When Peeperkorn dies and Clawdia departs again, he experiences the ennui and stagnation of a staleness, a "Stumpfsinn," on the mountain. Seeking to repress his awareness of "life as dead" (vii.627/872) at the Berghof, he plays "patience" (vii.632/879), but Settembrini perceives in his eyes, "that you [Hans Castorp] are conscious of your state" (vii.633/880). Indeed, as Mann informs us, he even fears an impending "catastrophe" that must inevitably "snatch life beyond the 'dead point'" (vii.634/881). Thus for him death has lost its charm. The mountain has lost its magic.

In desperation he resorts to the enchantment of music, but within his favorite world of Schubert's "Lindenbaum" he quickly discovers the now familiar sphere of death (vii.652/905). In his ascent through the years of "hermetic-pedagogic discipline, of ascent from one stage of being to another" (vii.651/904), he has acquired the ability to perceive in music the "spiritual backsliding" that Settembrini has characterized as "disease" (vii.652/906). Having long ago renounced his love of death and advanced to an admiration of life, he experiences serious misgivings regarding Schubert's song as a temptation against which conscience should function with decisive restraint (vii.653/907). Therefore, his newly acquired love of music, the response to a siren that Settembrini also characterized as "politically suspect" (iv.114/163) and especially "dangerous" for him personally, becomes at this stage in his formation a scruple of conscience.

Ultimately he escapes one last temptation to yield to death in the séance, which, like the "Snow" dream, unfolds in two phases: Holger's lovely poem of the sea (vii.663-64/921-22), followed the next night by the horrifying apparition of a warlike Joachim (vii.680-81/945-47). But in a crucial departure from the "Snow" dream he deprives this sequence of its subsequent "dream of thoughts" by flooding the room with the same white light of reason that Settembrini had once brought to bear on sickness, now death. Unlike the X-ray vision of his own grave which he had piously relished near the end of volume I, this penetration into the supernatural world so near the conclusion of volume II abruptly repulses him from the last entanglement of death's allure. As Pascal describes this final rupture, he "leaves the room with a 'threatening nod' to Krobowski; he has chosen for life, light, responsibility."[56] Although his initial attitude toward the séance overcame aversion with curiosity (vii.657/913), in the end antipathy triumphs. Death holds no further sway over his attitude toward life.

When the thunderclap of war resounds, Mann's "Seven-Sleeper," summoned at last from the actual realm of death, stands and looks about him: "He saw himself released, freed from enchantment" (vii.711/988). Admittedly, external rather than internal powers have freed him from the mountain's fatal magic, and "his own liberation" is reduced to utter insignificance before the fate of Europe and the world. Nevertheless, life has chosen to receive again "her erring and 'delilcate' child" (vii.711/988). And suddenly awakened to the impulse of life, he departs sternly, solemnly, and willingly, indeed immune to a facile regression into the arms of the "Magic Mountain," which for him long ago has lost its charms. Discharged with Settembrini's blessings, he abandons the inert mountain of death, eagerly embracing the active plains of life.

In an ending that critics have considered "perplexing" and "inconclusive"[57] he volunteers for the front line of battle in the great World War. Raising the question of "why Hans Castorp finally leaves the magic mountain"--while rejecting motives of patriotism, concern for political and international affairs, and the anticipation of reunion with Hamburg relatives--Hirschbach argues that he beholds in the war "the great opportunity to commit an honorable suicide. Nothing else could explain Hans' presence on the battlefield. He desires death.... With a song of death on his lips, he stumbles into his uncertain, certain future."[58]

I do not believe that Hans Castorp solicits death in the trenches of Flanders. Such an interpretation radically violates the prevalent tenor of the argument in the second volume, as if this apprentice had inexplicably regressed to the illusions that bound him in volume I. The mountain, never the flatland, represents death's enticing appeal. The flatland symbolizes the community of the living. And, as Seidlin so appropriately remarks, "even if this community is engulfed in a deadly war, which Hans Castorp may or may not survive," he has not forgotten the lesson of the "Snow." There remains an "obvious difference whether someone loses his life in the fight to stay alive (and this is the last glimpse we have of him), or whether one embraces the principle of death."[59]

Mann himself approaches the question of his hero's survival "without great concern," leaving it intentionally "open" (vii.716/994). For just as his prospects are small, so should be our concern. He in his apprenticeship has with certainty prepared himself for life. He has also fulfilled an apprenticeship to death.

A proper interpretation of the ending stands or falls on the hero's mental attitude. "The final outcome of 'The Magic Mountain,'" Lindsay insists, "is positive." Escaping the bonds of a seven-year trance, Hans Castorp "returns to face the difficulties and dangers of life, spiritually enriched and strengthened by his Alpine sojourn." To substantiate his claim, Lindsay cites the youth's "assertion of life at the end of the book."[60] In his attitudes toward both life and death Hans Castorp recognizes positive values. Two-fold death--the "res bina" (vii.511/705 and 596/827)--represents a means rather than an end to life. Indeed, his apprenticeship educates him concomitantly to life's positive values and to the relative merits of death.

The Magic Mountain ends with his ultimate release from a life-stifling fascination with death. He differs perhaps from previous heroes of the apprenticeship novel, not according to any change in the protagonist's attitude as he enters the world, but consequent to an alteration in the world that receives him. If Mann remains uncertain about the outcome of his modern parody of the older German "Wilhelm Meisterly apprenticeship novel,"[61] then such an evasion of the issue may reflect, as Pascal suggests, his own confrontation with "a world infinitely more bewildering than that awaiting the other heroes" in the apprenticeship tradition: "what has changed" is not the hero but "society itself, which now propounds infinitely more puzzling and difficult problems."[62] Perhaps the most clearly positive explanation of the inconclusive ending of The Magic Mountain springs from the multifarious character of the hero himself. Emerging from the bewildering experiences of the Sanatorium, having completed a three-stage apprenticeship to life and death, he enjoys an attitude of mind fully adaptable to coping with all the exigencies, ecstasies, and agonies of either peace or war, of both life and death. Whether he lives or dies is irrelevant. He is throughly prepared for either contingency.[63]

We advanced none to the rank of Masters but such as clearly felt and recognized the purpose they were born for, and had got enough of practice to proceed along their way with a certain cheerfulness and ease.

--Johann Wolfgang von Goethe,
Wilhelm Meister's Apprenticeship,
trans. Thomas Carlyle

10. THE COMPLETE APPRENTICESHIP

In a "priceless" conversation (vii.593/822) on the Magic Mountain Hans Castorp informs Clawdia Chauchat that "there is such a thing as alchemistic-hermetic pedagogy, transubstantiation, from lower to higher, ascending degrees, if you understand what I mean. But of course matter that is capable of taking those ascending stages by dint of outward pressure must have a little something in itself to start with."

"You are a quaint philosopher," Clawdia replies. "I will not assert that I have understood all your involved German ideas; but it sounds human and good, and you are good, a good young man" (vii.596/827).

In an equally priceless exchange in the Society of the Tower the country clergyman informs Wilhelm Meister, that a good young man who drains error to its dregs--if he be not "wahnsinnig," that is, "crazy" (VII.ix.61/122)--will turn from his error onto a path of his own choosing that is his own.

In the first stage of a good young man's apprenticeship to life and death the hero embarks on a singular path that to all appearances alienates him from the social community. This is the individual stage of his cultivation. In it he gains his freedom to a great extent from bondage to illusion.

In the second stage of his formation he is reintegrated with the community. This is the social stage, which serves to heighten inherent values that then thrive unconstrained in his newfound grasp of reality.

Although alienation and reintegration comprise a course of human cultivation that may be viewed as circuitous, the journey proves necessary to a viable, dynamic concept of growth and development. In the fall from childhood's paradisal unity into the anguished division between individual and community, alienation becomes an indispensable first step in the progression toward a second and higher step that reunites the individual with the outer world.

A third step even loftier than the heightening of life's inherent values encompasses the metaphysical world of death. This phase of relating death to life resolves the social tension between individual and community by transcending its limits and powers. In _The Magic Mountain_ it evolves as a by-product of stages one and two. For in securing freedom from life's illusions the apprentice at first succumbs to a strong bondage of death. He escapes this sympathy with death through the rededication of his inherent energies and heightened talents to life. In the Goethean sense of renunciation, he loses himself in the service of others, wherein he finds himself.

Therefore, the three stages--in stressing the individual, the social, and the metaphysical worlds--entail confrontations, respectively, with life's illusions, its values, and death. And in their essential functions as preparations for life and death each encounter proves necessary to a fully realized apprenticeship. Philip Carey completes the first of these stages; Wilhelm Meister, the second; and Hans Castorp, the third. Yet both Maugham and Goethe permit the open-ended possibility of a further stage of development, and each of their candidates stands ripe on its threshhold.

In the course of the argument of this book I have emphasized particularly the positive nature of the apprenticeship's preparatory stage with an eye to providing a valid perspective on Maugham's Of Human Bondage. When bracketed between the "archetype" and the "last" of the popularly and critically hailed German masterpieces in the apprenticeship tradition, Maugham's novel reveals positive values that clearly distinguish a masterpiece among English representatives of the type. I cannot sanction myopic criticism ascribing to the work a lingering negative impression, for in the context of the German apprenticeship novel it portrays a necessary and positive individual grade of culture.

We must certainly regard Of Human Bondage--some seventy years after its publication as "not dated."[1] In contrast to Wilhelm Meister it remains--as Maugham himself has observed concerning the novel of a contemporary--"eminently readable." And in a notable aside he adds, "I should not mention a merit that is so obvious except that many great books do not possess it."[2] In support of the tenor of Maugham's argument Eduard Spranger remarks concerning Wilhelm Meister, "Readers belonging to a different mental atmosphere cannot automatically enter into the spirit of this story which has a peculiar background--German life in the second half of the eighteenth century. Even we Germans have to modify our mental outlook. . . . It must be admitted that there are many educated Germans who have never read Wilhelm Meister."[3]

Charges leveled against all three works--Maugham's, Goethe's, and Mann's--have frequently focused on their supposed effect on adolescent readers. Judged unfit for the education of youth, these apprenticeship novels are censured primarily because of their immorality, and many admirers of these works when they first appeared were hard pressed to defend their affective as well as cognitive influence. For example, during the century after its publication, "no 'gentleman,' we hear in certain circles, could have written [Wilhelm Meister]; few real gentlemen, it is insinuated, can like to read it; no real lady, unless possessed of considerable courage, should profess having read it at all."[4] The basis for such objections, in all three of the above mentioned instances, rests primarily on the attitude of the author. Bad actions are not condemned; goods ones escape praise. The author adopts an ironic posture of detachment.

In our own time, in an age still witnessing the dregs of realism and naturalism, such considerations may appear ingenuous, even anachronistic. Part and parcel to the mode of narration in the modern novel is the author's impartiality. What once was attacked as a vice, his destitution of moral bias, is more profoundly seen as a virtue, his avoidance of enthusiastic or indignant didacticism. Even today's moralists, when confronted with the question of a novel's morality, are less likely to attack its author's detached tolerance of evil than his active sympathy with it.

Of more profound concern, however, than the issue of a novel's or its author's morality, is the same moral focus on specific characters, scenes, and incidents that depict vice in all its charms, and the effect of these impressions on a youthful reader. Accusations on these grounds point out Philip Carey's affairs with Miss Wilkinson and Mildred, Wilhelm Meister's relations to Mariane and the alluring Philine, and Hans Castorp's "adventure in evil" with Clawdia Chauchat. There are also many incidents that occur during Philip's sojourn in Paris, Wilhelm's association with the players, and Hans Castorp's self-abandonment to forbidden realms during his entire stay on the mountain.

Standard defenses, in responding to these and similar questions of the morality of a work of art, frequently consider the questions utilitarian, their answers irrelevant. The work is an aesthetic entity, a little world created as a second nature or a mirror reflective of our own, and hence not subject to historical, moral, or philosophical judgment. This autonomous view of art lifts the burden of responsibility for the moral use or abuse of a particular work of fiction off the shoulders of the author, indeed away from the work itself, resting it squarely on the back of the reader. Note the brilliantly witty conclusion to Boccaccio's Decameron. Or, on a more serious note, Milton's Areopagitica.

As it relates to our own argument in our own time, the objective realist Theodore Dreiser claims, regarding Of Human Bondage, that "to begin with it is unmoral, as a novel of this kind must necessarily be."[5] Certainly as early as 1855 George Henry Lewes was arguing that

> Wilhelm Meister is not a moral story. . . . The consequence is that it is frequently pronounced immoral; which I conceive to be an absurd judgment; for if it have not express moral purpose, guiding and animating all the scenes, neither has it an immoral purpose. It may not be written for the edification of virtue; assuredly it is not written for the propogation of vice.

In extending his argument Lewes asserts categorically that, although the book is "in no respect a Moral Tale, I am bound to declare that deep and healthy moral meaning lies in it."[6] Even D. J. Enright, whose unmercifully frank evaluation of the work unearths many "incredibly bad" faults, admits that it is "characterized by a kind of moral passion which, spasmodic though it may be, is yet too intense to be disregarded."[7]

One of the best replies to public concern over R. D. Boylan's new translation of Wilhelm Meister's Apprenticeship (1855) was George Eliot's realistic assessment of its potential for affecting the youth of English society:

> Ask nineteen out of twenty moderately educated persons what they think of Wilhelm Meister, and the answer will probably be--'I think it an immoral book; and besides, it is awfully

> dull: I was not able to read it'. Whatever truth there may be in the first half of this judgment, the second half is a sufficient guarantee that the book is not likely to do any extensive injury in English society. Parents may let it lie on the drawing-room table without scruple, in the confidence that for youthful minds of the ordinary cast it will have no attractions, and that the exceptional youthful mind which is strongly arrested by it is of too powerful and peculiar a character to be trained according to educational dogmas.[8]

Such assurances can also be applied, with little or no opposition, to Mann's *Magic Mountain*. But *Of Human Bondage* has been, and still is, very much in the hands of European and American youth. Hence its exposure to the more basic concern.

From a practical perspective of education Maugham's, Goethe's, and Mann's novels can be employed effectively to supplement the successive stages in an actual apprentice's introduction to life and death. *Of Human Bondage* inspires many of the "questions about good and evil, justice and injustice, fact and superstition, the good life and the wasted life"[9] that *Wilhelm Meister*--while adding queries of fate, character, the value of error, and education--seeks to answer. It then remains for *The Magic Mountain* to confront the final, inescapable issue of death.

After leading a youth through such a sequence of stages, if it be found that one or more of these novels is a significant cause of the supposed failure of his apprenticeship to life or death, then to him that is of that opinion, let the amended words of Horace suffice:

iubeas stultum esse, libenter[10]

for the apprenticeship novel, like error, is the companion of youth--indeed of us all.

NOTES

Preface

1. "The Validity of Literary Definitions," PMLA, 39 (1924), 736, 734, 728.
2. See Susanne Howe's Wilhelm Meister and His English Kinsmen, Apprentices to Life (New York, 1930); Jerome Buckley's Season of Youth: The Bildungsroman from Dickens to Golding (Cambridge, Mass., 1974); G. B. Tennyson's "The Bildungsroman in Nineteenth-Century English Literature," in Rosario Armato and John Spalek, eds., Medieval Epic to the "Epic Theater" of Brecht (Los Angeles, 1968), pp. 135-46; and Martin Swales' The German Bildungsroman from Wieland to Hesse (Princeton, 1978). See also Christine Touaillon's "Bildungsroman," in P. Merker and W. Stammler, Hrsg., Reallexikon der deutschen Literaturgeschichte (Berlin, 1925-31), I, 141-45; E. L. Stahl's dissertation, Die religiöse und die humanitätsphilosophische Bildungsidee und die deutschen Bildungsromans im 18. Jahrhundert (Bern, 1932), in SuD, Bd. 56 (Bern, 1934); Berta Berga's dissertation, Der moderne deutsche Bildungsroman (Bern, 1937), in SuD, Bd. 69 (Bern, 1942); Hans Borcherdt's "Der deutsche Bildungsroman," in G. Fricke, F. Koch, u. K. Lugowski, Hrsg., Von deutscher Art in Sprache und Dichtung, 5 (Stuttgart, 1941), 3-55, "Der Bildungsroman der Hochklassik und Hochromantik," in Der Roman der Goethezeit (Urach und Stuttgart, 1949), S. 261-382, and "Bildungsroman," in W. Kohlschmidt und W. Mohr, Hrsg., Reallexikon der deutschen Literaturgeschichte, 2. Aufl. (Berlin, 1955), I, 175-78; Hans Rudolf Wagner's dissertation, Der englische Bildungsroman bis in die Zeit des ersten Weltkrieges (Bern, 1949), in SAA, Bd. 27 (Bern, 1951); Fritz Martini's "Der Bildungsroman: Zur Geschichte des Wortes und der Theorie," DVLG, 35 (1961), 44-63; Lothar Köhn's "Entwicklungs- und Bildungsroman: Ein Forschungsbericht," in DVLG, 42 (Aug. 1968), 427-73, (Okt. 1968), 590-632; François Jost's "La Tradition du 'Bildungsroman,'" CL, 21 (1969), 97-115; and Jürgen Jacobs' Wilhelm Meister und seine Brüder: Untersuchungen zum deutschen Bildungsroman (München, 1972). One further useful source for definitions and characteristics is Jürgen Scharfschwerdt's Thomas Mann und der deutsche Bildungsroman (Stuttgart, 1967). Cf. also the list of unpublished dissertations in the Bibliography below. One of these by Judy R. Rogers, "The Evolution of the Bildungsroman" (Chapel Hill, 1973), offers five basic characteristics of the type through a focus on seven representatives from twentieth-century English and American literatures; and another one by Preston Fambrough, "The Apprenticeship Novel in Nineteenth-Century England and France" (Chapel Hill, 1979), through a similar focus on five representatives and two parodies from nineteenth-century English and French literatures, seeks to distinguish the term "apprenticeship novel" from "Bildungsroman" as "distinctly broader in scope," a distinction based on the studies of Howe, Tennyson, Buckley,

Jost, and Fambrough's own study.

3. English terminology poses a troublesome dilemma. I use the term "genre" in the sense that René Wellek and Austin Warren define it: the three "ultimate categories" of the first order (poetry, fiction, and drama) are subdivided into groups or "genres" (lyric poem, novel, short story, epic, play, etc.) of the second order. [See Wellek and Warren, "Literary Genres," Theory of Literature, rev. ed. (New York, 1956), ch. 17. See also R. S. Crane, ed., Critics and Criticism (Chicago, 1952), pp. 12-24, 546-63, for a defense of the utility of the distinction between genres.] I consider "genre," "literary tradition," "literary species," "literary form," "kind," and "type"--for the purpose of my argument--equivalent. [Irwin Ehrenpreis in The "Types" Approach to Literature (New York, 1945), pp. 4-5, arbitrarily equates "genre" in literary scholarship with "kind" in literary criticism and "type" in the teaching of literature. For these terms N. H. Pearson in "Literary Forms and Types," English Insititute Annual, 1940 (New York, 1941), pp. 61-72, employs "form," designating the "gross divisions" or ultimate categories of the first order as "types." A. Owen Aldridge in his editorial introduction to "Literary Forms," Comparative Literature: Matter and Method (Urbana, 1969), pp. 148-60, defines "genre" as meaning a "kind" or "species." M. H. Abrams in his revised Glossary of Literary Terms, 3rd ed. (New York, 1971), pp. 67-68 and 110-14, employs interchangeably the labels "genre," "literary species," "literary form," "kind," and "type" in his definition of the word "genre."] For a term to designate fictional subdivisions of the third order (Gothic novel, epistolary novel, Bildungsroman, Erziehungsroman, historical novel, "le nouveau roman," etc.)--rather than adopt the more accurate term "subgenre" or "genus" (the Germans employ the term "Art")--I favor use of the word "type," if only to countenance the right to view the "subgenre" as a "genre" in itself. Thus, in a progressively distinguishing scale I recognize the category (fiction), the genre (novel), and the type (Bildungsroman, apprenticeship novel) as classifying groups of the first, second, and third orders, respectively.

1. The Origin of the Term

1. See Hans Borcherdt, "Bildungsroman," in Werner Kohlschmidt und Wolfgang Mohr, Hrsg., Reallexikon der deutschen Literaturgeschichte, 2. Aufl. (Berlin, 1955), I, 175. The well-known passage from Dilthey's work asserts, "I wish to call the novels, which constitute the school of Wilhelm Meister (for Rousseau's kindred art form had no strong influence on it): 'Bildungsromane.' Goethe's work portrays human cultivation in different stages, forms, epochs of life. It fills with pleasure, since it does not depict the whole world together with its malformations and the struggle of evil passions for existence; the difficult material of life is excluded." [Das Leben Schleiermachers (Berlin, 1870), S. 317.]

2. Published in Dörptsche Beyträge für Freunde der Philosophie,

Literatur und Kunst, III (1816), 1. Hälfte. For Martini's article see "Der Bildungsroman: Zur Geschichte des Wortes und der Theorie," DVLG, 35 (1961), 44-63. See also Lothar Köhn, Entwicklungs- und Bildungsroman: Ein Forschungsbericht (Stuttgart, 1969), S. 5.

3. Published in Inländisches Museum, I, Heft 4 (1820-21); II, Heft 5 und 6 (1821).
4. Published in Neues Museum der teutschen Provinzen Rußlands, I, Hefte 1-3 (1824-25).
5. Leipzig und Liegnitz. See Martini, S. 58-60.
6. "La tradition du 'Bildungsroman,'" CL, 21 (1969), 102.
7. Cf. Hans Wagner, Der englische Bildungsroman bis in die Zeit des ersten Weltkrieges, Diss. Bern 1949, in SAA, 27 (Bern, 1951), 13: "In English there is no strictly adequate expression for it."
8. The English Novel in Transition, 1885-1940 (Norman, Okla., 1942), pp. 193 ff.
9. Confrontations (Princeton, 1965), p. 14. See also Anthony Thorlby, ed., The Penguin Companion to Literature (Baltimore, 1969), II, 114.
10. Wilhelm Meister and His English Kinsmen, Apprentices to Life (New York, 1930), pp. 4, 6, 127. See also Werner Friederich, History of German Literature (New York, 1948), pp. 18, 222.
11. See ch. 2 of this book, concerning the apprenticeship novel as a regulative type, for a more detailed discussion of these boundaries and their validity. The German language, for example, clearly distinguishes between "Erziehung" and "Bildung." Therefore, the two types of the novel borrowing their names from these terms logically express differing ideas. [See below, exp. pp. 8 f.]
12. or critics writing in English, as is here the case
13. See Howe, p. 6: "The German passion for categories, as opposed to the English preference for vagueness in these matters, has enabled the 'Bildungsroman' to remain in Germany something distinct from the more definite 'Erziehungsroman,' the pedagogic or educational novel," and "distinct also from the 'Entwicklungsroman.'"
14. There is some question here as to genus and species. The English often translate "Erziehungsroman" and "Bildungsroman" as "educational novel," a generic term subsuming both. On the other hand the Germans often regard "Erziehungsroman" as either wholly separate or a subclass of the generic term "Bildungsroman," which itself can be classed under "Entwicklungsroman." Cf. Jürgen Jacobs Wilhelm Meister und seine Brüder: Untersuchungen zum deutschen Bildungsroman (München, 1972), S. 14; and Melitta Gerhard, Der deutsche Entwicklungsroman bis zu Goethes "Wilhelm Meister" (Halle, 1926), S. 1. See also Jost, p. 100, for the specific to general progression of "Erziehungs-," "Bildungs-," and "Entwicklungsroman."
15. Cf. Werner Friederich and David Malone, Outline of Comparative Literature (Chapel Hill, 1954), p. 275: The "Bildungsroman" or apprenticeship novel places "emphasis upon the subjective quest of the hero for a philosophy of life and upon the psychological crisis and personal experiences of the hero alone."
16. A conceivable alternative source for Howe's use of the term is the title of George Henry Lewes' novel, Apprenticeship of Life (1850), to which Howe refers; but Lewes knew Carlyle's work too.

17. Cf. Friederich and Malone, pp. 179, 275-76, 281, 421, and 423. See also Wagner, S. 13: "Perhaps the best expression is 'apprenticeship novel,' derived from Goethe's 'Wilhelm Meisters Lehrjahre.'"
18. See Heinrich Meyer's "Introductory Remarks" to Helmut Germer, *The German Novel of Education, 1792-1805*, Diss. Vanderbilt 1966 (Bern, 1968), p. [i]: "'Bildung' is self-formation and involves the development, growth and maturing of innate, native gifts and needs. 'Bildung,' as Goethe meant it, had a biological component of the naturally given that takes on its varied shapes. 'Formation' is therefore a better translation than 'education.' The latter term implies too much our later connotations, connected with schooling and purpose and social standing, all of which were not meant when the word 'Bildung' originated and became fashionable at first." See also Germer, p. 1, and M. H. Abrams, *Glossary of Literary Terms*, 3rd ed. rev. (New York, 1971), p. 112.
19. Trevor Jones, "Bildungsroman," *Harraps' Standard German and English Dictionary* (London, 1963).
20. This term was adopted by François Jost in his article on "La tradition du 'Bildungsroman'" and by R.-M. Albérès in his *Histoire du roman moderne* (Paris, 1962), p. 114.
21. Fernand Baldensperger, *Goethe en France* (Paris, 1920), p. 176.
22. *Ibid.*, pp. 184, 177 (quoting Janin in the *Débats* of January 2, 1830), 185.
23. For the dearth of representatives of the type in France, see below, ch. 4, for concrete manifestations of the type.
24. Thorlby, p. 114; Jost, p. 114; Howe, p. 6; Mann, "[Geist und Wesen der Deutschen Republik]" und "Betrachtungen eines Unpolitischen," in *Gesammelte Werke* (Frankfurt, 1960), XI, 855, und XII, 505; Kornbluth, "The Reception of Wilhelm Meister in America," *Symposium*, 13 (1959), 128; Shipley, *Dictionary of World Literary Terms* (London, 1955), p. 30; Wilpert, *Sachwörterbuch der Literatur* (Stuttgart, 1955), S. 132; Friederich and Malone, p. 275; Wundt, *Goethes Wilhelm Meister und die Entwicklung des modernen Lebensideals* (Berlin, 1913), S. 68.
25. *Confrontations*, p. 14.
26. Howe, p. 24. See Kornbluth, p. 128.

2. The Concept of the Type

1. M. H. Abrams, *A Glossary of Literary Terms*, 3rd ed. rev. (New York, 1971), p. 110.
2. See Royal A. Gettmann, "novel, Types of," in Shipley, *Dictionary of World Literary Terms* (London, 1955).
3. See *Handbuch der Weltliteratur von den Anfängen bis zur Gegenwart*, 3. Aufl. (Frankfurt, 1960), Anh. II ("Schriftennachweis zu einzelnen Formen, Gattungen, Fragen und Stoffkreisen der Literatur"), S. 782-84 ("Roman").
4. See Levin's article on "novel" in Shipley.
5. *Goethes Wilhelm Meister und die Entwicklung des modernen Lebensideals* (Berlin, 1913), S. 54, 55-68.
6. "Vom Abenteuer- zum Bildungsroman," *GRM*, 14 (1926), 339, 346,

339, 340, 345.

7. Die religiöse und die humanitätsphilosophische Bildungsidee und die Entstehung des deutschen Bildungsromans im 18. Jahrhundert, Diss. Bern 1932, in SuD, 56 (Bern, 1934), 115-16.
8. "La Tradition du 'Bildungsroman,'" CL, 21 (1969), 99.
9. See Walter Rehm's and Werner Kohlschmidt's article on the "Abenteuerroman" in the Reallexikon der deutschen Literaturgeschichte, 2. Aufl. (Berlin, 1955), I, 1-4.
10. New York, 1950, p. 146.
11. Jost, p. 101.
12. Outline of Comparative Literature (Chapel Hill, 1954), p. 275.
13. Jost, p. 108.
14. Ibid.
15. Stuttgart, 1955, S. 132, 59-60.
16. Stahl, S. 116-17. See also Jost, p. 100: "The manuals of literature very often, alas, give as synonyms of our type [apprenticeship novel]: the novel of development (Entwicklungsroman) and the novel of education (Erziehungsroman). Of these two expressions the first says more than 'Bildungsroman,' the second says less."
17. See Shipley, "Bildungsroman," and the use of the term "Erziehungsroman" in the article on "Epiphany."
18. The German Novel of Education, 1792-1805, Diss. Vanderbilt 1966 (Bern, 1968), p. 4.
19. Germer defines the "Novel of Education" generally as "a novel that attempts to improve and educate its reader" [p. 1].
20. See Meyer's "Introductory Remarks" to Germer, p. [i]. Meyer regrets that "in English, 'novel of education' serves equally to cover the 'Bildungsroman' in the sequence of Rousseau and Goethe."
21. Philosophische Versuche über die menschliche Natur und ihre Entwickelung (Leipzig, 1777), II, 601. See also Jost's remarks concerning this distinction on p. 108 of his article.
22. "Rede an mein Haus," Sämtliche Werke (Liegnitz, 1899 ff.), XIII, 177, also noted in Jost, pp. 108-9.
23. Stahl, S. 117.
24. See Germer, p. 1. See also Martin Swales, The German Bildungsroman from Wieland to Hesse (Princeton, 1978), p. 14.
25. Jost, p. 101.
26. Cf. Meyer in Germer, pp. [i-ii].
27. Jost, pp. 101, 113.
28. Thomas Mann's Novel: Der Zauberberg (New York, 1933), p. 4.
29. See Stahl, S. 117: "'Entwicklung' must also in the sphere of the novel be differentiated from 'Bildung.'"
30. New York, 1952, p. 70.
31. Der moderne deutsche Bildungsroman, Diss. Bern 1937, in SuD, 69 (Bern, 1942), 4.
32. Wilhelm Meister and His English Kinsmen, Apprentices to Life (New York, 1930), p. 6.
33. Stahl, S. 117.
34. Wilpert, S. 59-60. Cf. also G. B. Tennyson, "The Bildungsroman in Nineteenth-Century English Literature," in Rosario Armato and John Spalek, eds., Medieval Epic to the "Epic Theater" of Brecht (Los Angeles, 1968), p. 142. Tennyson defines the

"Entwicklungsroman" as "merely the novel of development" but the apprenticeship novel as "the novel of harmonious cultivation of the whole personality."

35. For a more extensive consideration of the goal of culture, see the appropriate section of ch. 3's concern with fundamental principles, pp. 26 ff. below.
36. Der englische Bildungsroman bis in die Zeit des ersten Weltkrieges, Diss. Bern 1949, in SAA, 27 (Bern, 1951), 14.
37. One exception might be Emil Strauß's Freund Hein (Death the Comforter) from the list on p. 31 below, for the hero of this work commits suicide. Cf. also Thomas Mann's Zauberberg (Magic Mountain) as discussed below. But the main thrust of the distinction resides in the hero's capacity for the achievement, not the achievement itself, of his goal before his death.
38. Stahl, S. 117.
39. Wagner, S. 104.
40. Jost, p. 99.
41. Hrsg. Paul Merker und Wolfgang Stammler (Berlin, 1925-31), S. 141: "Bildungsroman."
42. Jost, p. 100. For further consideration of the similarities and differences between the apprenticeship novel and the autobiography, see Roy Pascal, "The Autobiographical Novel and the Autobiography," EIC, 9 (1959), 134-50.
43. For more detail on this aspect of the apprenticeship novel, see the section of ch. 3 below, treating the goal of the apprenticeship, p. 27.
44. See the chapter on Friedrich Hölderlin in Das Erlebnis und die Dichtung, 6. Aufl. (Leipzig, 1919), S. 395.
45. "Bildungsroman," in Werner Kohlschmidt und Wolfgang Mohr, Hrsg., Reallexikon der deutschen Literaturgeschichte, 2. Aufl. (Berlin, 1955), I, 177.
46. M. H. Abrams considers the "Künstlerroman" (artist-novel) "an important subtype of the 'Bildungsroman.'" [See Abrams, p. 113.] "It represents the development of a novelist or other artist into the stage of maturity in which he recognizes his artistic destiny and achieves mastery of his artistic craft." Abrams includes several twentieth-century instances of this subtype: Proust's Remembrance of Things Past, Joyce's A Portrait of the Artist as a Young Man, Mann's Tonio Kröger and Dr. Faustus, and Gide's The Counterfeiters. In addition, Maurice Beebe discusses artist novels of the nineteenth and early twentieth centuries. [Ivory Towers and Sacred Founts: The Artist as Hero in Fiction from Goethe to Joyce (New York, 1964), pp. 71 and 117-71.] Beebe considers artist novels that follow the "Sacred Fount tradition": Mme de Staël's Corinne, Hans Christian Andersen's The Improvisatore: or, Life in Italy, George Sand's Consuelo, Henry Murger's Scènes de la vie de Bohème, George du Maurier's Trilby, and Ernest Hemingway's The Sun Also Rises. He then traces the development of the "Ivory Tower tradition" of the artist as manifested in Edgar Allan Poe's "The Fall of the House of Usher," in Baudelaire himself and in other French writers of the second half of the nineteenth century, and in representatives of the Aesthetic Movement in England during the same period, beginning with Ruskin and climaxed by

Joyce. Beebe designates four writers--Balzac, James, Proust, and Joyce--who have achieved an effective balance between the two traditions. The artist tradition in Germany stems from Goethe's fragmentary Sendung, includes "Künstlerromane" and "-novellen" of the nineteenth and early twentieth century, and culminates in the artist novels of Thomas Mann. [See enumerations by H. Heckel in the Reallexikon, II, 172-75, and by Wilpert in the Sachwörterbuch, S. 298-99.]

47. History of German Literature (New York, 1948), p. 211.
48. "Der Bildungsroman: Zur Geschichte des Wortes und der Theorie," DVLG, 35 (1961), 57.
49. See Howe, p. 4. See also the section in ch. 3 below, concerning the nature of the apprenticeship, pp. 17 f.
50. "Der Bildungsroman der Hochklassik und Hochromantik," Der Roman der Goethezeit (Urach und Stuttgart, 1949), S. 266, 267. The organic aspect of the apprentice's striving would appear to dissolve Berta Berger's distinction between the goals of cultivation, "Bildung," and development, "Entwicklung," as noted above (p. 11), for the goal of cultivation here incorporates the more restricted organic goal of development.
51. Ibid., S. 268-69.
52. Jost, p. 100, n. 4. See also Beebe, Ivory Towers and Sacred Founts.
53. Whether by the term "la trame" Jost means the thread of the novel's plot or the thread of the hero's process of development, in either case the basic distinction between the foci applies.

3. Fundamental Principles

1. See Wilhelm Meister and His English Kinsmen, Apprentices to Life (New York, 1930), p. 4.
2. As Goethe acknowledges in a letter to Schiller, Wilhelm Meister, who notifies Werner of his decision to change his name (See bk. V, ch. iii), would have been more appropriately called "Wilhelm Schüler." [Goethes Werke (Weimar, 1887-1919), Abt. IV, Bd. 10, S. 212, 6. Dezember 1794.]
3. "La Tradition du 'Bildungsroman,'" CL, 21 (1969), 114.
4. The Magic Mountain, trans. H. T. Lowe-Porter (New York: Knopf, 1982), p. 596; Der Zauberberg, S. 827, in Gesammelte Werke (Frankfurt, 1960), Bd. III.
5. Hermann Weigand asserts that in the particular case of The Magic Mountain genius is indeed involved. Cf. Weigand, Thomas Mann's Novel: Der Zauberberg (New York: 1933), p. 4: "Hans Castorp has it 'in sich' [in himself]--to an extraordinary degree"; or p. 5: "It is the development of genius!" Roy Pascal, however--in providing a parallel to Wilhelm Meister, who becomes "a representative, not an exceptional, human being"--claims that Hans Castorp also "at the end of the novel . . . has become a representative German." [The German Novel (Manchester, 1956), pp. 8, 96.] See also Martin Swales, Thomas Mann: A Study (Totowa, N. J., 1980), who stresses Mann's repeated assertions of his hero's "mediocrity," his "Mittelmäßigkeit," as a "representative

German" [pp. 60, 59].

6. Weigand, p. 156.
7. "Ferneres über Weltliteratur," in Goethes Werke, Bd. 42, Abt. 2 (Weimar, 1907), S. 504. See also Goethe, "Bis 1786," Tag- und Jahreshefte in Goethes Werke, Bd. 35, Tl. 1, S. 8: The beginnings of Wilhelm Meister "sprang from an obscure feeling of great truth: that man often wishes to attempt something for which talent is denied him by Nature, wishes to undertake and practice what he cannot complete . . . yet it is possible that all the false steps lead to an inestimable good: a presentiment that unfolds itself more and more in Wilhelm Meister, clears up, and proves true, indeed in the end declares in distinct words: 'To my mind you resemble Saul, the son of Kish, who went out to seek his father's asses, and found a kingdom.'"
8. Goethe alludes to this question of aspiration in the Apprenticeship, bk. VII, ch. ii, p. 6/13, where the Abbé exclaims that, if one considers what endless operations nature and art must perform to produce a "cultured" human being, then one must be tempted to despair when he sees, "how lightly mortals will destroy themselves, will blamelessly or blamably expose themselves to be destroyed." One way in which a human being can ruin his endowment is indeed through lack of genuine concern about his "cultivation." As Jarno observes in bk. VIII, ch. v, p. 106/213: "The formation of his character is not the chief concern with every man. Many merely wish to find a sort of recipe for comfort, directions for acquiring riches, or whatever good they aim at." The problem here appears to involve, not potentiality or capability, but aspiration. [The above references are to the following editions: Wilhelm Meister's Apprenticeship, trans. Thomas Carlyle (London: J. M. Dent, 1912), 2 vols; and Wilhelm Meisters Lehrjahre in Goethes Werke (Weimar, 1887-1919), Abt. I, Bde. 21-23, respectively. A slash separates the page reference to the English translation from the page of the original, which follows.]
9. Weigand, p. 5.
10. The apparent paradox posed by items 15 and 16 is thoroughly discussed in the section below, concerning formation as open ended within the goal of the apprenticeship, esp. p. 27.
11. Howe, p. 4.
12. "Bildungs- und Entwicklungsromane," Der Roman (Essen, 1912), S. 140.
13. Die religiöse und die humanitätsphilosophische Bildungsidee und die Entstehung des deutschen Bildungsromans im 18. Jahrhundert, Diss. Bern 1932, in SuD, 56 (Bern, 1934), 115.
14. Das Erlebnis und die Dichtung, 6. Aufl. (Leipzig, 1919), S. 393. See also S. 322-23.
15. Ibid., S. 395.
16. Jost, p. 114.
17. "Bildungsroman," in Reallexikon der deutschen Literaturgeschichte, 2. Aufl. (Berlin, 1955), I, 176, 175-77.
18. "Bildungsroman," in Goethe-Handbuch, hg. Alfred Zastrau (Stuttgart, 1961), I, 1210. Stefan Fleischer's dissertation on "The Theme of Bildung in The Prelude, Hyperion, and Wilhelm Meisters Lehrjahre," DAI, 28 (1967), 1433-A (Cornell), argues that the

pattern of the "Bildungsroman" is not, "as the Goethe Handbuch suggests, a dialectic of 'Ich' and 'die Welt,'" that is, a process of growth which may be called 'socialization.'" Fleischer, however, in retaining the notion of a dialectic, simply substitutes personal and cultural history (time) for "die Welt" and individual consciousness (feeling) for "Ich." The final emphasis remains on the adjustment, though mental, rather than the conflict.

19. "Bildungsroman," Reallexikon, 2. Aufl., I, 177.
20. "Epiphany," Dictionary of World Literary Terms (London, 1955). See also Sidney Feshbach, "Hunting Epiphany-Hunters," PMLA, 87 (March, 1972), 304-6; and Morris Beja, Epiphany in the Modern Novel (Seattle, 1971).
21. Howe, p. 4.
22. "Goethe as a Representative of the Bourgeois Age," in Essays of Three Decades, trans. H. T. Lowe-Porter (New York, 1948), 83, 89, 67; "Goethe als Repräsentant des bürgerlichen Zeitalters," Gesammelte Werke, IX, 321, 328, 298. Mann's characterization of the universal bourgeois finds support in two salient passages of the Apprenticeship: Wilhelm's letter of reply to Werner (bk. V, ch. iii) and his subsequent meeting with Werner (bk. VIII, ch. i), where the old and the new objectives are vividly contrasted.
23. "The Development of Goethe's Concept of the Calling in Wilhelm Meisters Lehrjahre and the Wanderjahre," GQ, 32 (1959), 218.
24. "Classics Revisited: Goethe," SatR, April 19, 1969, p. 21.
25. "Die Formen des Wissens und die Bildung," Philosophische Weltanschauung (Bern, 1954), S. 32. This statement as it applies to specific values is thoroughly treated by Scheler in his book, Der Formalismus in der Ethik und die materiale Wertethik, 4. Aufl. (Bern, 1954), S. 113 f.
26. Scheler, S. 32-33. See also "The Forms of Knowledge and Culture," in Philosophical Perspectives, trans. Oscar Haac (Boston, 1958), pp. 31-32.
27. "Goethe's 'Wilhelm Meister' as a Picture and a Criticism of Society," PEGS, n.s., 9 (1933), 44.
28. Cf. Wilhelm Meister's Apprenticeship, bk. VII, ch. ix, pp. 59/119-20, Jarno to Wilhelm: "It is right that a man, when he first enters upon life, should think highly of himself, should determine to attain many eminent distinctions, should endeavor to make all things possible: but when his education has proceeded to a certain pitch, it is advantageous for him that he learn to lose himself among a mass of men, that he learn to live for the sake of others, and to forget himself in an activity prescribed by duty. It is then that he first becomes acquainted with himself; for it is conduct alone that compares us with others."
29. Pascal, p. 11.
30. "Bildungsroman," Das kleine Lexikon der Weltliteratur (Stuttgart, 1958), S. 201.
31. Weigand, pp. 4, 5.
32. Cf. Stahl, S. 52: "Philosophical humanitarian culture is the development of the aggregate of individual human talents brought about through the influence of worldly forces, in that the individual adapts to those worldly forces and develops his innately endowed powers."

33. See Der moderne deutsche Bildungsroman, Diss. Bern 1937, in SuD, 69 (Bern, 1942), 2. See also Thomas Mann, "Betrachtungen eines Unpolitischen" (Reflections of a Nonpolitical Man), in Gesammelte Werke (Frankfurt, 1960), XII, 501: "The opposite of godly fanaticism has yet another name . . . culture is this name, and the anti-fanatic, anti-medieval, the Renaissance and Humanist ideal, which it intends, is closely bound to the intellectual rise out of the bourgeois--that is, a new or renewed reference to the relations between the middle class and art. For cultivation means something passive as well as active."
34. Keiter und Kellen, S. 144, 146.
35. Jost, p. 105.
36. Howe, p. 11.
37. Jost, p. 114.
38. Hans Rudolf Wagner, Der englische Bildungsroman bis in die Zeit des ersten Weltkrieges, Diss. Bern 1949, in SAA, 27 (Bern, 1951), 14.
39. "Bildungsroman," in Paul Merker und Wolfgang Stammler, Hrsg., Reallexikon der deutschen Literaturgeschichte (Berlin, 1925-31), I, 141.
40. Ibid., S. 142.
41. "Der Bildungsroman der Hochklassik und Hochromantik," Der Roman der Goethezeit (Urach und Stuttgart, 1949), S. 266.
42. Cf. William Blake's ultimate goal of "redintegration" as the culminating by-product of the direct attempts of imagination, reason, emotion, and sensation to lose their bodies or put off their selfhoods. In "Night the Ninth" of The Four Zoas Urizen, by casting off at last his claim to dominance, induces the onset of a four-fold redintegration of the Eternal Family. And Blake's Milton, by annihilating his Selfhood, facilitates a similar reentry of the Immortal Four into the bosom of Albion.
43. Wagner, S. 104.
44. Howe, p. 11.
45. Meyer, in Helmut Germer, The German Novel of Education, 1792-1805, Diss. Vanderbilt 1966 (Bern, 1968), p. [ii].
46. Jost, p. 99. Cf. M. H. Abrams, Natural Supernaturalism (New York, 1971), p. 191: Abrams similarly alludes to the circuitous "story form of a 'Bildungsreise' [cultural journey] whose end is its own beginning." This circular-story form of the pilgrimage and quest, perhaps more than any other potential aspect of the apprenticeship novel, directly relates it to the period (particularly the German period) of Romantic literature. The form emerges as the imagined product of the cultural history, "Bildungsgeschichte," of the Romantic philosophy of consciousness, as Abrams characterizes it. [See pp. 192-95, 255.] Werner Friederich insists that "it was the publication of Wilhelm Meisters Lehrjahre (Wilhelm Meister's Apprenticeship, 1795), that helped to initiate Romanticism in Germany," for in this work "men like Friedrich Schlegel, Tieck, and Wackenroder found what they formulated into the principles of Romanticism." [Outline of Comparative Literature (Chapel Hill, 1954), p. 279.]
47. Natural Supernaturalism, p. 243.
48. For the quote in full see above, p. 17.

4. Concrete Representatives

1. See M. H. Abrams, Natural Supernaturalism (New York, 1971), p. 244.
2. See, respectively, François Jost, "La Tradition du 'Bildungsroman,'" CL, 21 (1969), p. 114; Susanne Howe, Wilhelm Meister and His English Kinsmen, Apprentices to Life (New York, 1930), p. 6; and Gero von Wilpert, Sachwörterbuch der Literatur (Stuttgart, 1955), S. 132. See also René Wellek, Confrontations (Princeton, 1965), p. 14; Werner Friederich and David Malone, Outline of Comparative Literature (Chapel Hill, 1954), p. 275; Joseph Shipley, Dictionary of World Literary Terms (London, 1955), p. 30; R.-M. Albérès, Histoire du roman moderne (Paris, 1962), p. 114; M. L. Kornbluth, "The Reception of Wilhelm Meister in America," Symposium, 13 (1959), 128; et al.
3. Howe, p. 24.
4. Jost, p. 105.
5. See Deutsche Literaturgeschichte in Tabellen, Tl. II: 1450-1770 (Frankfurt, 1960), S. 215. See also Tafel IV, S. 232, and F. W. Schroeder's dissertation, Wielands Agathon und die Anfänge des modernen Bildungsromans (Königsberg, 1904).
6. See "Der Bildungsroman: Zur Geschichte des Wortes und der Theorie," DVLG, 35 (1961), 61.
7. Handbuch der Weltliteratur von den Anfängen bis zur Gegenwart, 3. Aufl. (Frankfurt, 1960), Anhang II.
8. Friederich and Malone, p. 276.
9. New York, 1948, p. 222.
10. A Glossary of Literary Terms, 3rd ed. (New York, 1971), p. 113.
11. Friederich and Malone, p. 276.
12. Cf. Inge D. Halpert, "Wilhelm Meister and Josef Knecht," GQ, 34 (1961), 12-15; and Kurt May, "'Wilhelm Meisters Lehrjahre,' ein Bildungsroman?" DVLG, 31 (1957), 8 and 12. See the discussion of the subordinate nature of guidance in ch. 6 below, pp. 60 f., for a rebuttal of this charge against the role of the Society of the Tower within the novel.
13. Jost, p. 105.
14. Wilpert, S. 132.
15. Touaillon, "Bildungsroman," Reallexikon der Literaturgeschichte (Berlin, 1925-31), I, 143.
16. Jürgen Jacobs, Wilhelm Meister und seine Brüder: Untersuchungen zum deutschen Bildungsroman (München, 1972), S. 39-63.
17. Touaillon, S. 142-43.
18. Howe, p. 2. Two Renaissance prodigal sons who anticipate the apprenticeship theme are the heroes of John Lyly's Euphues (1578, 1580) and Robert Greene's Groatsworth of Wit Bought with a Million of Repentance (1592). [Howe, p. 16]
19. Touaillon, S. 145. Concerning the situation of the apprenticeship novel in France, see above, pp. 4-5, and below, p. 33, n. 29. As for England, the apprenticeship novel faced competition with the social novel or "Gesellschaftsroman," which achieved no significance in Germany until the advent of Theodor Fontane's later works. [See Wilpert, S. 200.]
20. See Touaillon, S. 144-45; Donner, Der Einfluss Wilhelm Meisters

auf den Roman der Romantiker (Diss. Helsingfors 1893), S. 33; Howe, Wilhelm Meister and His English Kinsmen; Borcherdt, "Der deutsche Bildungsroman," in Von deutscher Art in Sprache und Dichtung, 5 (Stuttgart, 1941), 4; Friederich and Malone, p. 276; Wilpert, S. 132; Köhn, "Entwicklungs- und Bildungsroman--Ein Forschungsbericht," DVLG, 42 (1968), 427-73 und 590-632; Jost, p. 106; Eppelsheimer, S. 783; and Jacobs, S. 106 f.

21. Subtitled "ein Schelmenroman" (picaresque novel)
22. Die Kindheit des Paracelsus, 1917; Das Gestirn des Paracelsus, 1921; Das dritte Reich des Paracelsus, 1925.
23. Both Jacobs and W. H. Bruford consider Wilhelm Meisters Wanderjahre (Wilhelm Meister's Travels), 1821, 1829, as an apprenticeship novel but qualify it as "far less concerned with the development of individual personalities than with that of man in society" [See Bruford, The German Tradition of Self-Cultivation: "Bildung" from Homboldt to Thomas Mann (Cambridge, Eng., 1975), p. 98]; indeed, it takes a turn from apprenticeship novel, "Bildungsroman," to novel of society, "Gesellschaftsroman" and should be viewed as an apprenticeship novel only "against the background of the Lehrjahre" [Jacobs, S. 93, 95]. Jacobs offers as a further candidate Goethe's autobiographical Dichtung und Wahrheit (Poetry and Truth), 1811-33.
24. See Der englische Bildungsroman bis in die Zeit des ersten Weltkrieges, Diss. Bern 1949, in SAA, 27 (Bern, 1951), 14; G. B. Tennyson, "The Bildungsroman in Nineteenth-Century English Literature," in Rosario Armato and John Spalek, eds., Medieval Epic to the "Epic Theater" of Brecht (Los Angeles, 1968), pp. 135-46; and Jerome Buckley, Season of Youth: The Bildungsroman from Dickens to Golding (Cambridge, Mass., 1974).
25. Howe argues that Dickens' David Copperfield and Great Expectations and Thackeray's Pendennis deal with young men who learn from experience and mature "but more by accident than design." Their "essential nature has not been modified. They have not developed through any inner realization of their own powers and the resolve to make their experience function" [Howe, p. 14]. Jost and Buckley include both works by Dickens. Indeed Tennyson remarks, "To my mind the most complete expression of the English 'Bildungsroman' is Great Expectations" [Tennyson, p. 143]. Concerning Thackeray's Pendennis, Gordon N. Ray calls it "the first true 'Bildungsroman' in English fiction" [See Thackeray: The Age of Wisdom (New York, 1958), p. 110], while Buckley rejects it as too conventional.
26. Wagner characterizes this work as the "first modern 'Bildungsroman'" [See Wagner, S. 53]; Buckley lists it; but Howe rejects it, Edmund Gosse's Father and Son, and Mrs. Humphrey Ward's Robert Elsmere as "so preoccupied with religious matters that their apprenticeships have become highly specialized." They are "novels of religious controversy." [Howe, pp. 13-14, 260-61]
27. The Early History of Jacob Stahl (1911), A Candidate for Truth (1912), and The Invisible Event (1915)
28. Jeremy (1919), Jeremy and Hamlet (1923), Jeremy at Crale (1927)
29. The more popular and broader literary tradition in France was perhaps the adolescent novel, "le roman de l'adolescence," which

Justin O'Brien defines in The Novel of Adolescence in France (New York, 1937). The list of works of this type from 1890-1930, on pages 213-15, includes both Rolland and Gide. Works of the type in English, German, Italian, and Spanish are listed on p. 14 and include many of the apprenticeship novels noted above.

30. Buckley regards Henri Brulard as "the only real Bildungsroman of the century in France" [See Buckley, p. 14]. Jacobs rejects Le Rouge et le Noir as leading to isolation rather than a "harmonious goal of the development of life" [Jacobs, S. 156].
31. Albérès, p. 114. Buckley also lists Père Goriot.
32. The original and simpler version of this work, published earlier in 1942 as "The Bear," certainly appears in itself to qualify as a short yet effective novel of apprenticeship.
33. Thomas Mann's Novel: Der Zauberberg (New York, 1933), p. 6.
34. Cf. Jürgen Scharfschwerdt, Thomas Mann und der deutsche Bildungsroman (Stuttgart, 1967), S. 248 f.
35. Touaillon, S. 144.
36. See Heinrich Keiter und Tony Kellen, "Bildungs- und Entwicklungsromane," Der Roman (Essen, 1912), S. 142.

Introduction

1. "Goethe als Repräsentant des bürgerlichen Zeitalters," Gesammelte Werke (Frankfurt, 1960), IX, 310.
2. Roy Pascal, The German Novel (Manchester, 1956), p. 76. Pascal, in limiting his study to the "most eminent examples" of the German "Bildungsroman," considers the work of Mann as more widely accepted and more significant among the moderns than the work of Hesse, whose Glasperlenspiel (Magister Ludi) might otherwise qualify as the last important German "Bildungsroman." [See Pascal, pp. vii-viii.] Certainly Mann's Zauberberg is the "last" of the most widely acknowledged and critically acclaimed representatives of the type.
3. History of German Literature (New York, 1948), p. 222. Hermann Weigand extols it as "the supreme 'Bildungsroman' of the world's literature." [Thomas Mann's Novel: Der Zauberberg (New York, 1933), p. 141.]
4. Susanne Howe, Wilhelm Meister and His English Kinsmen, Apprentices to Life (New York, 1930), p. 287. The immediate parallel between the English and the German versions of the apprenticeship, as Howe demonstrates, derives from the fact that Philip in Of Human Bondage is the only modern English apprentice who, like Wilhelm in Wilhelm Meister's Apprenticeship, "deliberately accepts the commonplace instead of the romantic destiny" [Howe, p. 290].
5. Somerset Maugham, A Biographical and Critical Study (Bloomington, Ind., 1961), p. 252.

5. Of Human Bondage

1. See "Of Human Bondage--Foreward (1915)," in W. Somerset

Maugham, Selected Prefaces and Introductions of W. Somerset Maugham (New York, 1963), pp. 36-39; and Richard A. Cordell, Somerset Maugham, A Biographical and Critical Study (Bloomington, Ind., 1961), pp. 87-89. The quotation in Isaiah actually reads as follows: "Give unto them beauty for ashes, the oil of joy for mourning, the garment of praise for the spirit of heaviness."

2. Of Human Bondage (New York: Grosset & Dunlap, 1915), ch. 85, p. 447. Subsequent quotations from this edition will appear in the text with reference to chapter and page.
3. "Of Human Bondage, or of the Strength of the Affects," in W. Hale White and Amelia H. Stirling, trans., Ethic, by Spinoza (London, 1927). Cf. "Of Human Servitude, or the Strength of the Emotions," in Andrew Boyle, trans., Spinoza's Ethics (London, 1963). See also Dean Doner, "Spinoza's Ethics and Maugham," University of Kansas City Review, 21 (Summer, 1955), 261-69, for Spinozan concepts underlying the novel's structure as well.
4. White and Stirling, trans., p. 176.
5. For a thorough definition of leitmotif, see ch. 9, n. 17, below.
6. Somerset Maugham (London, 1964), pp. 17-18.
7. An interesting guide to Philip's intellectual development is the leitmotif, as it alters, of the books he reads. At Blackstable Philip favors The Thousand and One Nights; at Heidelberg, where he throws off religious hypocrisy, he reads Renan's La Vie de Jésus; the affair with Miss Wilkinson and the sojourn in Paris center around La Vie de Bohème; at Blackstable again, where he seeks to rid himself of conscience, he concentrates on Darwin's Origin of Species; at the home of the Athelnys in London, where Athelny introduces him to the spirit of old Spain and the paintings of El Greco, he finds satisfaction with Don Quixote; and at Blackstable, while awaiting the death of his uncle, he reads again The Thousand and One Nights. When he dreams of traveling to Spain after receiving his diploma from the medical school, he engrosses himself in Smollett's Peregrine Pickle; but this whim quickly passes with his marriage to Sally.
8. Cordell, p. 94.
9. W. Somerset Maugham, A Candid Portrait (New York, 1959), p. 44. Pfeiffer claims that the theme of "the death of love" became a favorite of Maugham after his Mrs. Craddock in 1902.
10. Cordell, p. 94. Cf. above, p. 44, for quote in full.
11. New York, 1938, pp. 305-7.
12. Ibid., p. 306.
13. Ibid., p. 305.
14. Ibid., p. 78.
15. Ibid., p. 194.
16. W. Somerset Maugham (Norman, Okla., 1966), p. 56.
17. William Somerset Maugham (London, 1937), pp. 159, 188.
18. Season of Youth: The Bildungsroman from Dickens to Golding (Cambridge, Mass., 1974), p. 23.
19. Cordell, p. 96.
20. See next page below.
21. Cf. The Summing Up, p. 114.
22. Cordell, p. 96. See previous page above for quote in full.
23. Ch. 122, p. 647. To question the permanence of the conviction

itself would be to indulge in vain speculation. If Philip's revelation in the British Museum is not modeled after, it certainly parallels the enlightenment of Gautama Buddha under the Bo tree. The Buddha's enlightenment climaxed a six-year quest, in which Philip himself spent five years. Huston Smith in his illuminating study, The Religions of Man, draws a revealing parallel between the Buddha and Spinoza--both of whom Maugham highly revered--in claiming, "Of all the philosophers of the West, Spinoza stands closest to Buddha on this question of the mind's potential. 'To understand something is to be delivered of it'--these words come close to summarizing Spinoza's entire ethic. Buddha would have agreed completely." [New York, 1961, p. 117] The permanence of the conviction fostered by Philip's revelation provides, therefore, a question, not of thematism, but of epistemology.

24. For a more comprehensive treatment of the idea of the normal as an ideal, see Maugham, The Summing Up, pp. 68-69.
25. Bk. VII, ch. iii, p. 10, in Carlyle's translation; in Goethes Werke (Weimar, 1887-1919): Abt. I, Bd. 23, S. 20. See Maugham's acknowledgment of this debt to Goethe in W. Somerset Maugham, "The Three Novels of a Poet," Points of View (London, 1958), p. 38.

6. Wilhelm Meister's Apprenticeship

1. Critics generally designate the first four books of the Apprenticeship as comprising the entire Mission; but the Mission overflows into the fifth book both in fact and in plan. Roy Pascal remarks that "the Sendung closes with [Wilhelm's] signing a contract with Serlo [i.e., bk. V, ch. iii of the Lehrjahre]; it was to be concluded by the account of the production of Hamlet, and probably the establishment of a National Theater." [The German Novel (Manchester, 1956), p. 4]
2. "Wilhelm Meister and Josef Knecht," GQ, 34 (1961), 11.
3. "Über Goethes Meister," Athenaeum (Berlin, 1798), Bd. I, St. 2, S. 178.
4. A History of German Literature (London, 1966), p. 306. See also J. Rausch, who separates books I-V from book VIII as representing two stages of life, "Lebensstufen," while books VI and VII function solely as a "passage from the first to the second stage." ["Lebensstufen in Goethes 'Wilhelm Meister,'" DVLG, 20 (1942), 113]
5. Wilhelm Meister and His English Kinsmen, Apprentices to Life (New York, 1930), p. 65.
6. "The Three Novels of a Poet," Points of View (London, 1958), p. 36.
7. "On Some Images in Wilhelm Meisters Lehrjahre," PEGS, n.s., 20 (1951), 114.
8. "'Wilhelm Meister' and the Ambiguity of Goethe," Cambridge Journal, 6 (1952-53), 664.
9. "Phasen der Bildungsidee im 'Wilhelm Meister,'" Goethe, 5 (1962), 73.
10. See Reiss, "Wilhelm Meisters Lehrjahre," Goethes Romane (Bern,

1963), S. 74. See also Wundt, Goethes Wilhelm Meister und die Entwicklung des modernen Lebensideals (Berlin, 1913), S. 171.

11. Pascal, p. 3.
12. Wilhelm Meister's Apprenticeship, trans. Thomas Carlyle, Everyman's Library (London, 1912), Vol. I, bk. VI, p. 345; Wilhelm Meisters Lehrjahre, in Goethes Werke (Weimar, 1887-1919), Abt. I, Bd. 22, S. 332. Subsequent quotations from vols. 1-2 of the English translation and from vols. 21-23 of the German original will appear in the text with reference to book, chapter, and page, a slash separating the page reference to the English translation from the page of the original that follows.
13. Ethic, trans. W. Hale White and Amelia H. Stirling (London, 1927), p. 176. Cf. above, p. 41, for quote in full.
14. "Sense and Nonsense in Wilhelm Meisters Lehrjahre," DBGÜ, 5 (1965), 57.
15. "Wilhelm Meister's Interpretation of Hamlet," MP, 23 (1925-26), 89, 92.
16. Blackall, p. 62.
17. Pascal, p. 8.
18. Blackall, p. 62.
19. Ibid. The crisis, or "turning-point," appears elsewhere, as I shall endeavor to demonstrate on pp. 59f. below.
20. Here the country clergyman, rather than reverse the stranger's earlier contention, supplements it. Contrast Blackall, pp. 54-55, who argues with convincing logic that "the first conversation had asserted the primacy of an inner force, the second stresses the importance of outer forces. In content as in form the second conversation is the reverse of the first."
21. Rausch, S. 74.
22. Ibid., S. 92, 76.
23. Wundt, S. 240.
24. Halpert, pp. 12, 15. Halpert's disparagements of Wilhelm are drawn in contrast to Hermann Hesse's Josef Knecht.
25. Cf. Halpert, pp. 12-15. See also Kurt May's distinctions in "'Wilhelm Meisters Lehrjahre,' ein Bildungsroman?" DVLG, 31 (1957), esp. 8 and 12, as noted above, ch. 4, n. 12.
26. Wundt, S. 282-83. See also Rosemarie Haas, Die Turmgesellschaft in Wilhelm Meisters Lehrjahren (Bern, 1975).
27. Halpert, p. 14.
28. "Classicism," in J. M. Ritchie, ed., Periods in German Literature (London, 1966), p. 115.
29. Pascal, p. 13.
30. "A View of Wilhelm Meister's Apprenticeship," PMLA, 72 (1957), 99.
31. J. P. Eckermann, Gespräche mit Goethe in den letzten Jahren seines Lebens (Jena, 1905), I, 172, 18. Januar 1825. Contrast Joachim Müller, who disputes Goethe's inference [Müller, S. 72].
32. Howe, p. 66.
33. Müller, S. 72.
34. Cf. Robert T. Clark, Jr., "Personality and Society in Wilhelm Meisters Lehrjahre," Southwest Goethe Festival: A Collection of Nine Papers (Dallas, 1949), pp. 90-91, for a summary of the bibliography on Mignon as a hermaphrodite, including the

etymology of her name.
35. *Ibid.*, p. 95.
36. *Ibid.*
37. Blackall, p. 57.
38. *Mignon, Ein Beitrag zur Geschichte des Wilhelm Meister* (München, 1909), S. 175.
39. "Goethe. I.--Wilhelm Meister," *Fortnightly Review*, n.s., 43 (1888), 778-79.
40. Pascal, p. 19.

7. The First Stage

1. New York, 1938, p. 246.
2. "Goethe's 'Wilhelm Meister' as a Picture and a Criticism of Society," *PEGS*, n.s., 9 (1933), 27.
3. Susanne Howe, *Wilhelm Meister and His English Kinsmen, Apprentices to Life* (New York, 1930), p. 290.
4. Richard H. Ward, *William Somerset Maugham* (London, 1937), p. 134.
5. *Ibid.*
6. *W. Somerset Maugham* (Norman, Okla., 1966), p. 55. Cf. also D. Zhantiyeva, "'Some Points of View' and 'Summing-Ups': The Aesthetic Views and Creative Path of Somerset Maugham," *Inostrannaja Literatura*, 2 (Feb. 1960), 185-92; and G. V. Viswanath, "The Novels of Somerset Maugham," *Quest* (Bombay), 23 (Oct.-Nov. 1959), 50-52.
7. Boston, 1932, p. 381.
8. *A Short History of the English Novel* (London, 1951), p. 259.
9. "Somerset Maugham," *EJ*, 29 (1940), 524.
10. W. Somerset Maugham, "The Three Novels of a Poet," *Points of View* (London, 1958), p. 36.
11. "On Some Images in Wilhelm Meisters Lehrjahre," *PEGS*, n.s., 20 (1951), 117, 137.
12. *Goethes Wilhelm Meister und die Entwicklung des modernen Lebensideals* (Berlin, 1913), S. 278.
13. New York, 1939, p. 5.
14. "The Exoticism of Somerset Maugham," *Revue Anglo-Américaine*, 10 (1932-33), 315.
15. *The Summing Up*, pp. 56, 285.
16. Spencer, pp. 531-32.
17. *Somerset Maugham, A Biographical and Critical Study* (Bloomington, Ind., 1961), pp. 87, 97.
18. *W. Somerset Maugham, A Candid Portrait* (New York, 1959), p. 62.
19. *W. Somerset Maugham et ses romans* (Paris, 1928), p. 85.
20. *The Summing Up*, p. 310.
21. "Of Human Bondage--Foreword (1915)," *Selected Prefaces and Introductions of W. Somerset Maugham* (New York, 1963), p. 39.
22. P. 192.
23. See Pfeiffer's claim above, p. 69.
24. Cordell, p. 55.
25. *Das Erlebnis und die Dichtung*, 6. Aufl. (Leipzig, 1919), S. 395, as quoted also above, p. 20.

8. The Second Stage

1. Tagebücher, in Goethes Werke (Weimar, 1887-1919), Abt. III, Bd. I (1775-87), S. 61.
2. Goethes Wilhelm Meister und die Entwicklung des modernen Lebensideals (Berlin, 1913), S. 210.
3. Friedrich Schiller, Briefe (München, 1955), S. 427, 8. Juli 1796 an Goethe.
4. Wundt, S. 278.
5. "On Some Images in Wilhelm Meisters Lehrjahre," PEGS, n.s., 20 (1951), 137-38.
6. Wundt, S. 208-39.
7. See D. J. Farrelly, Goethe and Inner Harmony: A Study of "Schoene Seele" in the "Apprenticeship of Wilhelm Meister" (New York, 1973).
8. Cf. Spinoza, as quoted in ch. 5 above, p. 41.
9. Susanne Howe, Wilhelm Meister and His English Kinsmen, Apprentices to Life (New York, 1930), p. 56.
10. "Lebensstufen in Goethes 'Wilhelm Meister,'" DVLG, 20 (1942), 91.
11. Irvin Stock, "A View of Wilhelm Meister's Apprenticeship," PMLA, 72 (1957), 93.
12. Schiller, S. 418, 3. Juli 1796 an Goethe.
13. Ibid.
14. Rausch, S. 91. Rausch also notes in passing, "That the ideal would be published and conceived in a female character is quite Goethean."
15. The German Novel (Manchester, 1956), p. 27.
16. "Phasen der Bildungsidee im 'Wilhelm Meister,'" Goethe, 5 (1962), 61.
17. Ibid.
18. A dissertation by G. E. Gockley appears to support this observation, for Gockley concludes in his study of Goethe's style, "As regards Natalie, the usual categories which appear over and over in connection with the other women can no longer be clearly distinguished. Throughout the entire Natalie action Goethe fuses indirect and direct characterization in the scenes, in her speech and in reports by other characters, thereby reflecting the fusion of all the desirable qualities of womanhood within her." ["Goethe's Stylistic Presentation of the Main Women Characters in Wilhelm Meisters Lehrjahre," in DAI, 25 (1964), 472 (Indiana).]
19. "Sense and Nonsense in Wilhelm Meisters Lehrjahre," DBGÜ, 5 (1965), 69.
20. Tag- und Jahres-Hefte, in Goethes Werke (Weimar, 1887-1919), Tl. I, Bd. 35 (1749-1806), S. 8.
21. The Life of Goethe (London, 1938), p. 408.
22. See "Wilhelm Meister's Interpretation of Hamlet," MP, 23 (1925-26), 93.
23. Pascal, p. 11.
24. Stock, pp. 93-94.
25. Cf. Martin Swales' argument on the open-endedness of Wilhelm Meister, for "Wilhelm does not know all the answers by the end of the novel." [The German Bildungsroman from Wieland to Hesse (Princeton, 1978), p. 72.]

26. "The Three Novels of a Poet," Points of View (London, 1958), p. 36.
27. Pascal is a case in point. Cf. Pascal, p. 28.
28. New York, 1938, pp. 278-79.
29. Ibid., p. 291.
30. New York, 1950, p. 30.
31. P. 108.
32. P. 41.
33. Somerset Maugham, A Biographical and Critical Study (Bloomington, Ind., 1961), p. 235.
34. Points of View, p. 41.
35. Howe, p. 287.

9. The Third Stage: The Magic Mountain

1. "Der Zauberberg," Modern German Literature: The Major Figures in Context (New York, 1967), p. 95.
2. Thomas Mann's Novel Der Zauberberg: A Study (New York, 1933), p. 24.
3. Ibid., p. 20.
4. The Magic Mountain, trans. H. T. Lowe-Porter (New York: Knopf, 1982), ch. ii, p. 34; Der Zauberberg, in Gesammelte Werke (Frankfurt, 1960), Bd. III, S. 52. Subsequent quotations from these volumes will appear in the text with references to chapter and page, a slash separating the page reference to the English translation from the page of the original that follows.
5. See Joseph Brennan, Thomas Mann's World (New York, 1962), p. 28 and n. 66.
6. Although music represents a Circean pleasure appropriately classed with other narcotics that lull Hans Castorp into an inactive stupor, ensuring his release from an unconditional reverence for work, it also serves as a leitmotif relating the first and the third stages of his apprenticeship to life and death. Therefore, a detailed consideration of music as an all-embracing theme will follow later in this chapter. Concerning music's relevance to the present discussion of work, suffice it to note that its combination with porter's beer and the Maria Mancini cigar provide soothing opiates tempting him to doze. Note also Settembrini's infernal triad: "Beer, tobacco, and music. Behold the Fatherland" (iv.112/159)!
7. See Werner P. Friederich, History of German Literature (New York, 1948), p. 221.
8. Thomas Mann: The World as Will and Representation (Boston, 1957), p. 101.
9. Joseph G. Brennan, "Heard and Unheard Speech in The Magic Mountain," Novel, 3 (1970), 135.
10. "The Magic Mountain," Thomas Mann: The Mediation of Art (Oxford, 1956), p. 110.
11. Thomas, p. 91.
12. For a more detailed discussion of Settembrini's influence, see the section of this chapter concerning heightened inherent values in the social stage of an apprenticeship, pp. 94 f.
13. See Thomas, p. 101, and Weigand, p. 154, also p. 22.

14. Thomas, pp. 101, 104.
15. In employing these three quotations I follow the order of Jürgen Scharfschwerdt's argument in Thomas Mann und der deutsche Bildungsroman (Stuttgart, 1967), S. 117.
16. Abstractly defined, a leitmotif--as Weigand depicts its use in The Magic Mountain--constitutes "a focal point from which lines extend in a multitude of directions, linking a great variety of elements in a complex network of relations." Dependent on the leitmotif's successful function as a "code" word in Mann's novel, "the interpenetration of themes forms so close a web that the whole of the 'Zauberberg' tends to be present at every moment of the flow of its narrative." In a second reading the novel aspires "to be 'all there' at any given moment," an experience only vaguely felt in the first reading. "It grows upon us," Weigand contends, "as we read it a second time with the memory of our first experience freshly in mind. Only then, of course, can the interpenetration of themes be appreciated as pointing forward, as well as backward." [Weigand, pp. 91, 95.]
17. See Brennan, Thomas Mann's World, p. 147. Brennan distinguishes four basic and four supplementary "time-categories" in Mann's Magic Mountain: "clock time ('seven minutes'); subjective or psychological time ('seems long'); objective time or duration (nails grow; the world situation deteriorates); and eternity, the realm of death, which is entirely untouched by time. These categories do not include the 'historical' time of the novel (1907-1914), or the years it took for the novelist to write the book (1912-1924), the year of Our Lord in which the reader peruses the work, or the time it takes him to complete his reading. Forced by her husband of the time to acquire culture, motion-picture actress Ava Gardner filed suit for divorce, 'He made me read The Magic Mountain,' she complained. 'I thought I'd never finish that damn book.'"
18. Cf. Joachim's "One's ideas get changed" (i.7/16).
19. Cf. Settembrini's "Our smallest unit is the month" (iii.58/85).
20. For a thorough discussion of Mann's use of "recurrence" (Hippe-Clawdia, etc.) and of the leitmotif ("Kirghiz" eyes, anonymous and communal, fanatic, etc.) to suggest timelessness, see Brenan, Thomas Mann's World, pp. 149-50.
21. "The Promise and Blessing," in Charles Neider, ed., The Stature of Thomas Mann. A Critical Anthology (New York, 1947), p. 406. I have deferred the discussion of death's role in Mann's Magic Mountain until the section of this chapter concerning the metaphysical stage, that is, preparation for death. See pp. 97 ff.
22. Hinton Thomas lucidly clarifies the process of "Steigerung" in Hans Castorp's development of his inherent qualities. See Thomas, pp. 107-8. See also Georg Lukács, Thomas Mann (Berlin, 1949), S. 36; and Mann's "Einführung in den 'Zauberberg,'" Gesammelte Werke (Frankfurt, 1960), XI, 612.
23. I am not disturbed in the following analysis by critical indictments of volume II's abstractness. Henry Hatfield properly observes that "after Clavdia's departure, The Magic Mountain becomes more abstract, more obviously the novel of ideas." [Thomas Mann (Norfolk, Conn., 1951), p. 77. See also Scharfschwerdt, S. 114-15, 152 (quoting Hatfield).] René Wellek believes that this

over-weight of thought, i.e., philosophy of ideas, artistically weakens or mars volume II, rendering it inferior to the first volume. [Wellek and Austin Warren, Theory of Literature, rev. ed. (New York, 1956), p. 123.] But the same charge can be--indeed has been--leveled against books VI-VIII of Wilhelm Meister (See p. 77 above), and in a very real sense abstractness can be considered inherently characteristic of an apprentice's search for values. The abstractions of The Magic Mountain's second volume may therefore be indispensable. They appropriately portray the second stage in Hans Castorp's apprenticeship to an idealistically deeper awareness of life. Christine Touaillon offers support for this contention in her assertion: "The language of the apprenticeship novel requires as much talent in realistic miniature painting as in idealistic preoccupation: hence it cannot do without the aptitude for abstraction." ["Bildungsroman," in Paul Merker und Wolfgang Stammler (Hrsg.), Reallexikon der deutschen Literaturgeschichte (Berlin, 1925-31), I, 142.]

24. See p. 86 f.
25. Roy Pascal, "Thomas Mann: The Magic Mountain," The German Novel (Manchester, 1956), p. 84.
26. Cf. Thomas, p. 90: "Naphta's outlook illuminates the deeper implications of Joachim's scheme of values."
27. Thus Mann prepares his reader for the introduction of Peeperkorn immediately in chapter 7.
28. Brennan, crediting Peeperkorn with giving "the heaviest tip toward the instinctive and infrarational side of the pedagogical balance," calls him "the ambassador of Feeling." ["Heard and Unheard Speech," p. 136.]
29. "The Lofty Game of Numbers: The Mynheer Peeperkorn Episode in Thomas Mann's Der Zauberberg," PMLA, 86 (Oct., 1971), 932.
30. Thomas, p. 98.
31. Seidlin, p. 932.
32. The Ironic German: A Study of Thomas Mann (London, 1958), p. 209. Cf. Thomas, p. 98, who affirms that vitalism alone cannot suffice but leads instead to decadence and suicide.
33. "Heard and Unheard Speech," p. 137.
34. The Polish "affair of honor" (vii.685/956) foreshadows this duel, which Hans Castorp properly characterizes as "intellectual" (vii.699/971), taking place wholly "in the intellectual sphere" and having "nothing to do with the personal." For an intellectual duel it is only natural that he select as meeting-place the "scene of his retreat and stock-taking activities" (vii.701/974), where formerly he has habitually resolved the Settembrini-Naphta debates.
35. Weigand, pp. 126-27.
36. Schlegel, as quoted in Josef Körner, Romantiker und Klassiker. Die Brüder Schlegel in ihren Beziehungen zu Schiller und Goethe (Berlin, 1924), S. 90.
37. "An Epic of Illness," New Statesman, 24 (17 Sept. 1927), 715; Robert M. Lovett, "The Epic of Decay," New Republic, 51 (6 July 1927), 180-81; and Lewis Mumford, "The Magic Mountain," in Neider, ed., p. 152, respectively.
38. The Concept and Function of Death in the Works of Thomas Mann (Philadelphia, 1932), p. 3. Baer suggests two further terms

descriptive of Hans Castorp's attitude in volume I: wandering in death, "Todesvagabundage," and the romantic yearning for death, "Todessehnsucht," of Friedrich Schlegel, Novalis, Heinrich Heine, Nikolaus Lenau, Conrad Ferdinand Meyer, and Theodor Storm.

39. Thomas Mann (Oxford, 1954), p. 44.
40. Settembrini's opinion of disease closely parallels Maugham's view in The Summing Up: suffering does not turn men into saints, but only into sick animals. [New York, 1938, pp. 63-64.]
41. See p. 57 above.
42. Thomas, p. 87.
43. "Von Deutscher Republik," in Gesammelte Werke (Frankfurt, 1960), XI, 851, as quoted in Thomas, p. 87.
44. Weigand, p. 21.
45. Ibid., p. 23.
46. Scharfschwerdt, S. 142-43.
47. See Seidlin's notation of this salient feature, in "The Lofty Game of Numbers," p. 935.
48. "The Education of Hans Castorp," Monatshefte, 46 (Jan. 1954), 26, 25, 28, 32. Martin Swales argues that Hans Castorp forgets the abiding insights of the "Snow" scene; he "forgets both the substance and the import of his dream of humanity" [Thomas Mann: A Study (Totowa, N.J., 1980), p. 58], but only because he is mediocre, that is, wholly human [The German Bildungsroman from Wieland to Hesse (Princeton, 1978), p. 124].
49. Pascal, p. 88.
50. Seidlin, p. 939, n. 33.
51. Baer, pp. 50, 59-60.
52. "Von Deutscher Republik," in Gesammelte Werke, XI, 851.
53. "Tischrede bei der Feier des fünfzigsten Geburtstags," in Gesammelte Werke, XI, 368.
54. Thomas Mann (New York, 1967), p. 16.
55. Baer, p. 54.
56. Pascal, p. 81.
57. See Butler Waugh, Thomas Mann's The Magic Mountain: A Critical Commentary (New York, 1967), p. 66, and Friederich, p. 221. T. E. Apter regards the ending as "naïve and sentimental," as "unsatisfactory, as untrue to the substance of this work" [See Apter's chapter on "The Fascination of Disgust," in his Thomas Mann: The Devil's Advocate (New York, 1978), pp. 76-77].
58. Hirschbach, p. 32. See also pp. 26-27.
59. Seidlin, p. 939, n. 33.
60. Lindsay, pp. 127, 128.
61. See his "Lübeck als geistige Lebensform" (Lübeck as a Spiritual Way of Life), in Gesammelte Werke, XI, 393-95.
62. Pascal, p. 97.
63. Cf. Mann's own speculation regarding Hans Castorp as a survivor of the war: "In the swarm of the World War I have lost sight of him, but, if he still lives, I believe he will not have changed much. Perhaps, yes surely, he has grown more earnest, self-assured, composed, but he will still continue to be the apprentice, the respectful and cheerfully attentive, examining, discarding, selecting, no man's servant, his own and most good-natured friend." ["Die Schule des Zauberbergs" (The School

of the Magic Mountain), in Gesammelte Werke, XI, 601.]

10. The Complete Apprenticeship

1. L. Brander, Somerset Maugham, A Guide (New York, 1963), p. 27.
2. Ibid. The only available English translation of Wilhelm Meister on the American market today is H. M. Waidson's 3-volume rendering of 1979, obtainable in either cloth or paperback. The Collier single-volume paperback edition of the Carlyle translation went out of print in 1976.
3. "Goethe's Wilhelm Meister," Indian Literature, 8, no. 1 (1965), 31.
4. Thomas Carlyle, summarizing reactions in "Goethe," Critical and Miscellaneous Essays (London, 1899), I, 229. See also Francis Jeffrey [Contributions to the Edinburgh Review (London, 1844), I, 263] and Thomas DeQuincey [Collected Writings, ed. D. Masson (London, 1890), II, 222-58], who ridicule Wilhelm Meister as immoral, vulgar, and absurd.
5. "As a Realist Sees It," New Republic, 5 (1915-16), 202.
6. The Life of Goethe (London, 1938), p. 414.
7. "'Wilhelm Meister' and the Ambiguity of Goethe," Cambridge Journal, 6 (1952-53), 664, 665.
8. "The Morality of Wilhelm Meister," in Thomas Pinney, ed., Essays of Eliot (London, 1963), p. 144.
9. Richard A. Cordell, Somerset Maugham, A Biographical and Critical Study (Bloomington, Ind., 1961), p. 55. Cordell reports, "It has an especial appeal to young men and is widely used in English courses in the schools" [See p. 98], a claim to which Maugham himself, with perceptive misgivings, responds, "It has gained the doubtful honor of being required reading in many educational institutions. If I call it a doubtful honor, it is because I am not sure you can read with pleasure a book you have to read as a task." [From an address by Maugham entitled "Of Human Bondage, with a Digression on the Art of Fiction" (20 April 1946), in Klaus W. Jonas, The Maugham Enigma (New York, 1954), p. 127.]
10. Satires, I, I, 63: "Bid him be a fool, since that's his choice."

BIBLIOGRAPHY

This bibliography provides a selected list of works related to a consideration of the apprenticeship novel's definition. For a more general coverage of studies of the apprenticeship type see "Novel and Short Story" under "Literary Genres" in Fernand Baldensperger's and Werner Friederich's Bibliography of Comparative Literature (Chapel Hill, 1950), pp. 195-98. Their work is continued in the annual bibliographies in the Yearbook of Comparative and General Literature (1952 ff.), vols. 1-9 (Chapel Hill, University of North Carolina) and subsequent vols. (Bloomington, Indiana University). Lothar Köhn in his "Entwicklungs- und Bildungsroman--Ein Forschungsbericht," Deutsche Vierteljahrsschrift für Literaturwissenschaft und Geistesgeschichte, 42 (1968), 427-73 and 590-632 [also available in expanded book form (Stuttgart, 1969)], has compiled in two parts a superior comprehensive review of the research concerning definitions, history, etc., of the "Bildungsroman."

Klaus W. Jonas' A Bibliography of the Writings of W. Somerset Maugham (South Hadley, Mass., 1950) comprises a fairly complete bibliography of Maugham's works. A more recent publication, Charles Sanders' W. Somerset Maugham: An Annotated Bibliography of Writings About Him (DeKalb, Ill., 1970), considers writings from 1897 through 1968.

The standard bibliography of Goethe's works is Carl Diesch's and Paul Schlager's Goethe Bibliography, 1912-50 (Berlin, 1957-60), Bd. IV, Abt. V, Lfg. 1-3, of Karl Goedeke's Grundriss zur Geschichte der deutschen Dichtung aus den Quellen, 15 Bände (Berlin, 1884-1966). But Hans Pyritz's Goethe-Bibliographie (Heidelberg, 1965) [particularly for the purposes of this book, pp. 455-58 and 751-58] and Band II, 1955-64 (Heidelberg, 1968) [pp. 121 and 230-34] have more recently earned critical respect.

Klaus W. Jonas' Fifty Years of Thomas Mann Studies: A Bibliography of Criticism (Minneapolis, 1955) lists 3,010 items concerning Mann, including 164 references to "Der Zauberberg" alone (see pp. 149-59). And Klaus W. and Ilsedore B. Jonas' Thomas Mann Studies: A Bibliography of Criticism, Volume II (Philadelphia, 1967) contemporizes the previous volume from 1954-1965, adding 3,500 items to Fifty Years. Harry Matter's Die Literatur über Thomas Mann; eine Bibliographie 1898-1969 (Berlin, 1972) in two volumes lists a formidable total of 14,426 items, of which 439 apply directly to "Der Zauberberg." The most recent complete compilation is Jonas' Die Thomas-Mann-Literatur, 2 Bde. (Berlin, 1972, 1979). Vol. I covers 1896-1955; vol. II, 1956-75.

As the above bibliographies alone indicate, the mass of related critical material--particularly pertaining to the works of Goethe and Mann--precludes both the possibility and the practicality of an inclusive examination of the available data. However, a restriction of the focus primarily to the three works treated in the second part of this book renders the source material more manageable. Yet even then this bibliography presumes to contain only those studies that may be considered the principal publications relating to the subject of this book, including several works of special but peripheral interest.

For instance, this book does not acknowledge many of the unpublished dissertations on the topic of "Definitions and Distinctions," such as the folowing:

Ankele, Felicitas Charlotte. "Thomas Mann's 'Zauberberg' als Bildungsroman." Thesis: Seattle, 1926.

Arnold, Ludwig. "Stifters 'Nachsommer' als Bildungsroman." Gießen, 1939.

Baumann, Hanny Elizabeth. "Die bildende Kunst im deutschen Bildungsroman Literatur." Bern, 1933.

Beddow, Michael. "Thomas Mann's 'Felix Krull' and the Traditions of the Picaresque Novel and the Bildungsroman." Cambridge, Eng., 1975.

Berger, Georg. "Die Romane Jean Pauls als Bildungsromane." Leipzig, 1923.

Cocalis, Susan L. "The Early German 'Bildungsroman' and the Historical Concept of 'Bildung': Thematic, Structural, and Formal Characteristics of the 'Bildungsroman' in the 'Age of Goethe.'" Princeton, 1974. [Cocalis concludes, "The Bildungsroman therefore can be regarded as a definite literary genre with specific norms . . . ."]

Edelmüller, Hildegard. "Der Bildungsroman des Arbeiters." Wien, 1942.

Fambrough, Preston. "The Apprenticeship Novel in Nineteenth-Century England and France." Chapel Hill, 1979.

Fleischer, Stefan. "The Theme of Bildung in the Prelude, Hyperion, and Wilhelm Meisters Lehrjahre." Ithaca, 1967.

Gadway, John Francis. "The Castle in the Bildungsroman." New Orleans, 1972.

Gottbrath, K. "Der Einfluß von Goethes 'Wilhelm Meister' auf die englische Literatur." Münster, 1934.

Heesch, Käthe. "Gottfried Kellers 'Grüne Heinrich' als Bildungsroman des deutschen Realismus." Hamburg, 1939.

Hoffmann, Kurt. "K. Ph. Moritz' Anton Reiser und seine Bedeutung in der Geschichte des deutschen Bildungsroman." Breslau, 1923.

Kehr, Charlotte. "Der deutsche Entwicklungsroman seit der Jahrhundertwende. Ein Beitrag zur Geschichte des Entwicklungsroman." Leipzig, 1938.

Linke, Wolfgang. "Die Arbeit in den Bildungsroman des poetischen Realismus." Erlangen, 1952.

Majstrak, Manfred. "Das Problem von Individuum und Gemeinschaft in den großen nachklassischen Bildungsromanen Stifters und Kellers." Bonn, 1954.

Pielow, Winfried. "Die Erziehergestalten der großen deutschen Bildungsromane von Goethe bis zur Gegenwart." Münster, 1951.

Rogers, Judy R. "The Evolution of the Bildungsroman." Chapel Hill, 1973.

Schötz, Alfred. "Gehalt und Form des Bildungsromans im 20. Jahrhundert." Erlangen, 1950.

Thomet, Ulrich. Das Problem der Bildung im Werke Thomas Manns.

Bern, 1975.
Treffer, Günther. "Studien zum Problem der Bildung in Thomas Mann's Roman Der Zauberberg." Wien, 1956.
Walter, Barbara. "Der moderne deutsche Bildungsroman." Berlin, 1948.
Wildstake, Karl. "Wielands Agathon und der französische Reise- und Bildungsroman von Fénélons Telemach bis Barthélemys Anacharsis." München, 1933.

ONE/ Definitions and Distinctions

Abrams, M. H. "Genre" and "Novel." *A Glossary of Literary Terms*. 3rd ed. (New York, 1971), pp. 67-68 and 110-14.
———. *Natural Supernaturalism: Tradition and Revolution in Romantic Literature*. New York, 1971.
Albérès, R.-M. *Histoire du roman moderne*. Paris, 1962.
Aldridge, A. Owen. "Editor's Introduction to Literary Forms." *Comparative Literature: Matter and Method* (Urbana, 1969), pp. 158-60.
Baldensperger, Fernand. *Goethe en France*. Paris, 1920. Esp. pp. 171-85.
Berger, Berta. *Der moderne deutsche Bildungsroman*. Diss. Bern, 1937. In *Sprache und Dichtung*, Bd. 69. Bern, 1942.
Borcherdt, Hans H. "Bildungsroman." In Kohlschmidt, Werner, und Wolfgang Mohr, Hrsg. *Reallexikon der deutschen Literaturgeschichte*, 2. Aufl. (Berlin, 1955), I, 175-78.
———. "Der Bildungsroman der Hochklassik und Hochromantik." *Der Roman der Goethezeit* (Urach und Stuttgart, 1949), S. 261-382.
———. "Der deutsche Bildungsroman." In *Von deutscher Art in Sprache und Dichtung*. Hrsg. von G. Fricke, F. Koch u. K. Lugowski, 5 (Stuttgart, 1941), 3-55.
Bruford, W. H. *The German Tradition of Self-Cultivation: "Bildung" from Homboldt to Thomas Mann*. Cambridge, Eng., 1975.
Buckley, Jerome. *Season of Youth: The Bildungsroman from Dickens to Golding*. Cambridge, Mass., 1974.
Crane, R. S., ed. *Critics and Criticism*. Chicago, 1952. Esp. pp. 12-24, 546-63.
Davis, Fitzroy K. "Bildungsroman." *Saturday Review of Literature*, 18 (24 Sept. 1938), 9. [Focuses on Mann's *Joseph in Egypt*]
Dilthey, Wilhelm. *Das Erlebnis und die Dichtung*. 6. Aufl. Leipzig, 1919.
———. *Das Leben Schleiermachers*. 2. Aufl. Berlin, 1922. Bd. 1.
Donner, J. O. E. *Der Einfluss Wilhelm Meisters auf den Roman der Romantiker*. Diss. Helsingfors, 1893.
Ehrenpreis, Irwin. *The "Types" Approach to Literature*. New York, 1945.
Eppelsheimer, Hanns W. *Handbuch der Weltliteratur von den Anfängen bis zur Gegenwart*. 3. Aufl. Frankfurt, 1960. Anhang II: "Bildungsroman."
Friederich, Werner P. *History of German Literature*. New York, 1948.

Friederich and David H. Malone. Outline of Comparative Literature. Chapel Hill, 1954.
Frierson, William C. The English Novel in Transition, 1885-1940. Norman, Okla., 1942.
Gerhard, Melitta. Der deutsche Entwicklungsroman bis zu Goethes "Wilhelm Meister." Halle, 1926.
Germer, Helmut. The German Novel of Education, 1792-1805. Diss. Vanderbilt, 1966. Bern, 1968. "Introductory Remarks" by Heinrich Meyer.
Howe, Susanne. Wilhelm Meister and His English Kinsmen, Apprentices to Life. New York, 1930.
Jacobs, Jürgen. Wilhelm Meister und seine Brüder: Untersuchungen zum deutschen Bildungsroman. München, 1972.
Jenisch, Erich. "Vom Abenteuer- zum Bildungsroman." Germanisch-romanische Monatsschrift, 14 (1926), 339-51.
Jones, Trevor, ed. Harrap's Standard German and English Dictionary. London, 1963.
Jost, François. "La Tradition du 'Bildungsroman.'" Comparative Literature, 21 (1969), 97-115.
Keiter, Heinrich, und Tony Kellen. "Bildungs- und Entwicklungsromane." Der Roman (Essen/Ruhr, 1912), S. 136-46.
Kindermann, Heinz, und Margarete Dietrich. Lexikon der Weltliteratur. Wien, 1950.
Kirsch, Edgar. "Hans Grimms 'Volk ohne Raum' als Bildungsroman." Dichtung und Volkstum, 38 (1937), 475-88.
Kornbluth, M. L. "The Reception of Wilhelm Meister in America." Symposium, 13 (1959), 128-34.
Krüger, Hermann Anders. "Der neuere deutsche Bildungsroman." Westermanns Monatshefte, 101, I. Teil (1906), 257-72.
McInnes, Edward. "Zwischen Wilhelm Meister und Die Ritter vom Geist: zur Auseinandersetzung zwischen Bildungsroman und Sozialroman im 19. Jahrhundert." Deutsche Vierteljahrsschrift für Literaturwissenschaft und Geistesgeschichte, 43 (1969), 487-514.
Martini, Fritz. "Der Bildungsroman: Zur Geschichte des Wortes und der Theorie." Deutsche Vierteljahrsschrift für Literaturwissenschaft und Geistesgeschichte, 35 (1961), 44-63.
Miles, David H. "The Picaro's Journey to the Confessional: The Changing Image of the Hero in the German Bildungsroman." Publications of the Modern Language Association, 89, no. 5 (1974), 980-92.
Pascal, Roy. "The Autobiographical Novel and the Autobiography." Essays in Criticism, 9 (1959), 134-50.
————. The German Novel. Manchester, 1956.
Pearson, N. H. "Literary Forms and Types." English Institute Annual, 1940 (New York, 1941), pp. 61-72.
Pei, Mario A., and Frank Gaynor, eds. Liberal Arts Dictionary. New York, 1952.
Pongs, Hermann. "Bildungsroman." Das kleine Lexikon der Weltliteratur. Stuttgart, 1958.
Scharfschwerdt, Jürgen. Thomas Mann und der deutsche Bildungsroman. Stuttgart, 1967.
Scheler, Max. "Die Formen des Wissens und die Bildung" und "Spinoza." Philosophische Weltanschauung (Bern, 1954), S. 16-48

und 49-61. Trans. Haac, Oscar. Philosophical Perspectives. Boston, 1958.

Schilling, Bernard. "Realism in 19th Century Fiction: Balzac, Dickens and the Bildungsroman." In Nicolas Banasević, ed., Actes du V-e Congrès de l'Association Internationale de Littérature Comparée (Belgrade, 1969), pp. 251-59.

Schmitt, Fritz, und Gerhard Fricke. Deutsche Literaturgeschichte in Tabellen. Teil II: 1450-1770. Frankfurt, 1960.

Schrader, Monika. Mimesis und Poiesis: Poetologische Studien zum Bildungsroman. Rev. Diss. Berlin, 1975.

Schroeder, F. W. Wielands Agathon und die Anfänge des modernen Bildungsroman. Diss. Königsberg, 1904.

Seidler, Herbert. "Wandlungen des deutschen Bildungsroman im 19. Jahrhundert Wirk." Wort, 11 (1961), 148-62.

Shipley, Joseph, ed. Dictionary of World Literary Terms. London, 1955.

Sieburg, Friedrich. "Auch ein Bildungsroman." Gegenwart, 9 (25 Sept. 1954), 622-23. [Focuses on Mann's Felix Krull]

Smith, Horatio, ed. Columbia Dictionary of Modern European Literature. New York, 1947.

Stahl, Ernst Ludwig. Die religiöse und die humanitätsphilosophische Bildungsidee und die Entstehung des deutschen Bildungsroman im 18. Jahrhundert. Diss. Bern, 1932. In Sprache und Dichtung, Bd. 56. Bern, 1934.

Swales, Martin. The German Bildungsroman from Wieland to Hesse. Princeton, 1978.

Tennyson, G. B. "The Bildungsroman in Nineteenth-Century English Literature." In Armato, Rosario, and John Spalek, eds. Medieval Epic to the "Epic Theater" of Brecht (Los Angeles, 1968), pp. 135-46.

Tetens, Nicolas. Philosophische Versuch über die menschliche Natur und ihre Entwickelung. Leipzig, 1777.

Thorlby, Anthony, ed. The Penguin Companion to Literature. Baltimore, 1969. Vol. II.

Touaillon, Christine. "Bildungsroman." In Merker, Paul, und Wolfgang Stammler, Hrsg. Reallexikon der deutschen Literaturgeschichte (Berlin, 1925-31), I, 141-45.

Wagner, Hans Rudolf. Der englische Bildungsroman bis in die Zeit des ersten Weltkrieges. Diss. Bern, 1949. In Schweizer Anglistische Arbeiten, Bd. 27. Bern, 1951.

Wellek, René. Confrontations: Studies in the Intellectual and Literary Relations Between Germany, England, and the United States During the Nineteenth Century. Princeton, 1965.

——— and Austin Warren. Theory of Literature. Rev. ed. New York, 1956.

Whitmore, Charles E. "The Validity of Literary Definitions." Publications of the Modern Language Association of America, 39 (1924), 722-36.

Wilpert, Gero von. Sachwörterbuch der Literatur. Stuttgart, 1955.

Wundt, Max. Goethes Wilhelm Meister und die Entwicklung des modernen Lebensideals. Berlin, 1913.

Yelland, H. L., et al. Handbook of Literary Terms. New York, 1950.

Zastrau, Alfred, Hrsg. "Bildungsroman." Goethe-Handbuch

(Stuttgart, 1961), I, 1210-11.
Ziolkowski, Theodore. The Novels of Hermann Hesse. A Study in Theme and Structure. Princeton, 1965. [Pp. 89-91 give a succinct definition of the "Bildungsroman."]

TWO / Three Classic Apprenticeship Novels

GOETHE

A. Primary Sources

Goethes Werke. 133 Bde. in 143. Weimar: H. Böhlau, 1887-1919.
Wilhelm Meister's Apprenticeship. Trans. Carlyle, Thomas. London: Everyman's Library, 1912. 2 vols.
Wilhelm Meisters Lehrjahre. In Goethes Werke (Weimar: H. Böhlau, 1887-1919), Abt. I, Bde. 21-23.

B. Secondary Sources

Beharriell, F. J. "The Hidden Meaning of Goethe's 'Bekenntnisse einer schönen Seele." In Sammons, J. L., and E. Schürer. Lebendige Form: Fest. Henel (München, 1970), S. 37-62.
Berendt, Hans. Goethes "Wilhelm Meister," ein Beitrag zur Entstehungsgeschichte. Dortmund, 1911.
Berger, Albert. Ästhetik und Bildungsroman: Goethes "Wilhelm Meisters Lehrjahre." Diss. Wien, 1977.
Beriger, Hanno. Goethe und der Roman. Studien zu "Wilhelm Meisters Lehrjahre." Zürich, 1955.
Blackall, Eric A. "Sense and Nonsense in Wilhelm Meisters Lehrjahre." Deutsche Beiträge zur Geistigen Überlieferung, 5 (1965), 49-72.
Bollnow, Otto F. "Vorbetrachtungen zum Verständnis der Bildungsidee in Goethes 'Wilhelm Meister.'" Sammlung, 10 (1955), 445-63.
Braemer, Edith. "Zu einigen Problemen in Goethes Roman 'Wilhelm Meisters Lehrjahren.'" In Thalheim, H. G., und U. Wertheim. Studien zur Literaturgeschichte und Literaturtheorie: Fest. Scholz (Berlin, 1970), S. 143-200.
Bruford, W. H. "Goethe's 'Wilhelm Meister' as a Picture and a Criticism of Society." Publications of the English Goethe Society, n.s., 9 (1933), 20-45.
Carlyle, Thomas. "Goethe." Critical and Miscellaneous Essays (London, 1899), I, 198-257.
Clark, Robert T., Jr. "Personality and Society in Wilhelm Meisters Lehrjahre." Southwest Goethe Festival: A Collection of Nine Papers (Dallas, 1949), pp. 85-100.
Diamond, William. "Wilhelm Meister's Interpretation of Hamlet." Modern Philology, 23 (1925-26), 89-101.
Dieckmann, Liselotte. "Wilhelm Meisters Lehrjahre." Johann Wolfgang Goethe (New York, 1974), pp. 120-131.
Dowden, Edward. "Goethe. I.--Wilhelm Meister." Fortnightly Review, n.s., 43 (1888), 768-89.
Eaton, John W. "Goethe's Contribution to Modern Education."

Germanic Review, 9 (1934), 145-55.
Eckermann, J. P. Gespräche mit Goethe in den letzten Jahren seines Lebens. Bd. I. Jena, 1905.
Eliot, George. "The Morality of Wilhelm Meister." In Pinney, Thomas, ed. Essays of George Eliot (London, 1963), pp. 143-47.
Enright, D. J. "'Wilhelm Meister' and the Ambiguity of Goethe." Cambridge Journal, 6 (1952-53), 664-78.
Ermatinger, Emil. "Goethes Frömmigkeit in Wilhelm Meisters Lehrjahre." Zeitwende, 3, Nr 1 (1927), 152-71.
Fairley, Barker. A Study of Goethe. Oxford, 1947.
Farrell, R. B. "Classicism." In Ritchie, J. M., ed. Periods in German Literature (London, 1966), pp. 99-120.
Farrelly, D. J. Goethe and Inner Harmony: A Study of "Schoene Seele" in the "Apprenticeship of Wilhelm Meister." New York, 1973.
Fleischer, Stefan. "Bekenntnisse einer schönen Seele: Figural Representation in Wilhelm Meisters Lehrjahre." Modern Language Notes, 83 (1968), 807-20.
Gerhard, Melitta. "Goethes 'Wilhelm Meister' und der moderne Bildungsroman." Der deutsche Entwicklungsroman bis zu Goethes "Wilhelm Meister" (Halle, 1926), S. 121-66.
Gille, Klaus F. "Wilhelm Meister" im Urteil der Zeitgenossen. Assen, 1971.
————, Hrsg. Goethes Wilhelm Meister: Zur Rezeptionsgeschichte der Lehr- und Wanderjahre. Königstein/Ts., 1979.
Gray, Ronald D. Goethe the Alchemist. Cambridge, Eng., 1952.
————. "Wilhelm Meister." Goethe, A Critical Introduction (Cambridge, Mass., 1967), pp. 186-200.
Haas, Rosemarie. Die Turmgesellschaft in Wilhelm Meisters Lehrjahren. Bern, 1975.
Halpert, Inge D. "Wilhelm Meister and Josef Knecht." German Quarterly, 34 (1961), 11-20.
Harris, W. T. "Goethe's Wilhelm Meister." In Dudley, Marion V., ed. Poetry and Philosophy of Goethe (Chicago, 1887), pp. 12-37.
Hass, Hans-Egon. "Goethe. Wilhelm Meisters Lehrjahre." In Wiese, Benno von, ed. Der deutsche Roman. Vom Barock bis zur Gegenwart. Struktur und Geschichte (Düsseldorf, 1963), I, 132-210.
Hatch, Mary Gies. "The Development of Goethe's Concept of the Calling in 'Wilhelm Meisters Lehrjahre.'" German Quarterly, 32 (1959), 217-26.
Henkel, Arthur. "Versuch über den 'Wilhelm Meister.'" Ruperto-Carola, 31 (1962), 59-67.
Hatfield, Henry C. Goethe: A Critical Introduction. Cambridge, Mass., 1963.
Hesse, Hermann. "Wilhelm Meisters Lehrjahre." Dank an Goethe (Zürich, 1946), S. 51-82.
Hohlfeld, A. R. Fifty Years with Goethe, 1901-51: Collected Studies. Madison, Wis., 1953.
Immerwahr, Raymond. "Friedrich Schlegel's Essay 'On Goethe's Meister.'" Monatshefte für deutschen Unterricht, deutsche Sprache und Literatur, 49 (1957), 1-21.
Jaloux, Edmond. "Lecture de Wilhelm Meister." Revue d'Allemagne, 6 (1932), 97-114.

Kahn, Ludwig W. "Goethes 'Wilhelm Meister' und das Religiöse." Monatshefte für deutschen Unterricht, deutsche Sprache und Literatur, 52 (1960), 225-33.
Larrett, W. "Wilhelm Meister and the Amazons. The Quest for Wholeness." Publications of the English Goethe Society, n.s., 39 (1969), 31-56.
Lewes, George Henry. Life of Goethe. London, 1938.
Lukács, Georg. "Wilhelm Meisters Lehrjahre." Goethe und seine Zeit (Bern, 1947), S. 31-47. Trans. Anchor, Robert. Goethe and His Age (New York, 1969), pp. 50-67. Also in Lange, Victor, ed. Goethe: A Collection of Critical Essays (Englewood Cliffs, N.J., 1968), pp. 86-98.
Mann, Thomas. "Goethe als Repräsentant des bürgerlichen Zeitalters." Gesammelte Werke (Frankfurt, 1960), IX, 297-332.
———, ed. The Permanent Goethe. New York, 1948.
Martin, David M. "Thematic Structure of Goethe's Wilhelm Meister's Apprenticeship." Criticism, 3 (1961), 201-5.
Maugham, W. Somerset. "The Three Novels of a Poet." Points of View (London, 1958), pp. 1-55.
May, Kurt. "Weltbild und innere Form der Klassik und Romantik im 'Wilhelm Meister' und 'Heinrich von Ofterdingen.'" Form und Bedeutung (Stuttgart, 1957), S. 185-203.
———. "'Wilhelm Meisters Lehrjahre,' ein Bildungsroman?" Deutsche Vierteljahrsschrift für Literaturwissenschaft und Geistesgeschichte, 31 (1957), 1-37.
Meusch, Robert. "The Ethical Development of Wilhelm Meister." Publications of the English Goethe Society, 5 (1890), 83-97.
Miller, R. D. Wilhelm Meisters Lehrjahre. An Interpretation. Harrogate, 1969.
Müller, Günther. Gestaltung-Umgestaltung in Wilhelm Meisters Lehrjahre. Halle, 1948.
Müller, Joachim. "Phasen der Bildungsidee im 'Wilhelm Meister.'" Goethe, Neue Folge des Jahrbuchs der Goethe-Gesellschaft, 24 (1962), 58-80.
Pascal, Roy. "'Bildung' and the Division of Labour." German Studies (London, 1962), pp. 14-28.
———. "Wilhelm Meister's Apprenticeship." The German Novel (Manchester, 1956), pp. 3-29.
Rausch, Jürgen. "Lebensstufen in Goethes 'Wilhelm Meister.'" Deutsche Vierteljahrsschrift für Literaturwissenschaft und Geistesgeschichte, 20 (1942), 65-114.
Reiss, H. S. "On Some Images in Wilhelm Meisters Lehrjahre." Publications of the English Goethe Society, n.s., 20 (1951), 111-38.
———. "Wilhelm Meisters Lehrjahre." Goethes Romane (Bern, 1963), S. 72-142. Rev. and trans. as Goethe's Novels (Coral Gables, Fla., 1969).
Rexroth, Kenneth. "Classics Revisited: Goethe." Saturday Review, 52 (19 April 1969), 21.
Robertson, J. G. Goethe. New York, 1927.
———. "Wilhelm Meisters Lehrjahre." History of German Literature (London, 1966), pp. 303-6.
Röder, G. Glück und glückliches Ende im deutschen Bildungsroman.

Eine Studie zu Goethes Wilhelm Meister. München, 1968.
Ross, Flora. *Goethe in Modern France*. Urbana, Ill., 1937.
Saine, Thomas P. "Über Wilhelm Meisters Bildung." In Sammons, J. L., und E. Schürer. *Lebendige Form: Fest. Henel* (München, 1970), S. 63-82.
———. "Wilhelm Meister's Homecoming." *Journal of English and Germanic Philology*, 69, no. 3 (July 1970), 450-69.
Schiller, Friedrich. *Briefe*. München, 1955.
Schlegel, Friedrich. "Über Goethes Meister." *Athenaeum*, I, St. II (Berlin, 1798), 147-78.
Schneider, Margret. *Etüdien zum Lesen sprachlicher Formen in Goethes Wilhelm Meister*. Zürich, 1970.
Schütze, Martin. "Das zusammenbrennende, zusammentreffende Ganze in 'Wilhelm Meister.'" *Modern Philology*, 26 (1928-29), 481-97.
Seidler, Herbert. "Wandlungen des deutschen Bildungsroman im 19. Jahrhundert." *Wirkendes Wort*, 11 (1961), 148-62.
Spranger, Eduard. "Goethe's Wilhelm Meister." *Indian Literature*, 8, no. 1 (1965), 30-35.
Staiger, Emil. "Wilhelm Meisters Lehrjahre." *Goethe* (Zürich, 1952), II, 128-74.
Steiner, Jacob. *Goethes Wilhelm Meister: Sprache und Stilwandel*. Stuttgart, 1966.
Stock, Irvin. "A View of Wilhelm Meister's Apprenticeship." *Publications of the Modern Language Association*, 72 (1957), 84-103.
Storz, Gerhard. "Zur Komposition von Wilhelm Meisters Lehrjahre." In Gaiser, Konrad. *Das Altertum und jedes neue Gute: Fest. Wolfgang Schadewaldt* (Stuttgart, 1970), S. 157-65.
Strelka, Joseph. "Goethes 'Wilhelm Meister' und der Roman des zwanzigsten Jahrhunderts." *German Quarterly*, 41 (1968), 338-55.
Thode, Henry. "Goethe der Bildner." *Goethe-Jahrbuch*, 27 (1906), 1-26.
Thüsen, Joachim von der. "Der Romananfang in 'Wilhelm Meisters Lehrjahre." *Deutsche Vierteljahrsschrift für Literaturwissenschaft und Geistesgeschichte*, 43 (1969), 622-30.
Viëtor, K. "Goethe: 'Wilhelm Meisters Lehrjahre.'" In Schillemeit, J., Hrsg. *Interpretationen* (Frankfurt, 1965), III. 30-48.
———. *Goethe, the Poet* [Part I of *Goethe: Dichtung, Wissenschaft, Weltbild*]. Trans. Hadas, Moses. Cambridge, Mass., 1949.
———. *Goethe, the Thinker* [Parts II and III of *Goethe: Dichtung, Wissenschaft, Weltbild*]. Trans. Morgan, Bayard Q. Cambridge, Mass., 1950.
Wagman, Frederick H. *Goethe's Conception of Personality*. Philadelphia, 1933.
Weigand, Hermann J. "Shakespeare in German Criticism." In Schuller, Herbert M., ed. *Persistence of Shakespeare Idolatry* (Detroit, 1964), pp. 105-33.
Weiss, G. H. "An Interpretation of the Miners' Scene in Goethe's Wilhelm Meisters Lehrjahre." In Sammons, J. L., and E. Schürer. *Lebendige Form: Fest. Henel* (München, 1970), S. 83-88.
Wolff, Eugen. *Mignon, Ein Beitrag zur Geschichte des Wilhelm Meister*. München, 1909.
Wundt, Max. *Goethes Wilhelm Meister und die Entwicklung des modernen Lebensideals*. Berlin, 1913.

A. Primary Sources

"Einführung in den 'Zauberberg.'" In Gesammelte Werke (Frankfurt, 1960), XI, 602-17. Trans. "The Making of the Mountain." Atlantic Monthly, 191 (Jan. 1953), 41-45.
Gesammelte Werke. 12 Bde. Frankfurt: S. Fischer, 1960.
The Magic Mountain. Trans. Lowe-Porter, H. T. New York: Knopf, 1982.
"Die Schule des Zauberbergs." In Gesammelte Werke (Frankfurt, 1960), XI, 599-601.
Der Zauberberg. In Gesammelte Werke (Frankfurt, 1960), Bd. III.

B. Secondary Sources

Altenberg, Paul. Die Romane Thomas Manns. Homburg, 1961.
Apter, T. E. Thomas Mann: The Devil's Advocate. New York, 1978.
Arntzen, Helmut. "Thomas Mann: Der Zauberberg." Der moderne deutsche Roman (Heidelberg, 1962), pp. 37-57.
Baer, Lydia. The Concept and Function of Death in the Works of Thomas Mann. Philadelphia, 1932.
Bauer, Arnold. Thomas Mann. Trans. Henderson, A. and E. New York, 1971.
Bendow, Bruce. "The Meaning of 'The Magic Mountain.'" Apprentice, 17 (Dec. 1953), 10-15.
Berger, Berta. "Der Held des Bildungsromans--ein Exponent des bürgerlichen Verfalls und Kriegsgeschehens." Der moderne deutsche Bildungsroman (Bern, 1942), S. 22-27.
Blackmur, R. P. "Hans Castorp, Small Lord of Counterpositions: Notes on the Prophecy of Mann's 'The Magic Mountain.'" Hudson Review, I (1948), 318-39.
Boyd, Ernest. "Der Zauberberg." Nation, 120 (13 May 1925), 552.
Brennan, Joseph G. "Heard and Unheard Speech in The Magic Mountain." Novel: A Forum of Fiction, 3 (1970), 129-39.
———. Thomas Mann's World. New York, 1962.
———. "Three Novels of 'Dépaysement.'" Comparative Literature, 22, no. 3 (Summer 1970), 223-36.
———. Three Philosophical Novelists: James Joyce, André Gide, Thomas Mann. New York, 1964.
Brewster, Dorothy, and Angus Burrell. "The Magic Mountain." Modern Fiction (New York, 1934), pp. 332-35.
Cleugh, J. Thomas Mann: A Study. New York, 1968.
Eichner, Hans, and J. A. Asher. "Thomas Mann and Goethe." Publications of the English Goethe Society, n.s., 26 (1957), 81-98.
Eickhorst, William. ["Thomas Mann."] Decadence in German Fiction (Denver, 1953), pp. 50-57.
Einsiedel, Wolfgang von. "Thomas Manns Zauberberg: Ein Bildungsroman?" Zeitschrift für Deutschkunde, 42 (1928), 241-53.
Eloesser, Arthur. Thomas Mann: Sein Leben und sein Werk. Berlin, 1925.
Enders, Horst. "Der doppelte Beginn mit Hans Castorp. Zu Thomas Manns 'Der Zauberberg.'" In Miller, Norbert, Hrsg. Romananfänge.

Versuch einer Poetik des Romans (Berlin, 1965), S. 289-316.
"An Epic of Illness." New Statesman, 24 (17 Sept. 1927), 715.
Fougère, Jean. Thomas Mann; ou, La séduction de la mort. Paris, 1947.
Gorman, Herbert. "The Magic Mountain." Saturday Review (London), 144 (6 Aug. 1927), 200-1.
Gray, Ronald D. "The Magic Mountain." The German Tradition in Literature (Cambridge, Eng., 1965), pp. 157-72.
Guthke, Karl S. "Thomas Mann on His 'Zauberberg.' An Unpublished Letter to Hans M. Wolff (25. Nov. 1950)." Neophilologus, 44 (April 1960), 120-22.
Hallamore, Joyce. "Zur Siebenzahl in Thomas Manns 'Zauberberg.'" German Quarterly, 35 (Jan. 1962), 17-19.
Harrington, M. "Last Bourgeois." Nation, 214 (17 April 1972), 506-7.
Harvey, William John. "Thomas Mann." Character and the Novel (Ithaca, N.Y., 1965), pp. 100-8.
Hatfield, Henry C. "The Achievement of Thomas Mann." Germanic Review, 31 (1956), 206-14.
———. From The Magic Mountain: Mann's Later Masterpieces. Ithaca, N.Y., 1979.
———. "Recent Studies of Thomas Mann." Modern Language Review, 51 (1956), 390-403.
———. Thomas Mann. Norfolk, Conn., 1951.
———. Thomas Mann: A Collection of Critical Essays. Englewood, N.J., 1964.
———. "Der Zauberberg." Modern German Literature: The Major Figures in Context (New York, 1967), pp. 94 ff.
Heller, Erich. "Form als Mass und Übermass: Ein Gespräch über Thomas Manns 'Zauberberg.'" Monat, 2, Nr 131 (1959), 40-60; Nr 132 (1959), 60-67.
———. The Ironic German: A Study of Thomas Mann. London, 1958.
Heller, Peter. Dialectics and Nihilism: Essays on Lessing, Nietzsche, Mann, and Kafka. Amherst, 1966.
Hirschbach, Frank D. "The Education of Hans Castorp." Monatshefte für deutschen Unterricht, deutsche Sprache und Literatur, 46 (Jan. 1954), 25-34.
Hoffmann, Gerd. "Bildungseinflüsse auf Hans Castorp im Zauberberg." In Wenzel, G. Thomas Mann zum Gedenken (Potsdam, 1956), S. 134-48.
Hollingdale, R. J. Thomas Mann: A Critical Study. Lewisburg, Pa., 1971.
Hunt, Joel A. "The Stylistics of a Foreign Language: Thomas Mann's Use of French." Germanic Review, 32 (1957), 19-34.
———. "The Walpurgisnacht Chapter: Thomas Mann's First Conclusion." Modern Language Notes, 76 (Dec. 1961), 826-29.
Kahler, Erich. The Orbit of Thomas Mann. Princeton, 1969.
Kaufmann, Fritz. Thomas Mann: The World as Will and Representation. Boston, 1957.
Kiehl, Bruno. "Der Schatz im Zauberberg." Zeitschrift für deutsche Bildung, 4 (1928), 527-34.
Koopmann, Helmut. Die Entwicklung des "intellektualen" Romans bei Thomas Mann. Bonn, 1962.

Krutch, Joseph W. "Spring Novels and the Magic Mountain." Nation, 124 (8 June 1927), 638.
Lesser, J. "Thomas Mann's Change of Mind." German Life and Letters, n.s., 2 (1949), 165-71.
Lewisohn, Ludwig. "The Magic Mountain." New York Herald Tribune Book Review, 5 May 1927, p. 1.
———. "Thomas Mann." English Journal, 22 (Sept. 1933), 527-35.
Lindsay, J. M. Thomas Mann. Oxford, 1954.
Lion, F. Thomas Mann: Leben und Werk. Zürich, 1947.
Lovett, Robert M. "The Epic of Decay." New Republic, 51 (6 July 1927), 180-81.
Lukács, Georg. Thomas Mann. Berlin, 1949.
"The Magic Mountain." Living Age, 333 (15 Aug. 1927), 375.
"The Magic Mountain." Review of Reviews, 77 (1929), 278.
"The Magic Mountain Mouse." New Masses, 19 (June 1934), 25.
Martin, John S. "Circean Seduction in Three Works by Thomas Mann." Modern Language Notes, 78 (1963), 346-52.
Mauer, Warren R. "Names from 'The Magic Mountain.'" Names, 9, no. 4 (Dec. 1961), 248-59.
Muir, Edwin. "The Magic Mountain." Nation and Athenaeum, 41 (2 July 1927), 452.
Muller, Herbert J. "The Magic Mountain." South Atlantic Quarterly, 36 (July 1937), 302-13.
———. "Thomas Mann." Modern Fiction: A Study in Values (New York, 1937), pp. 314-82.
Neider, Charles, ed. The Stature of Thomas Mann. A Critical Anthology. New York, 1947.
Norman, Arthur M. Z. "Seven Symbolism in 'The Magic Mountain.'" Monatshefte für deutschen Unterricht, deutsche Sprache und Literatur, 47 (Nov. 1955), 360.
Pascal, Roy. "Thomas Mann: The Magic Mountain." The German Novel (Manchester, 1956), pp. 76-98.
Passage, Charles E. "Hans Castorp's Musical Incantation." Germanic Review, 38 (1963), 238-56.
Peacock, Ronald. Das Leitmotiv bei Thomas Mann. Bern, 1934.
Priestley, J. B. "Thomas Mann: The Magic Mountain." Literature and Western Man (New York, 1960), pp. 420-23.
Puckett, Hugh W. "Dangerous Heights." Saturday Review, 3 (16 July 1927), 972-73.
Randall, A. W. G. "A New Novel: Der Zauberberg." Saturday Review, 1 (23 May 1925), 777.
Rebelsky, Freda Gould. "Coming of Age in Davos: An Analysis of the Maturation of Hans Castorp in Thomas Mann's The Magic Mountain." American Imago, 18 (1961), 413-21.
Reed, T. J. Thomas Mann: The Uses of Tradition. Oxford, 1974.
Sauereßig, Heinz. Die Entstehung des Romans "Der Zauberberg": Zwei Essays und eine Dokumentation. Biberach, 1965.
Scharfschwerdt, Jürgen. Thomas Mann und der deutsche Bildungsroman. Stuttgart, 1967.
Schultz, H. Stefan. "On the Interpretation of Thomas Mann's Der Zauberberg." Modern Philology, 52 (1954), 110-22.
Scott, Dawson. "The Magic Mountain." Bookman (London), 74 (1928), 267.

Seidlin, Oskar. "The Lofty Game of Numbers: The Mynheer Peeperkorn Episode in Thomas Mann's Der Zauberberg." Publications of the Modern Language Association, 86 (Oct. 1971), 924-39.
Slochower, Harry. "Bourgeois Liberalism: Thomas Mann's Magic Mountain." Three Ways of Modern Man (New York, 1937), pp. 50-105.
Stern, Joseph P. Thomas Mann. New York, 1967.
Streit, Konrad. "Der Bildungsroman des 20. Jahrhunderts." Schweizer Journal, 11, Nr 7/8 (1945), 42-43.
Stresau, Hermann. Thomas Mann und sein Werk. Frankfurt, 1963.
Struc, Roman S. "The Threat of Chaos. Stifter's 'Bergkristall' and Thomas Mann's 'Schnee.'" Modern Language Quarterly, 24 (Dec. 1963), 323-32.
Stuckenschmidt, Dierk. "'Schlüsselbilder' in Thomas Manns 'Zauberberg.'" Monatshefte für deutschen Unterricht, deutsche Sprache und Literatur, 58 (Dec. 1966), 310-20.
"A Study in Degeneration." Times (London) Literary Supplement, 26 (7 July 1927), 469.
Swales, Martin. Thomas Mann: A Study. Totowa, N.J., 1980.
Thomas, R. Hinton. "The Magic Mountain." Thomas Mann: The Mediation of Art (Oxford, 1956), pp. 85-111.
Waugh, Butler. Thomas Mann's The Magic Mountain: A Commentary. New York, 1967.
Weigand, Hermann J. "Thomas Mann and Goethe; A Supplement and a Correction." Germanic Review, 32 (Feb. 1957), 75-76.
———. Thomas Mann's Novel Der Zauberberg: A Study. New York, 1933.
Zinberg, Dorothy S. and Norman E. "Hans Castorp: Identity Crisis Without Resolution." American Imago, 20 (1963), 393-402.

MAUGHAM

A. Primary Sources

Cakes and Ale. New York, 1950.
Of Human Bondage. New York: Grosset & Dunlap, 1915.
Selected Prefaces and Introductions of W. Somerset Maugham. New York, 1963.
The Summing Up. New York, 1938.

B. Secondary Sources

Aldington, Richard. W. Somerset Maugham, An Appreciation. New York, 1939.
Allen, Walter E. ["Somerset Maugham."] English Novel: A Short Critical History (New York, 1957), pp. 390-94.
Brander, Laurence. Somerset Maugham: A Guide. New York, 1963.
Brassilach, Robert. "Servitude Humaine de Somerset Maugham." Gringoire, 2 Juillet 1937, p. 4.
Brewster, Dorothy, and Angus Burrell. "Time Passes." Adventure or

Experience: Four Essays on Certain Writers and Readers of Novels (New York, 1930), pp. 37-75.
Brophy, J. Somerset Maugham. London, 1952.
Brown, Ivor. W. Somerset Maugham. London, 1970.
Collins, J. P. "W. Somerset Maugham: Playwright Novelist." Bookman (London), 57 (Oct. 1919), 12-15.
"A Compromise." Nation (London), 17 (21 April 1915), 684.
Cooper, Frederic T. "Some Novels of the Month." Bookman (New York), 42 (Sept. 1915), 104-5.
Cordell, Richard A. Somerset Maugham, A Biographical and Critical Study. Bloomington, Ind., 1961.
Doner, Dean. "Spinoza's Ethics and Maugham." University of Kansas City Review, 21 (June 1955), 261-69.
Dottin, Paul. W. Somerset Maugham et ses Romans. Paris, 1928.
Dreiser, Theodore. "As a Realist Sees It." New Republic, 5 (1915-16), 202-4.
Drew, Elizabeth A. ["Somerset Maugham."] The Modern Novel: Some Aspects of Contemporary Fiction (New York, 1926), pp. 93, 96, 98-100, 252.
Edgett, E. F. "The Bondage of a Youth." Boston Evening Transcript Book Section, 11 August 1915, p. 18.
"Fiction." Athenaeum, no. 4582 (21 Aug. 1915), 128.
Frierson, William C. ["Somerset Maugham."] English Novel in Transition: 1885-1940 (Norman, Okla., 1942), pp. 197-200.
Goodrich, M. A. "After Ten Years 'Of Human Bondage.'" New York Times Book Review, 25 January 1925, p. 2.
Gould, Gerald. "New Novels." New Statesman, 5 (25 Sept. 1915), 594.
Harris, Wendell V. "Molly's 'Yes': The Transvaluation of Sex in Modern Fiction." Texas Studies in Literature and Language, 10 (Spring 1968), 107-18, esp. 111-12.
Jonas, Klaus W. The Maugham Enigma: An Anthology. New York, 1954.
————. The World of Somerset Maugham, An Anthology. London, 1959.
Kuner, M. C. "Maugham and the West: The Human Condition--Bondage." In Jonas, Klaus, ed. The World of Somerset Maugham (New York, 1959), pp. 37-95.
Lovett, R. M., and H. S. Hughes. ["Somerset Maugham."] History of the Novel in England (Boston, 1932), p. 381.
McIver, C. S. Wilhelm Somerset Maugham, A Study of Technique and Literary Sources. Diss. Philadelphia, 1936.
Marchand, Leslie A. "The Exoticism of Somerset Maugham." Revue Anglo-Américaine, 10 (1932-33) 314-29.
Menard, Wilmon. The Two Worlds of Somerset Maugham. Los Angeles, 1965.
Morgan, Ted. Maugham. New York, 1980.
Muller, Herbert J. ["Somerset Maugham."] Modern Fiction: A Study of Values (New York, 1937), pp. 240-43.
Naik, M. K. W. Somerset Maugham. Norman, Okla., 1966.
Neill, S. Diana. ["Somerset Maugham."] Short History of the English Novel (London, 1951), pp. 258-59.
"The New Books." Independent, 83 (23 Aug. 1915), 268.
"The New Books." Outlook, 110 (11 Aug. 1915), 874.

"New Novels." Times (London) Literary Supplement, 12 Aug. 1915, p. 269.
O'Connor, W. Van. "Two Types of 'Heroes' in Post-War Fiction." Publications of the Modern Language Association, 77 (March 1962), 168-74.
"Of Human Bondage." New York Times Book Review, 1 Aug. 1915, p. 278.
"Our Booking-Office." Punch, 149 (25 Aug. 1915), 179-80.
Papejewski, Helmut. Die Welt-, Lebens- und Kunstanschauung Maughams. Köln, 1952.
Payne, W. M. "Recent Fiction." Dial, 59 (16 Sept. 1915), 220.
Pfeiffer, Karl G. W. Somerset Maugham: A Candid Portrait. New York, 1959.
"Reviews: Man in the Making." Saturday Review (London), 120 (4 Sept. 1915), 233-34.
Roberts, R. E. "The Amorist." Bookman (London), 48 (Sept. 1915), 171-72.
"Some of the New Fiction: Maugham Returns to the Novel." Springfield (Sunday) Republican (Mass.), 8 Aug. 1915, p. 15.
Spence, Robert. "Maugham's 'Of Human Bondage': The Making of a Masterpiece." Library Chronicle, 17 (Spring-Summer, 1951), 104-14.
Spencer, Theodore. "Somerset Maugham." English Journal, 29 (1940), 523-32. Also in College English, 2 (1940), 1-10.
Thiébaut, Marcel. "Parmi les livres." La Revue de Paris, 44ème année, 5 (15 Sept. 1937), 457-59.
Tindall, W. Y. ["Somerset Maugham."] Forces in Modern British Literature: 1885-1946 (New York, 1947), pp. 74-75, 132-33, 179-80.
VanDoren, Carl and Mark. "Maugham 1874--." American and British Literature Since 1890 (New York, 1925), pp. 205-8.
Ward, Richard H. William Somerset Maugham. London, 1937.
Weygandt, Cornelius. A Century of the English Novel (New York, 1925), pp. 168, 364-67, 430.

INDEX

STUDIENREIHE ZUR GERMANISTIK

Germanic Studies in America:

Bd. 1 Nordmeyer, Rubaijat von Omar Chajjam. 2. Aufl. 104 S., brosch. und Lwd., 1969.
Bd. 2 Richards, The German Bestseller in the 20th Century. A complete Bibliography and Analysis. 276 S., Lwd., 1968.
Bd. 3 Germer, The German Novel of Education 1792–1805. A complete Bibliography and Analysis. 280 S., Lwd., 1968.
Bd. 4 Gerlitzki, Die Bedeutung der Minne in «Moritz von Craun». 132 S., Lwd., 1970.
Bd. 5 Bowman, Life into Autobiography. A Study of Goethe's «Dichtung und Wahrheit». 162 S., Lwd., 1971.
Bd. 6 Putzel, Letters to Immanuel Bekker from Henriette Herz, S. Probenheim and Anna Horkel. 108 S., Lwd., 1972.
Bd. 7 Geldrich, Heine und der spanisch-amerikanische Modernismo. 304 S., Lwd., 1971.
Bd. 8 Friesen, The German Panoramic Novel in the 19th Century. 232 S., Lwd., 1972.
Bd. 9 Novak, Wilhelm von Humboldt as a Literary Critic. 142 S., Lwd., 1972.
Bd. 10 Shelton, The Young Hölderlin. 282 S., Lwd., 1973.
Bd. 11 Milstein, Eight Eighteenth Century Reading Societies. A Sociological Contribution to the History of German Literature. 312 S., Lwd., 1972.
Bd. 12 Schatzberg, Scientific Themes in the Popular Literature and the Poetry of the German Enlightenment, 1720–1760. 350 S., Lwd., 1973.
Bd. 13 Dimler, Friedrich Spee's «Trutznachtigall». 158 S., Lwd., 1973.
Bd. 14 McCort, Perspectives on Music in German Fiction. The Music-Fiction of Wilhelm Heinrich Riehl. 154 S., Lwd., 1974.
Bd. 15 Motsch, Die poetische Epistel. Ein Beitrag zur Geschichte der deutschen Literatur und Literaturkritik des achtzehnten Jahrhunderts. 218 S., Lwd., 1974.
Bd. 16 Zipser, Edward Bulwer-Lytton and Germany. 232 S., Lwd., 1974.
Bd. 17 Rutledge John, The Dialogue of the Dead in Eighteenth-Century Germany. 186 S., Lwd., 1974.
Bd. 18 Rutledge Joyce S., Johann Adolph Schlegel. 322 S., Lwd., 1974.
Bd. 19 Gutzkow, Wally the Skeptic. Novel. A translation from the German with an Introduction and Notes by Ruth-Ellen Boetcher Joeres. 130 S., Lwd., 1974.
Bd. 20 Keck, Renaissance and Romanticism: Tieck's Conception of Cultural Decline as Portrayed in his «Vittoria Accorombona». 120 S., Lwd., 1976.
Bd. 21 Scholl, The Bildungsdrama of the Age of Goethe. 80 S., Lwd., 1976.
Bd. 22 Bartel, German Literary History 1777–1835. An Annotated Bibliography. 230 S., Lwd., 1976.
Bd. 23 Littell, Jeremias Gotthelf's «Die Käserei in der Vehfreude»: A Didactic Satire. 122 S., Lwd., 1977.
Bd. 24 Carels, The Satiric Treatise in Eighteenth-Century Germany. 168 S., Lwd., 1976.
Bd. 25 Lensing, Narrative Structure and the Reader in Wilhelm Raabe's «Im alten Eisen». 118 S., Lwd., 1977.
Bd. 26 Profit, Interpretations of Iwan Goll's late Poetry with a comprehensive and annotated Bibliography of the Writings by and about Iwan Goll. 202 S., Lwd., 1977.
Bd. 27 Hollyday, Anti-Americanism in the German Novel 1841–1862. 212 S., Lwd., 1977.
Bd. 28 Horwath, Der Kampf gegen die religiöse Tradition. Die Kulturkampfliteratur Österreichs, 1780–1918. 295 S., Lwd., 1978.
Bd. 29 Pantle, Die Frau ohne Schatten – By Hugo von Hofmannsthal and Richard Strauss. An Analysis of Text, Music, and their Relationship. 256 S., Lwd., 1978.
Bd. 30 Leckey, Some Aspects of Balladesque Art and their Relevance for the Novels of Theodor Fontane. 114 S., Lwd., 1979.

Bd. 31 Thomas, Ordnung und Wert der Unordnung bei Bertolt Brecht. 141 S., Lwd., 1979.
Bd. 32 Emmel, Weltklage und Bild der Welt in der Dichtung Goethes. Zweite, durchgesehene Auflage. 223 S., Lwd., 1979.
Bd. 33 Stern, Hilde Domin: From Exile to Ideal. 93 S., Lwd., 1979.
Bd. 34 Gellinek, Herrschaft im Hochmittelalter. Essays zu einem Sonderproblem der älteren deutschen Literatur. 180 S., Lwd., 1980.
Bd. 35 Weeks, The Paradox of the Employee. Variants of a Social Theme in Modern Literature. 160 S., Lwd., 1979.
Bd. 36 Mittelmann, Die Utopie des weiblichen Glücks in den Romanen Theodor Fontanes. 125 S., Lwd., 1980.
Bd. 37 Manyoni, Langzeilentradition in Walthers Lyrik. 128 S., Lwd., 1980.
Bd. 38 Helbig, G.E. Lessing: Die Erziehung des Menschengeschlechts. 77 S., Lwd., 1980.
Bd. 39 Schrader, A Method of Stylistic Analysis Exemplified on C.M. Wieland's 'Geschichte des Agathon'. 240 S., Lwd., 1980.
Bd. 40 Whiton, Der Wandel des Polenbildes in der deutschen Literatur des 19. Jahrhunderts. 208 S., Lwd., 1981.
Bd. 41 Fairy Tales as Ways of Knowing. Essays on Märchen in Psychology, Society and Literature, ed. by Michael M. Metzger and Katharina Mommsen. 200 S., Lwd., 1981.
Bd. 42 Beckett, The Reception of Pablo Neruda's Works in the German Democratic Republic. 251 S., Lwd., 1981.
Bd. 43 Wiswall, A Comparison of Selected Poetic and Scientific Works of Albrecht von Haller. 432 S., Lwd., 1981.
Bd. 44 Cervantes, Struktur-Bezüge in der Lyrik von Nelly Sachs. 144 S., Lwd., 1982.
Bd. 45 Guthke, Erkundungen: Essais zur Literatur. 432 S. Lwd., 1983.
Bd. 46 Remak, Novellistische Struktur: Der Marschall von Bassompierre und die schöne Krämerin (Bassompierre, Goethe, Hofmannsthal). 130 S., Lwd., 1983.
Bd. 47 Laane, Imagery in Conrad Ferdinand Meyer's Prose Works. 258 S., Lwd., 1983.

DATE DUE
